The Practice of Moral Judgment

The Practice of
Moral Judgment

Barbara Herman

Harvard University Press
Cambridge, Massachusetts
London England   1993

Library of Congress Cataloging-in-Publication Data

Herman, Barbara.
  The practice of moral judgment / Barbara Herman.
    p.   cm.
  Includes bibliographical references and index.
  ISBN 0–674–69717–0 (alk. paper)
    1. Kant, Immanuel, 1724–1804—Ethics. 2. Ethics,
Modern—18th century.   3. Ethics, Modern—19th century.
I. Title.
B2799.E8H535 1993   92–20915
170′.92—dc20   CIP

To Mickey and Danny

Preface

KANT'S ethics has been the captive of its critics. The basic terms we use to describe it were introduced by J. H. Muirhead (c. 1930) when he sorted all of moral thought into two camps—the deontological and the teleological— for the purpose of explaining why any nonteleological system was misguided. Kantian ethics has ever since been presented as the defining example of a deontological theory, with those features highlighted that fit a preconceived, critical picture of deontology: rule-based, centered on duty rather than on good, without concern for the place of morality in a good human life, and so on. Of course this picture of Kant's ethics does not lack connection with what Kant says, but the portions taken to support the deontological reading often do not have the significance or play the role it assigns them. In these chapters I argue for a very different understanding of the Kantian project, sometimes on the grounds that it gives a better reading of key texts and other times, when the text does not speak to an issue, on the grounds that it simply makes better sense. My object has been not only to provide new insight into Kant's ethics, but also to develop a method of access to the untapped theoretical power and fertility of this alternative to consequentialist reasoning in ethics.

The practice of characterizing Kant's ethics in a way that sets the stage for criticism is so familiar it is hard to notice. But the effect of using hostile terms of interpretation is to replace the distinctive arguments Kant makes with rounds of futile altercation. Consider the Kantian motive of duty. The idea that we act best when we do the right thing from the motive of duty, indeed, from the motive of duty alone, is usually the first thing learned about Kant's ethics. Almost in the same breath comes a set of critical questions: Is a motive possible that is attached to principle and independent of any interest? If it were possible to act from the motive of duty, how could that be the best way to act? Would it not at least sometimes be better to act from love or sympathy or a passion for justice? Friends of Kant then argue that the motive of duty can do everything intuitively preferred motives do or that, when it cannot, the loss is exaggerated, or acceptable, given the importance of Kant's understanding of moral constraint. What gets missed in these skirmishes is the philosophical question to which the motive of duty was the answer. It gets missed, I believe, because the criticism frames the discussion in the terms of a supposedly self-evident empiricist understanding of motives—a view of motives that Kant rejects.

The motive of duty is part of an answer to a question about possible objects of rational assessment. Kant's argument is roughly this: if morality binds with practical necessity, it cannot work through the passive desires and interests that agents happen to have. Moral agents therefore cannot be described by an empiricist account of motivation. They must possess the capacity to be moved by principle (or by a conception of the good). A satisfactory grasp of the possibility of morality requires a revision of our understanding of agency. In arguing that willings of actions and ends (as described in maxims) are the appropriate objects of practical assessment, Kant not only introduces an alternative theory of action, but also argues for the methodological priority of a theory of value. It is not until the motive of duty is placed in the revised theory of action and agency that Kant's claims for it can make sense. For this reason, the familiar debate about the motive of duty must be futile.

The same pattern is at work in discussions of the Categorical Imperative. We are effectively blocked from thinking about the Categorical Imperative because what it is and does is supposed to be obvious: it is a principle of judgment for determining the permissibility of actions through a hypothetical universalization test. But knowing this, we take the next questions to be about the test (how it works, how to block strategies to defeat it, and so on), and miss the fact that we have taken the nature of judgment (in general and in the moral case) to be of no philosophical moment in Kant's ethics.

This book represents a sustained effort to break the grip of these interpretive givens. Of course it has not been possible either to identify them all or to break free of them all at once. In the course of the attempt, however, I have become convinced not only that Kantian ethics is itself more complex and supple than we think, but also that it depends on a radically different conception of action and agency than the one we tend to take for granted. Not surprisingly, many of the conclusions I reach are in effect programs for further investigation. This seems to me a welcome result.

I have tried to follow two interpretive guidelines: what I argue must make sense in terms of the text, and it must make the text make sense. If Kant's ethics is as radical as I think, then it is important to show that what one claims is there. This is not so much a program for extensive exegesis as it is a commitment to something like a continuous dialogue with the texts. Once we revise an interpretation to gain a better or more powerful argument, the best guarantee that we are proceeding correctly is the light the revision can shed on parts of the text that are otherwise intractable. For some, because the texts are difficult and often fail to address important questions, and because many of Kant's central concepts are unacceptable to us (such as the idea of "noumena"), it has been convenient to think of what they do as "Kantian" ethics. I am uneasy with this strategy, not because I would endorse everything Kant says but because the very things taken to be the separable core of Kantian ethics may be hostage to misleading interpretations. For instance, it seems to me that the popular Kant*ian* notion of respect for persons requires Kant's account of ends and persons to provide the basis for a distinctive mode of moral regard.

The value of a move back to the text is muted by the fact that the text underdetermines interpretation and by the fact that we do not want to accept or be responsible for everything Kant says. Thus the requirement that an interpretation must make the text make sense. This does not mean that the account decided on is the one that squares with intuition or some privileged set of cases, for they may be the source of interpretive distortion. Rather, where interpretation would lead away from intuition, we follow only if it also provides insight into other areas of theory or moral practice.

The essays develop two general themes. The first concerns moral judgment. As I noted, it has been one of the givens of Kant's ethics that everything there was to say about moral judgment belonged to the interpretation of the Categorical Imperative tests, and that all of the difficulties in this area were a species of problems about universalization: the difficulty of deriving content from a formal procedure and the problem of action description are the two most famous. I argue that it is much better to see the Categorical Imperative and its tests as an aspect of moral judgment— setting its terms, I would say—but needing to be placed in a framework that can explain moral perception, deliberation, and (internal) criticism. How the Categorical Imperative works cannot be understood apart from a reasoned view of the kind of results it is able to generate and of its place in the moral agent's complex field of response and deliberation. In the later chapters I argue for the unusual view that Kantian moral judgment depends on the availability of an articulated conception of value—in particular, of the value of the fully embodied person.

Casuistry is the bottom line in an account of moral judgment. Unless the account allows one to think fruitfully about hard cases, and to understand why hard cases are hard, it is not worth much. Although it is first necessary to get the account to work for the canonical examples (deceit, mutual aid, and so on), the only test that it is working is when the argument to a canonical result sets terms for practical thinking in other areas. The demands of casuistry also set a program for theory. Facts of context and subjective particularity need to find a way into moral judgment. I therefore do not treat the discussion of applications as in any way secondary; there is no sharp line between theory and practice.

The second large theme concerns what might be called "moral personality." A great deal of recent criticism of Kantian ethics has targeted its thin conception of the person, the inadequacy of its idea of character, its stultifying restriction on admissible moral motivation, and its mistaken views about the place of impartial moral requirement in a good human life. These criticisms live off the mistaken view of moral judgment as involving algorithmic employment of tests, and its attendant picture of the moral agent as seeking to bring her will into conformity with principles of duty. With this view of judgment out of the way, it becomes possible to see that Kant's notions of virtue and character are in no way peripheral to the understanding of moral judgment and action. We are able to consider the nature of a Kantian moral agent—what motives, feelings, thoughts, and commitments guide her deliberations and actions. There is then room to develop an account of moral personality that places moral activity within the ongoing practical commitments of a good life.

The Kant that emerges in these chapters may seem friendlier to our best wishes for moral philosophy than is credible. This is not in itself an argument. I believe that the mark of great figures in the history of philosophy is that they have important things to say about what matters, if we are able to read through the barrier of language and parochial concern. This has been my experience with Kant's ethics.

Versions of all but two (Chapters 7 and 10) of the essays collected here have been published elsewhere. I have made minor modifications throughout, mostly to unify vocabulary and to add notes that trace some of the connections among the chapters. There is a change in argument only in Chapter 1 ("On the Value of Acting from the Motive of Duty"). Various published criticisms of its central positive argument convinced me that I had not fully thought out the implications of my view or, therefore, given the best argument for it. There is a danger in patchwork repair, but I think the advantage of a more unified account outweighs the untidiness of the seams. It has been a privilege to participate in such an extended and thoughtful philosophical conversation. The only other change of note has been the combination of two published essays ("Rules, Motives and Helping Actions" and "Integrity and Impartiality") into one. They began as parts of the same project and seem more effective when trimmed and brought back together.

One thing I decided not to change was the use of the masculine pronoun in the earlier essays. It was natural for me then to write with it; now it is not. If, as I believe, the way one speaks affects what one can think, pronoun change is not cosmetic.

I should note that there may appear to be a change in my view of the role of the Categorical Imperative procedure in these chapters: a shift from the model of "maxim testing" in the first five essays to a model of establishing deliberative presumptions in the second five. It is more helpful to think of the second view as developing from questions arising in trying to make sense of the first. This is a nice instance of the methodology I recommend. Starting to think about Kant and moral judgment, one has no reason to question the package of the standard maxim-testing view and the criticisms (tailoring of maxims, empty formalism, and so on) that come with it. In trying to get the text and the view to make sense, however, one encounters questions that cannot be answered on the standard model (for example, the source of the moral terminology agents must use in describing their actions prior to assessment). In looking back at the first essays, it seems plain to me that the questions I was asking led me in each case to the view of the Categorical Imperative procedure that only became explicit later. The chapters together make an argument in practice for the revision of the standard view.

The same method lies behind my treatment of maxims—Kant's term of art for representing willings. Although one cannot say anything about moral judgment without using maxims (the objects of judgment), it is not possible to be clear about maxims or maxim content until a much-elaborated characterization of moral judgment is in hand to indicate the work maxims are to do. My account of maxims is therefore piecemeal and not completed until the last chapter. This is not a tidy method, but it respects the mutual dependence of theory of action and theory of judgment that is the key to understanding Kant's ethics.

Work on this volume was supported in part by a fellowship from the John Simon Guggenheim Memorial Foundation and by generous leave time from the University of Southern California.

I have been helped at all stages by many good friends and colleagues. I owe special gratitude to Tom Hill, Chris Korsgaard, Onora O'Neill, and Andy Reath for their efforts at making my work better, and also for what I have learned from reading their own work on Kant's ethics. I also want to thank Ann Davis, Ruth Gavison, Amélie Rorty, Jerome Schneewind, and Carol Voeller for making available their time and support as it was needed. Mickey Morgan provided a constant source of philosophical good sense—often understanding where an argument was going before I did—a sometimes daunting battery of counterexamples, and standards of clarity and good writing that have improved my work at every level. I count myself more than lucky to be living with such a good philosopher and generous man. Thanks also to my son Danny for special help he knows he has given.

Finally, I owe much to Stanley Cavell, John Rawls, and Judith Jarvis Thomson. In addition to their guidance and support, they imparted a sense of the value of philosophy, the importance of asking the right questions, and the need to take time to get things right.

Contents

The Practice of Moral Judgment

Note on Sources

All references to Kant are to *Kants gesammelte Schriften, herausgegeben von der Deutschen Akademie der Wissenschaften* (formerly *Königlichen Preussischen Akademie der Wissenschaften*), 29 vols. (Berlin: Walter de Gruyter, 1902–). References to *Critique of Pure Reason* are to the standard A and B pagination of the first and second Prussian Academy editions.

Kritik der reinen Vernunft (1st ed., 1781; 2nd ed., 1787), vols. 3 and 4.
> *Critique of Pure Reason,* trans. N. Kemp Smith (New York: St. Martin's Press, 1965). Abbreviated in text as KrV with page numbers.

Grundlegung zur Metaphysik der Sitten (1785), vol. 8.
> *Groundwork of the Metaphysics of Morals,* trans. H. J. Paton (New York: Harper and Row, 1964). Abbreviated G.

Kritik der praktischen Vernunft (1788), vol. 5.
> *Critique of Practical Reason,* trans. L. W. Beck (Indianapolis: Bobbs-Merrill, 1956). Abbreviated KpV.

Die Religion innerhalb der Grenzen der blossen Vernunft (1793), vol. 6.
> *Religion Within the Limits of Reason Alone,* trans. T. M. Greene amd H. H. Hudson (New York: Harper and Row, 1960).

Die Metaphysik der Sitten (1797), vol. 6 (in two parts: *Metaphysische Anfangsgründe der Rechtslehre* and *Metaphysische Anfangsgründe der Tugendlehre*).
> *The Metaphysics of Morals,* trans. Mary J. Gregor (Cambridge: Cambridge University Press, 1991). Second part *(The Doctrine of Virtue)* abbreviated DV.

Anthropologie in pragmatischer Hinsicht (1798), vol. 7.
> *Anthropology from a Pragmatic Point of View,* trans. Mary J. Gregor (The Hague: Martinus Nijhoff, 1974).

1

On the Value of Acting from the Motive of Duty

IT HAS quite reasonably been a source of frustration to sympathetic readers that Kant seems to claim that a dutiful action can have moral worth only if it is done from the motive of duty alone. The apparent consequence of this view—that an action cannot have moral worth if there is supporting inclination or desire present—is, at the least, troubling in that it judges a grudging or resentfully performed dutiful act morally preferable to a similar act done from affection or with pleasure. To many, sympathetic or not, it has in addition seemed contrary to ordinary judgment to withhold the accolade of moral worth from actions done from "good" motives other than the motive of duty. These concerns cut deeply, challenging the intuitive basis in ordinary moral knowledge that is essential to Kant's argument.

There are strategies that might be employed to disperse the problem of moral worth. One might note that the discussion of moral worth is brief and unique to the *Groundwork of the Metaphysics of Morals* where it plays a bridging role between the announcement of the unconditioned goodness of the good will and the Categorical Imperative as its principle. Kant may not have accorded moral worth the doctrinal importance we give it and so was not attentive to the kinds of cases that concern us. We might then amend his account. While it is indeed important to locate moral worth in the full argument of the *Groundwork,* Kant seems careful enough about the cases and quite clear about his conclusion: an act has moral worth if and only if it is done from the motive of duty.

Alternatively, one might accept this conclusion but seek to give it diminished importance within the general Kantian argument. It is because one takes the doctrine of moral worth to contain Kant's central claim about the moral goodness of persons that restriction of moral worth to actions done from the motive of duty seems so objectionable. Kant has much to say elsewhere—especially in *The Doctrine of Virtue* and *Religion Within the Limits of Reason Alone*—about virtue and the moral disposition that supports caution about the scope of the doctrine of moral worth. But one cannot, I think, avoid the importance of the idea that *one way* of acting—from one motive—is given moral preeminence. So even if Kant has an account of moral virtue that makes room for other motives and traits, if the virtuous disposition represents a good will, then it (its virtue) will be expressed in actions done from the motive of duty.

It is best to take a direct approach to the doctrine of moral worth: we need to understand the moral question that Kant thought required "dutiful action done from the motive of duty" as an answer. Both sympathetic and hostile critics of the doctrine take the question to be obvious: What motive (or motives) distinguish the actions of the good moral agent from those of the agent whose actions are merely morally correct? If the dour "the motive of duty alone" is Kant's response to *this* question, it is not surprising that it has provoked harsh reactions.[1] If, however, the question is not the one Kant asked, then these reactions may not be in order. Since we proceed against the grain of traditional interpretation, we will do well to go slowly.

I

Kant introduces the concept of moral worth in the *Groundwork* as part of the opening account of the good will. The paragraphs that precede its introduction present the two basic facts about the good will: it is unqualifiedly good (and the only thing that is), and it is good only because of its willing, not because of its success in producing effects. With this characterization of the good will, what is needed, Kant says, is "to elucidate the concept of a will estimable in itself and good apart from any further end."[2] That is, we need to see what good willing looks like. Kant proceeds by taking up

> the concept of duty, which includes that of a good will, exposed, however, to certain subjective limitations and obstacles. These so far from hiding a good will or disguising it, rather bring it out by contrast and make it shine forth more brightly. (G397)

What follows is the discussion of moral worth and the examples of "acting for the sake of duty."

---

1. And the reactions have been extremely harsh: from the mockery of Schiller's verse, to the dismissive arguments of philosophers responsive to the virtues, to the angry contempt of contemporary philosophical feminists. It has seemed incredible that Kant could have held such a view *and* claimed authority for it in ordinary moral knowledge.

2. *Groundwork of the Metaphysics of Morals*, p. 397; hereafter cited G with page numbers from the Prussian Academy edition.

The way the examples are set up suggests that they are offered as cases in which good willing is perspicuous, rather than as the only kinds of cases in which good willing is present or can be known. If this is correct, and it is good willing in an action that "moral worth" honors, we need to see exactly what the "subjective limitations and obstacles" reveal about good willing (and so about moral worth) before we can generalize to correct conditions of attribution of moral worth.

Staying with Kant's presentation: the key to good willing is to be found in an examination of the motive someone has in performing a dutiful act *for the sake of duty.* Kant seems to think that what is special about this motive is revealed by contrasting it to other motives that, in at least some circumstances, can also lead to dutiful actions. He proceeds by looking at examples of two kinds of action that are "according to duty" but are not performed from the motive of duty, and so are said not to have moral worth: (1) dutiful actions done because they serve the agent's self-interest (the shopkeeper example) and (2) dutiful actions that are just what the agent wants to do—those for which he is said to have an "immediate inclination" or interest (the sympathy, self-preservation, and happiness examples).

The crucial question, obviously, is: *why* is it not possible that these nonmoral motives give dutiful actions moral worth? We will look at the two most famous of Kant's examples to see whether they provide a clue to what Kant thinks is of value in the actions he says have moral worth.

The shopkeeper example. We want to see whether this example makes clear what significant moral difference there is between doing a dutiful action (treating people honestly, giving inexperienced customers the correct change) from the motive of self-interest (or profit) and doing the same action from the motive of duty. One may say: when you do a dutiful action from duty, you do it because it is what duty requires; when you do it from self-interest, you do it for some other reason. This is hardly wrong. But it is uninformative about *why* doing an action "because it is what duty requires" is of any moral importance.

The details of the example are instructive. The dutiful action is not to overcharge inexperienced customers. When there is considerable competition, Kant points out, it is good business not to overcharge, and so the sensible shopkeeper's business interests *require* him to act honestly in such circumstances. The message is plain: while it is *always* morally correct to serve people honestly (we can assume this for the example), acting from an interest in making a profit will require honest actions in only *some* circumstances—there may be times when honesty is not the best policy.

It seems, then, that the moral fault with the profit motive is that it is unreliable. When it leads to dutiful actions, it does so for circumstantial reasons. The businessman's interest in the dutiful action is controlled by (Kant says: mediated by) his interest in his business, and whether he acts well or not depends on the paths that circumstances open for the pursuit of his business goals. This example suggests the need for a motive that will guarantee that the right action will be done. But the sympathy example suggests that this is only part of the story.

The sympathy example.[3] Here is a person who would help others from an *immediate* inclination: he helps others because that is what he wants to do; helping others is not the means to some further end he has. In Kant's words, "there are many spirits of so sympathetic a temper that, *without any further motive of vanity or self-interest,* they find an inner pleasure in spreading happiness around them" (G398, emphasis added). Now if, following the shopkeeper example, the issue here is the reliability of the motive (wanting to help others), we have a problem. In the shopkeeper example it seemed plausible to argue that the interest in profit was inadequate as a moral motive[4] because the likelihood of such a motive producing morally correct action was dependent on contingent and changeable circumstances. But here, where the right action is given as helping another, and that is just what the person has an immediate inclination to do, there can be no complaint that this motive will lead to other sorts of action in changed circumstances. But if the motive of sympathy yields right actions, why isn't it judged to be a motive producing actions with moral worth?

Kant says that such an action,

> however right and amiable it might be, has still no genuinely moral worth. It stands on the same footing as [action from] the other inclinations—for example, the inclination for honor, which if fortunate to hit on something beneficial and right and consequently honorable, deserves praise and encouragement, but not esteem; for its maxim lacks moral content, namely, the performance of such actions, not from inclination, but *from duty.* (G398)

The inclination for honor is criticized in two ways: it is described as only "fortunate" to hit on something right; and the maxim of the action it prompts is said to lack moral content. Is the motive of sympathy only fortunate when it hits on a right action? Doesn't it necessarily prompt a person to help others? Suppose I see someone struggling, late at night, with a heavy burden at the backdoor of the Museum of Fine Arts. Because of my sympathetic temper I feel the immediate inclination to help him out. We

---

3. I consider here only the first part of the sympathy example, since it most clearly addresses the question of the moral value of the moral motive. The reading of the whole example comes after this question is resolved, and we have a clearer sense of what it is for an action to have moral worth (see section IV).

4. "The moral motive" and "the motive of duty" I use interchangeably. In asking whether something could be *a* moral motive I am asking whether it could be a motive that gives an action moral worth.

need not pursue the example to see its point: the class of actions that follows from the inclination to help others is not a subset of the class of right or dutiful actions.

In acting from immediate inclination, the agent is not concerned with whether his action is morally correct or required. That is why he acts no differently, and in a sense no better, when he saves a drowning child than when he helps the art thief. Of course we are happier to see the child saved, and indeed might well prefer to live in a community of sympathetic persons to most others, but the issue remains. The man of sympathetic temper, while concerned with others, is indifferent to morality. In Kant's language, the maxim of his action—the subjective principle on which the agent acts—has no moral content. If we suppose that the *only* motive the agent has is the desire to help others, then we are imagining someone who would not be concerned with or deterred by the fact that his action is morally wrong. And, correspondingly, the moral rightness of an action is no part of what brings him to act.

On this reading of the sympathy example it would seem that Kant did not reject such emotions as moral motives because they could not be steady and strong, or because they were essentially partial.[5] Even if, for example, sympathy could be strengthened to the force of habit, and trained (as Hume suggests) toward impartial response, it would still generate morally correct actions only by accident. For while sympathy can give an interest in an action that is (as it happens) right, it cannot give an interest in its being right.[6]

I said of the shopkeeper example that the person's motive was to make a profit, and so his hitting upon a right action was also, in this way, a matter of luck. The economic circumstances that happened to prevail required honest actions as the necessary means to business ends. So in this example, too, the denial of moral worth to an action is intended to mark the absence of interest in the morality of the action: that the shopkeeper's action was morally correct and required was not a matter of concern to him.

This suggests a more general thesis. Even if social institutions were arranged to guarantee that profit and honesty went together (through penalties, social sanctions, and so on), the performance of honest actions,

5. A sharply argued version of this criticism can be found in Bernard Williams, "Morality and the Emotions," in *Problems of the Self* (Cambridge: Cambridge University Press, 1973), pp. 226–228.

6. Whether *any* emotion could give an agent a moral interest in an action is a question that must look first to an account of the emotions (of what it is to say of a motive that it is an emotion). For Kant, the answer is clearly no; he holds that no emotion or inclination can make the moral law the determining ground of the will, since they determine the will according to the principle of happiness. See *Critique of Practical Reason* (hereafter cited KpV) 92–93 and G401n.

so motivated, would still be no more than "fortunate": that is, dependent on external and contingent circumstances. Maximizing the number of honest transactions is not what moral worth looks to. And a concern with moral worth will not encourage the social manipulation of circumstances so that people just find themselves doing what is right.

What can we conclude? This reading of the two examples does not (and is not intended to) give us an account of what moral worth is or a clear idea of the conditions for its correct attribution. It does suggest why Kant thought that there was something the matter with a dutiful action performed from a nonmoral motive: nonmoral motives may well lead to dutiful actions, and may do this with any degree of regularity desired. The problem is that the dutiful actions are the product of a fortuitous alignment of motives and circumstances. People who act according to duty from such motives may nonetheless remain morally indifferent.

Taking the limits of nonmoral motives as a guide, we can introduce a minimal claim. For a motive to be a moral motive, it must provide the agent with an interest in the moral rightness of his actions. And when we say that an action has moral worth, we mean to indicate (at the very least) that the agent acted dutifully from an interest in the rightness of his action: an interest that therefore makes its being a right action the nonaccidental effect of the agent's concern.

II

If we now see why a dutiful action does not have moral worth when done from a nonmoral motive alone, what can we say of the dutiful actions that *are* done from the motive of duty where the agent *also* has nonmoral interests in the action? This is the problem of the overdetermination of dutiful action.

The overdetermination of actions is a general phenomenon. It is quite common for us to have more than one motive for what we do, and even more than one motive that by itself would be sufficient to produce a particular action. Although Kant never explicitly discusses overdetermined moral cases, where an action is done from the motive of duty and from some other nonmoral motive, there is a tradition of reading Kant— especially the sympathy example—as holding that the mere presence of the nonmoral motive signifies a lack of moral worth. On this reading, the value that moral worth marks depends on the motive of duty acting alone.

The key text is in the second stage of the sympathy example. In the first stage of the example, Kant considers a man of sympathetic temper who does what is right (he helps others where he can) because he finds "an inner satisfaction in spreading joy and rejoice[s] in the contentment which [he has] made possible" (G398). As we have seen, Kant says that while such an action is "dutiful and amiable," it has no moral worth. In the second stage, Kant imagines "this friend of man" so overcome by sorrow that he is no longer moved by the needs of others. Kant continues:

> Suppose that, when no longer moved by any inclination, he tears himself out of this deadly insensibility and does the action without any inclination for the sake of duty alone; then for the first time his action has its genuine moral worth. (G398)

As one commentator responds: "Surely the most obvious way of generalizing from this remark yields the doctrine that only when one acts from duty alone—'without *any* inclination'—does his act have moral worth."[7] If one accepts this generalization—and it is traditional to do so—then one is faced either with the grim interpretation of moral worth or with the need to revise the doctrine to include cooperating nonmoral motives in a less stringent requirement. Although I think the generalization drawn from the passage is neither obvious nor necessary, there is insight to be gained from the difficulties that come with trying to accommodate it.

An instructive example is Richard Henson's attempt to take the sting out of the doctrine of moral worth by diminishing the significance of the *Groundwork* view. Drawing on the account of duties of virtue in the later *Metaphysics of Morals,* Henson argues that Kant can be seen as having another and benign conception of moral worth—he calls it the "fitness-report" model—according to which a dutiful act would have moral worth "provided that respect for duty was present and would have sufficed by itself [to produce the dutiful act], even though (as it happened) other motives were also present and might themselves have sufficed."[8] This is the model that is to do the basic work of crediting moral agents for doing the right thing in the right way. By contrast, Henson suggests we understand the *Groundwork*'s conception of moral worth on the analogue of praise acknowledging victory against great odds (say, powerful desires tempting one away from duty), calling it, appropriately, the "battle-citation" model. If the conditions of action include supporting inclinations, and especially if the inclinations are sufficient by themselves to produce the dutiful act, then there is no great victory and no reason for praise. And, as Henson remarks, in honoring a person who has struggled morally and won, "we mean of course to encourage others who find themselves in comparable straits: but

7. Richard Henson, "What Kant Might Have Said: Moral Worth and the Over-determination of Dutiful Action," *Philosophical Review* 88 (1979), 45.

8. Ibid., p. 48. The original version of this chapter was written in response to Henson's essay.

we emphatically do not mean to encourage anyone to try to *bring about* such situations"[9] in which this sort of praise is appropriate. It need not be a fault if one never earns a battle citation for one's dutiful actions.[10]

The two-model approach to moral worth leaves Kant acquitted of the damaging charge that he believes it morally desirable not to want to do the action you morally ought to do. And each of the models of moral worth captures a natural form of moral praise. But the success of the two-model strategy depends on the adequacy of either model to capture the moral point of Kant's account of moral worth: that a right or dutiful action is performed is the nonaccidental effect of the agent's moral concern.

According to the fitness-report model, overdetermined actions can have moral worth so long as the motive of duty is *sufficient by itself* to produce the dutiful action. But what it means for the moral motive to be "sufficient by itself" is unclear. It could mean sufficient if alone—that is, cooperating motives would not be required to bring about the dutiful action. Or it might be a stronger condition: if at the time of the action the agent had some conflicting motives, the moral motive was capable of bringing about the dutiful action without the aid of cooperating motives. Neither of these quite natural interpretations will support a satisfactory account of moral worth. It is instructive to see why they cannot.

Overdetermination involves cooperation between moral and nonmoral motives. Knowing this much does not reveal the conditions of cooperation. For the most part, two motives will cooperate to produce the same action only by accident.[11] As circumstances change, we may expect the actions the two motives require to be different and, at times, incompatible. But then, on either reading of sufficient moral motive, an agent judged morally fit might not have a moral motive capable of producing a required action "by itself" if his *presently* cooperating nonmoral motives were, instead, in conflict with the moral motive.[12] That is, an agent with a sufficient moral motive could, in different circumstances, act contrary to duty, from the *same* configuration of moral and nonmoral motives that in felicitous circumstances led him to act morally.

9. Ibid., p. 50.

10. The battle-citation metaphor suggests powerful, serious, difficult-to-control conflict. But the metaphor exaggerates the case. Dutiful action from a moral motive in the face of temptation is an ordinary and natural part of moral life. Indeed, the introduction of such conflict would be a necessary part of a moral education if its occurrence were not inevitable.

11. Part of the task of moral education is to shape a person's character so that the alignment of moral and nonmoral motives can be depended upon.

12. The weaker version may not yield a dutiful action in the presence of any conflicting motive. The stronger version takes care of only motives that in fact conflict with the moral motive at the time of the action. It is not set up to deal with motives that *might have* produced conflict.

Consider a shopkeeper whose honest actions are overdetermined. On the fitness model, a shopkeeper with a sufficient moral motive will perform honest actions even if the profit motive is absent. But the fact that the moral motive was sufficient by itself in the overdetermined case does not imply that he would perform honest actions when the profit motive clearly indicated that he should *not* act honestly. What does this tell us? Looking at the possible outcome of the original configuration of motives in altered circumstances introduces the suspicion that it might have been an accident that the agent acted as duty required in the *first* case: the explanation of his dutiful action might have been the absence of conflict with the profit motive. In what sense, then, was the shopkeeper morally fit? Surely to say that an action had moral worth we need to know that it was no accident that the agent acted as duty required.

There are two paths that can be taken here. (1) If the moral motive would have prevailed in altered circumstances (where the presently cooperating nonmoral motive instead indicated some other, incompatible, course of action), then the success of the moral motive in the case at hand was not dependent on the accident of circumstances that produced cooperation rather than conflict. This suggests a move to a greater-strength interpretation of sufficiency. While such a move solves the problem with the fitness model, it would pose a serious difficulty to an argument like Henson's for two models of moral worth.

On a greater-strength interpretation of the fitness model, an action can have moral worth only if the moral motive is strong enough to prevail over the other inclinations—without concern for whether they in fact cooperate or conflict. Henson's battle-citation model of moral worth differs only in that the moral motive has had to prevail. We do give different praise to the man who we know would be courageous than we do to the man who is (though why we do is a matter of some puzzlement), but there is no difference in the structure and strength of the two men's motives. Henson is right to point out that it is not morally desirable to be in circumstances where the moral motive has to win out, and so we are under no moral requirement to put ourselves in situations where we will earn such praise. But it is hardly plausible to see *this* difference in praise as marking a distinct notion of moral worth—since there is no difference in moral motive or the configuration of motives in the two cases. The only difference is in the circumstantial accident of cooperation or opposition of the nonmoral motives in the presence of an overpowering moral motive. A greater-strength interpretation of sufficiency would then undermine the claim that there were *two* notions of moral worth in Kant, and leave us with just the battle-citation model's powerful moral motive.

There are more substantive questions raised by a shift to a greater-strength interpretation of sufficiency, however. It is not at all clear that we should require of the moral motive that it be stronger or be able to prevail in altered circumstances in order to attribute moral worth to a given action. Even if circumstances tomorrow are such that the alignment of moral and nonmoral motives breaks down, and the dutiful action is as a result not done, it is surely possible that the dutiful action that *is* done today, when the motives are aligned, has moral worth. (In much the same way, succumbing to temptation only *raises* a question about motives in past cases.) Moral worth is not equivalent to moral virtue.

The problem is this: the experiment of imagining altered circumstances while holding fixed a given configuration of moral and nonmoral motives suggests that a dutiful action's being performed may be an accident of circumstances even with the presence of a sufficient moral motive (in Henson's original sense). While it seems reasonable to credit an action with moral worth only if its performance does not depend on an accident of circumstances, it seems equally reasonable to allow that failure in different circumstances does not require denial of moral worth to the original performance. With strength its only variable, the sufficiency account cannot satisfy both reasonable requirements.

(2) Both conditions could be met by a configuration of moral and nonmoral motives such that in acting dutifully it is the moral motive itself on which the agent acted. When this configuration holds, it would be no accident that the dutiful action was done, since it was just the agent's concern to act as duty required that determined his acting as he did. In different circumstances, if the configuration remains the same, the agent will again act dutifully. If he does not, it can only be from a different configuration of motives—one in which he is acting from some motive other than the motive of duty. But this failure to act dutifully would provide no reason to discredit the dutiful action in the original case. Thus the difficulties that emerge with the notion of sufficiency support a literal reading of Kant's requirement that dutiful actions be done *from* the motive of duty: the presence of a moral motive sufficient to produce the dutiful action does not show that the interest that in fact determined the action was a moral one.[13]

Support for this third alternative to strength and fitness can be found in the *Critique of Practical Reason* (92–93),[14] where Kant denies any necessary opposition between moral and nonmoral motives, including the "principle of happiness." What is required is that where there is a question of duty, we "take no account" of the claims of happiness; we are not required to renounce them. For an action to have moral worth, the nonmoral motives

13. Henson acknowledges such an account as an alternative to his fitness and battle-citation models of moral worth, but rejects it because he believes there are no adequate criteria for deciding the factual question of which of a number of motives an agent actually acted on (p. 44). By itself this is a weak argument. We often need to insist that although we had a motive we did not act on it. Unless this were so, there would be little room for moral insincerity.

14. See also G400–401 and *Theory and Practice* 278–279.

(which are empirical and therefore belong to the principle of happiness, not the moral law) "must be separated from the supreme practical principle and never be incorporated with it *as a condition*" (emphasis added). It seems natural to conclude that when an action has moral worth nonmoral motives may be present, but they may not be what moves the agent to act. But it is not obvious how a motive could be present and yet not operative. To make sense of the third alternative, we need to complicate our understanding of motives in Kant's theory of action.

From the perspective of a familiar empiricist account of motives, the third alternative is unintelligible. It is easy to see why. If one takes motives to be desires, and desires are a kind of cause, when a motive is present it should have an effect (direct or indirect) on choice or action.[15] In line with this, one would suppose that cooperating motives add force in a given direction of action, and conflicting motives interfere with or even cancel each other (at the extreme). A prudential or a moral motive would be just another kind of desire, distinguished, presumably, by its object. What moves an agent to act is the resultant of these vector-like forces.[16] On such an account of motives, it will seem that the only way to satisfy the moral-worth requirement—that acting from the motive of duty not be an accident—is to require that the outcome of the agent's present configuration of motives be invariant through changes in circumstances. The implausibility of the latter requirement then counts against the former one. We plainly cannot use this kind of account of motives to make sense of Kant's view.

The key to understanding Kant is in the idea that moral worth does not turn on the presence or absence of inclination supporting an action, but on its inclusion in the agent's maxim *as* a determining ground of action: as a motive. Kantian motives are neither desires nor causes. An agent's motives reflect his *reasons* for acting. An agent may take the presence of a desire to give him a reason for action as he may also find reasons in his passions, principles, or practical interests. All of these, in themselves, are "incentives" *(Triebfedern)*, not motives, to action. It is the mark of a rational agent that incentives determine the will only as they are taken up into an agent's

---

15. Holly Smith, canvassing this way of understanding moral worth, remarks, "Since I find problems in understanding the idea of a desire that exists but has no connection with the agent's choice, even though it is a desire to perform or to avoid performance of actions available for choice, I shall not discuss this suggestion." See "Moral Worth and Moral Credit," *Ethics* 101 (1991), 290–291n. Interestingly, she finds no issue in couching a claim about motives in the language of desires. A similar objection to the idea of motives not acted on can be found in Paul Benson, "Moral Worth," *Philosophical Studies* 51 (1987), 365–382.

16. This is of course a crude version of the empiricist view. In particular, it leaves out the complexity of structure that comes with second-order desires. Nevertheless, something very much like the crude version is at work in the critical debate about Kant's doctrine of moral worth.

maxim. Indeed, it is only when an agent has a maxim that we can talk about his motive.[17]

The man of sympathetic temper responds to suffering *and* takes that response to give him a reason to help. Only then does he act from the motive of sympathy. An action that is done from the motive of duty is performed because the agent finds it to be the right thing to do and takes its rightness or requiredness as his reason for acting. He acts from the motive of duty with a maxim that has moral content.

On this view of motives, an agent could act from more than one motive in more than one way. It may be that neither of two incentives alone gives the agent sufficient reason to act (assuming a "favorable balance of reasons" principle). Then the agent may act from a combined motive. Or an agent may have incentives that provide two independent sufficient reasons for an action. Clearly no dutiful action from a combined motive could have moral worth. The harder question is whether there is anything wrong with taking both moral and nonmoral incentives into one's maxim as independently sufficient motives. Since a dutiful action has moral worth because the agent takes the fact that an action is morally required to be his reason for action—it is morality that guides his will—the presence of a nonmoral motive in his maxim is disqualifying.[18]

What we should now say about the preferred (third) alternative is this: when an action has moral worth, nonmoral *incentives* may be present, but they may not be the agent's motives in acting. If the agent acts from the motive of duty, he acts because he takes the fact that the action is morally required to be the ground of choice. It does not follow from this that the action's moral worth is compromised by the presence of nonmoral feelings or interests, so long as they are not taken by the agent as grounds of choice: as motives. Thus one can say both that an agent's doing the right thing is nonaccidental because he acted from the motive of duty *and* admit that he might not have acted from this motive in altered circumstances. Strictly speaking, the doctrine of moral worth can accept the overdetermination of action with respect to *incentives,* not motives.

One might still object that, on this account of moral worth, it remains a matter of luck or accident that an agent acted in a morally worthy way. The strength of competing inclinations, the presence of circumstances that evoke competition, the strength of the moral motive itself may be affected

---

17. Evidence for this account of motives can be found throughout Kant's practical philosophy. It is perhaps most clearly laid out in the introduction to the *Metaphysics of Morals.*

18. I take the conjunction of motives in one maxim to imply a principle that makes each the condition of acting on the other. More puzzling is the disjunctive motive, "Do the right thing because it is right *or* because it promotes some nonmoral good." Here as well the motive of duty would not be the determining ground of the will, not because of some condition but because the principle is one of indifference.

by chance. The effect of chance, however, is on *who* is able to act in a morally worthy way. It poses a distributive problem that belongs to the theory of moral virtue and not to moral worth. It is *actions* and not agents that are credited with moral worth.[19] And although it may be a matter of luck *whose* actions have moral worth, what moral worth expresses is the relation of a motive to an action (through its maxim). When an agent does act dutifully from the motive of duty, when his maxim of action has moral content, it is not a matter of luck that the *action* has moral worth.[20]

III

The scope of the motive of duty is not restricted to morally worthy actions. It applies as well to actions that are merely correct or permissible: actions whose maxims satisfy the conditions set by the Categorical Imperative. Since it is possible to act in accordance with duty, but not from duty, it is obviously possible to have a morally correct action and only a nonmoral motive for acting on it. But for an action not required by duty, what can the moral motive add when the maxim already passes the Categorical Imperative's tests?

Our discussion of why *dutiful* actions should be done from the motive of duty suggests an answer: in acting from the motive of duty, the agent sets himself to abide by the moral assessment of his proposed actions. Suppose you have something you want (for whatever reason) to do. What the motive of duty provides is a commitment to do what you want only if the maxim of your action is judged morally satisfactory.[21] If it does pass

19. This may not seem so clear, for the moral worth of an action is said to be in its maxim (G399): the expression (in rule form) of an agent's volition (what the agent is moved to do and for what reason). Thus there is a sense in which moral worth *is* about agents—it is about their willings. The point of saying that it is actions that are credited with moral worth is to highlight the relationship between *an* action and *its* motive (via the action's maxim), which is where moral worth resides (and not in the permanent structure of an agent's motives: that is the matter of virtue —see DV46). The opposite view is argued in Keith Simmons, "Kant on Moral Worth," *History of Philosophy Quarterly* 6 (1989), 85–100.

20. Here I disagree with Thomas Sorrell, "Kant's Good Will," *Kant-Studien* 78 (1987), 87–101, who argues that if moral worth signifies good willing, and the good will is a will that can never be bad, an action cannot have moral worth unless it is done from a good will. This erases the distinction between moral worth and virtue that I would draw. I see no reason why good willing cannot be present in a will that is not altogether good. We do not always give moral concerns priority—and so our will is not good—but sometimes we do.

21. Motives other than duty can appear to produce this result: someone might believe that the road to salvation lies in satisfying the Categorical Imperative. The only difference here is in the motive: the end (satisfying the Categorical Imperative), and so the actions taken, will be the same. That is, the difference is in the nature of the agent's attachment to his end. In the one case, Kant could argue, it is the realization through the Categorical Imperative of the agent's dignity as a rational being; in the other, the attachment to the Categorical Imperative

the test, you are free to act, and the motive of duty as well as your original motive are satisfied. The difference introduced by the motive of duty is that one would *not* have acted on the original (nonmoral) motive had the maxim of action it prompted been morally unsatisfactory (failed the Categorical Imperative tests).

This aspect of the motive of duty fits a general pattern of motives that do not themselves have an object (in the ordinary way), but rather set limits to the ways (and whether) *other motives* may be acted upon. For example, a concern for economy is a motive that, by itself, does not normally lead one to do anything. It leads one to consider whether something that is wanted for other reasons is also a good value. That is, the motive to economy does not have a role to play unless another motive to action is already present. Then it says to act as you plan to only if what you would do is economical (as well as whatever else it is). If there is conflict between my desire for something and my more general concern for economy, that does not indicate what I will do: motives like that for economy may be easily (and sometimes appropriately) set aside for the satisfaction of other desires. (We often experience this as a kind of quasi-moral guilt; sometimes it is a release from inhibition.)

Following Kant, let us say that such motives provide *limiting conditions* on what may be done from other motives (usually primary, or initiating, motives).[22] Cooperation is then seen as the case in which the limiting condition sanctions acting on the primary motive; it does not merely, and independently, push along with it. Similarly, conflict does not consist in opposing tugs, but in the action suiting the primary motive failing to satisfy the limiting condition. What, in the end, will be done does involve an issue of strength. But the strength metaphor alone masks the complexity of the interaction.

When the motive of duty functions as a limiting condition, there is no lessening of the agent's moral commitment if he acts from the motive of duty *and* nonmoral motives, so long as the motive of duty is effective: its satisfaction is decisive in the agent's going on with his proposed action. Rather than posing a moral obstacle, the nonmoral motive is in most cases

depends on a desire to be saved. Giving up the idea of an afterlife might require that such a person remotivate his attachment to morality. The attachment to the Categorical Imperative that comes from the motive of duty does not depend on the maintenance of such extramoral beliefs (although such beliefs may be needed to reinforce moral commitment).

22. A primary motive is one that can, by itself, produce action. Limiting conditions may also be directed at other limiting conditions—lexically, or in some other structure (with or without conflict among them). Insofar as a motive functions as a limiting condition, all it can require is that the actions prompted by *other* motives satisfy its condition. The problem of disjunctive motives does not occur here because the moral motive is the condition of acting on the nonmoral motive.

necessary if the motive of duty (as a limiting condition) is to have an object of interest. As Kant sees it, moral deliberation characteristically begins with a nonmoral interest or motive that prompts consideration of an appropriate course of action.[23] Ordinary moral life is embedded in desires for ordinary things, desires that lead to different kinds of action in different circumstances. My need for money may send me to the bank, to work, or to a deceitful promise, depending on the situation in which I must act to meet my need. Whether I will be tempted to act in a morally impermissible way will likewise depend on contingent and variable circumstances. If we follow Kant, it is what happens next that is the crucial moment for the moral agent. Once I am aware of what I want to do, I must consider whether it is morally permissible. If I have an effective motive of duty, I will act only when I determine that it is. I then act in the presence of more than one motive, satisfying both my nonmoral desire *and* the motive of duty. This is the normal state of affairs for someone with a sincere interest in doing what is right.[24]

Although as a limiting condition the motive of duty can enter only when there is a proposed course of action based on another motive, it is unlike many other motives that impose limiting conditions since it can, by itself, move an agent to act. The clearest case of this is, of course, in morally worthy actions. There are also certain kinds of action that cannot be done at all unless done from the motive of duty (as a primary motive). For example, not every act of bringing aid is a beneficent act. It is beneficent only if the agent conceives of what he is doing as an instance of what *any* moral agent is required to do when he can help another, and acts to help for that reason. For Kant, only the motive of duty could prompt someone to act on a maxim with such content—for no other motive responds to a conception of action that regards the agent himself impersonally or is impartial in its application.

The motive of duty cannot, by itself (as a primary motive), prompt merely permissible actions, for it is by definition a matter of moral indifference whether they are performed. (We might say, with Kant, that the maxims of permissible actions have no moral content.) The role of the motive of duty here can only be in the background, as an effective limiting condition, requiring that the agent not act contrary to duty. If the agent loses interest in his proposed course of action, the motive of duty can have nothing to

---

23. This is clear in the way he presents instances of moral deliberation. For example: "[A person] finds himself driven to borrow money because of need. He well knows that he will not be able to pay it back; but he sees too that he will get no loan unless he gives a firm promise to pay it back . . . He is inclined to make such a promise; but he still has enough conscience to ask 'Is it not unlawful and contrary to duty to get out of difficulties in this way?' " (G422).

24. Such actions can be described as overdetermined in the sense that they satisfy more than one motive. They are not overdetermined in Henson's sense, where each motive must be sufficient by itself to produce the action.

say about what he should do until another course of action is proposed (other things morally equal). In other words, permissible actions cannot be done "from the motive of duty." Therefore merely permissible actions, even when they are performed on the condition that they are permissible (that is, even when the motive of duty is effective as a limiting condition in them), cannot have moral worth.[25]

For an action to be a *candidate* for moral worth, it must make a moral difference whether it is performed. (Only then is it even possible for the action to be done from the motive of duty.) For an action to *have* moral worth, moral considerations must determine how the agent conceives of his action (he understands his action to be what morality requires), and this conception of his action must then determine what he does. (It is when this condition is satisfied that a maxim of action has moral content.[26]) That is, an action has moral worth if it is required by duty and has as its primary motive the motive of duty. The motive of duty need not reflect the only interest the agent has in the action (or its effect); it must, however, be the interest that determines the agent's acting as he did.

Earlier we noted that the discussion of moral worth was introduced by Kant to illuminate the nature of good willing (good of itself, without regard to any further end). Now we can see why good willing is found in actions that have moral worth: in them, the agent need not be concerned with anything other than the morality of what he does in order to have sufficient motive to act. If the maxim of an action is an expression of an agent's will in acting, to say that the maxim of a dutiful action done from the motive of duty has moral content is to say of the agent's will that it is ultimately determined by "that preeminent good which we call moral" (G401).

---

25. One might want to say that, in permitting myself to act only when and because my maxim satisfies the Categorical Imperative, I *am* doing an action that has moral worth, since it is done from the motive of duty. But it is the permitting and not the action permitted that would have moral worth. (In permitting myself another glass of wine I am not acting on the same motive I will be acting on when I drink it.) Since it is not clear to me how there can be a *duty* to act on maxims that satisfy the Categorical Imperative (the Categorical Imperative tells you what your duty is), I would rather treat the permitting as acting on the moral motive in its limiting condition function, thereby indicating an attitude of virtue rather than moral worth.

26. Thus a dutiful action performed on the condition that it is permissible (that is, from the motive of duty as a limiting condition only), will not have moral worth, even if it is no accident of circumstances that the dutiful action is done. Its not being an accident is only a necessary condition for moral worth. In the case of a perfect duty, for example, only those maxims of inclination that include the required action will be permissible (G401n). So an agent with a policy of never acting impermissibly will (nonaccidentally) act as perfect duty requires. When inclination and duty coincide, however, he may act with no other conception of his action than as a permissible means of satisfying inclination. That is, he may act dutifully, with no sense that his action is required, from a maxim that has no moral content.

It is clear that the role of the motive of duty is considerably more extensive than the illustrative examples in the *Groundwork* might lead one to believe. This is especially important in providing some idea of the moral cast given to ordinary action in the theory. Although we should never act contrary to duty, the function of the motive of duty is not to press constantly for *more* dutiful actions, or to get us to see the most trivial actions as occasions for virtue: rather it is to keep us free of the effects of temptations in ordinary situations that can suggest morally prohibited courses of action. It is only in its function as a primary motive that one acts *from* the motive of duty at all, and only those actions that are required (by the Categorical Imperative) *can* have the motive of duty as a primary motive. As a limiting condition, the motive of duty can be present in (or satisfied by) an action, and yet that action have no moral import. Thus we can preserve the sense in which, for Kant, the motive of duty is ubiquitous—governing all our actions—without having to accept the view that all of our actions must be seen as matters of duty.

IV

At this point we need to return to the *Groundwork*'s sympathy example to see how our account of moral worth and the moral motive fares interpretively. That is, we want, in its terms, an analysis of the value of acting with moral worth that satisfactorily explains Kant's apparent insistence that only the action done from the motive of duty alone has moral worth.

Earlier I suggested that the problem with the natural motive of sympathy is that the interest it gives an agent in his action is not a moral interest. The man of sympathetic temper is one whose helpful actions, however steady and genuinely beneficial, are motivated by his natural response to the plight of others. He acts because he is moved by others' distress. As such there is no moral component in his conception of what he does. Therefore nothing in what motivates him would prevent his acting in a morally impermissible way if that were helpful to others, and it is to be regarded as a bit of good luck that he happens to have the inclination to act as morality requires.[27] What is missing is an effective and motivating moral interest in his action: the source of the action is not the moral motive itself (he is not acting

---

27. One might, of course, cultivate an inclination because of its recognized moral utility. In *Doctrine of Virtue* (hereafter cited DV) 125 Kant distinguishes between what we might call "natural" and "moral" sympathy: the latter appears to be the moral motive making use of our natural propensity to care about the welfare of others to promote "active and rational benevolence." The message for us is in the clear subordination of the natural to the moral motive. We are not morally better off without natural sympathy.

beneficently), nor is he committed to refraining from helpful actions that are not permissible. That is to say, his action neither has moral worth nor indicates an attitude of virtue.

If the moral motive *is* effective and motivating, it would seem that the presence of a nonmoral inclination should have no effect on the action's moral worth. That is, even if the moral motive expresses but *one* kind of interest the agent has in the helpful action, so long as it is the moral motive the agent acts on, the action should have moral worth. Indeed, what is morally valuable in actions judged to have moral worth seems prominently displayed in cases of this type: the dutiful act is chosen without concern for its satisfying other incentives the agent may have.

What, then, can we make of Kant's supposed insistence that only when there is no natural inclination to help can the helping action have moral worth? The key to the sympathy example is found in attending to the fact that it describes the moral situation of the *same man* in two different circumstances: the "friend of man," no longer moved by the needs of others, is the man of sympathetic temper with whom the discussion begins. Straightaway we should ask why Kant would think *this* change of circumstances for *this* man is revelatory. At the least, the emphasis on an individual should make us cautious about how we generalize from the case.

Let us follow Kant. The first part of the sympathy example looks at the helping act of the man of sympathetic temper. We concluded that there is good reason to find moral fault in the dutiful action done from inclination alone. Kant says that this action has no moral worth. In the second part of the example, we are to suppose that things change for the man, and his natural concern for others becomes ineffective. We need not imagine that his character changes—he is still a man of sympathetic temper; changed circumstances have called forth other, more powerful inclinations, which have made him unable to feel for others or disinclined to concern himself on their behalf. Looking to inclination *alone* for motivation, then, he cannot act to help. Kant supposes that he does act in the face of this "deadly insensibility," from the motive of duty. That such an action is judged to have moral worth is in no way problematic. What has seemed unwarranted is the claim that in acting "without any inclination—then for the first time the action has its genuine moral worth." And it would be if it were an instance of the generalization "only when there is no inclination to a dutiful action can it have moral worth." We come to a quite different conclusion, however, if we see the passage as a set of remarks about one (kind of) person, a man of sympathetic temper who normally helps others because he is stirred by their need but sometimes, when his feelings are dimmed, helps them because that is what duty requires. Of *him* it is then said: only when the inclination to help others is not available does *his* helping action have moral worth. For of him it was true that when he had the inclination he did not act from the motive of duty. This does not imply that no dutiful action can have moral worth if there is cooperating inclination. Nor does it imply that a sympathetic man could not act from the motive of duty when his sympathy was aroused. The account is of a kind of temperament we are tempted to value morally, designed to show how even dutiful actions done from apparently attractive motives might yet be morally wanting.

We should expect confirmation of this interpretation in the other examples Kant offers in this section, and it will be worth reminding ourselves of their detail to see it.[28] Immediately after the shopkeeper example, which describes an action "done neither from duty nor from immediate inclination," Kant considers the duty of self-preservation:

> to preserve one's life is a duty, and besides this everyone has also an immediate inclination to do so. But on account of this the often anxious precautions taken by the greater part of mankind for this purpose have no inner worth, and the maxim of their action is without moral content. They do protect their lives in conformity with duty, but not from the motive of duty. When on the contrary, disappointments and hopeless misery have quite taken away the taste for life; when a wretched man, strong in soul and more angered at his fate than fainthearted or cast down, longs for death and still preserves his life without loving it—not from inclination or fear but from duty; then indeed his maxim has a moral content. (G397–398)

I think that one reads this as *obviously* supporting the "no-inclination" generalization only by ignoring what Kant seems to be taking elaborate pains to say: most of the time people act to preserve their lives with no regard to its being a duty (and often with no regard to morality at all), simply because they have an inclination to self-preservation. This seems true enough. *If* it is a duty to preserve one's life, then Kant would surely be right in saying that most self-preserving acts have no moral worth. Here, as before, we could point to a lack of interest in the morality of such actions. There is a willingness, from the point of view of the inclination to self-preservation, to act in a morally impermissible way; and with the absence of such inclination, "when disappointments and hopeless misery have quite taken away the taste for life," no reason remains to preserve the life no longer cared about. The conclusion is that actions motivated by the inclination to self-preservation alone have no moral worth. And since, as a matter of fact, most self-preserving actions come from this source, "the

---

28. It is unfortunate that such exclusive attention has been lavished on the sympathy example, for it is difficult to see its point given the obvious attractiveness of the kind of person it criticizes. The striking similarity of detail in the self-preservation and happiness examples is easily overlooked once one is convinced that Kant has made the argument "if inclination, no moral worth" in the sympathy case.

often anxious precautions taken by the greater part of mankind for this purpose have no inner worth."

Now the contrast. We imagine a person who normally acts to preserve his life because he wants to keep living. Circumstances change, his "taste for life" is gone; death appears as a more attractive alternative to continued life.[29] If inclination were all that now prompted his actions, what once led him to self-preserving actions would now lead him to act contrary to duty. He then acts to preserve his life from the motive of duty; *that* self-preserving action has moral worth. The conclusion: for most of us, most of the time, self-preserving actions stem from inclination alone and have no moral worth. Sometimes, some people, when they have no inclination to preserve their lives, may yet do so from the motive of duty. For such a person, only then, and for the first time, would his self-preserving action have moral worth. Nothing in this account speaks against the possibility of an action with more than one incentive having moral worth. As with the sympathy example, what is being examined is the dutiful act done from immediate inclination *alone*. The point of the discussion is to reveal what is added, morally, when a person acts from the motive of duty. It is easier to see what is added when all inclination is taken away.[30]

We can see this structure of argument again in Kant's discussion of the indirect duty we have to promote our happiness. He begins with the observation that the motive for most of the actions that conform to this duty is the ordinary desire to be happy ("the universal inclination towards happiness"). Such actions, plainly, have no moral worth. As with the sympathy and self-preservation examples, the argument looks at the actions of a particular man (in this case someone suffering from gout), whose altered circumstances direct an inclination that ordinarily conforms to duty away from it. The gout sufferer is in the odd situation where he cannot act according to the (indirect) duty to promote his own happiness unless he acts from the motive of duty. This is so because the inclination toward happiness *in him,* in his special circumstances, is distracted by present pleasure, when,

29. There is surprising subtlety in this example. Why, one might wonder, does Kant insist on someone "strong in soul" and angered by his fate, rather than someone depressed or weak? Is it that a weaker person might turn to morality as a comfort? Or perhaps he is interested in cases where the choice against morality seems strongest, most rational. The resolution of this does not affect the larger interpretive question. The presence and the quality of the detail do suggest a kind of concern with a particular case that should quickly warn one off easy and large generalizations.

30. Beck notes that when Kant discusses the use of examples in *Second Critique* 92–93 he compares himself to a chemist separating a compound (of motives) into its elements: Kant's purpose in using cases that present conflict between moral and nonmoral motives is merely to precipitate the motive of duty, and not to present conflict as a condition for moral worth. See Lewis W. Beck, *A Commentary on Kant's Critique of Practical Reason* (Chicago: University of Chicago Press, 1960), p. 120n.

for the sake of happiness, he ought to abstain and seek good health. If he follows inclination, *in these circumstances,* he will act contrary to duty, although ordinarily he would not. (Pleasure and happiness frequently coincide.) Kant concludes that when the gout sufferer acts to promote his happiness from the motive of duty (choosing health over pleasure), "for the first time his conduct has a real moral worth." Here again the example directs us to refrain from giving moral value to inclination, however likely it is to promote dutiful actions, because of the accidental nature of the connection between *any* inclination and duty. When the inclination alone prompts a morally correct action, there is no moral worth because, in Kant's terms, there is no moral content or interest in the volition (maxim). Nothing in the example forces the reading that it is the mere *presence* of the inclination that is responsible for the denial of moral worth. The moral failure is seen when, in the absence of the motive of duty, and so of a moral interest in the action, circumstances may be such that inclination alone gives the agent no reason to do the dutiful action. Indeed, in acting from inclination alone, the agent *never had* a reason to do what morality required.

What can be said in summary about these three examples? They concern men motivated to dutiful actions by different kinds of inclination.[31] Exactly what normally motivates their acting according to duty leads them to act impermissibly when changed circumstances direct the inclination to something other than a dutiful action. It is said of *these* men that their dutiful actions have moral worth only when, in the altered circumstances (where inclination does not in fact support a dutiful action), they nonetheless act, from the motive of duty alone. Then, for the first time, they show a moral interest in their action. For it is only then that they act from the motive of duty at all. If there is any obvious generalization to be taken from these cases, it has to do with the moral inadequacy of nonmoral motives.

If an agent does not have an independently effective and motivating moral interest in an action, although he may act as duty requires, there remains a dependence on nonmoral interests that compromises his ability to act morally. One need not be indifferent to the possible satisfactions that a dutiful action may produce. It is just that the presence of such possibilities should not be the ground of the agent's commitment to acting morally. Overdetermined actions *can* have moral worth so long as the moral motive is the determining ground of action—the motive on which the agent acts.

---

31. Each of the examples deals with a different category of inclination: the inclination to self-preservation is an instinct; a sympathetic temper is a natural (to human beings) disposition; the desire for happiness is based on an empirically determined Idea.

Morality is not to be merely one of the things, among others, in which we have an interest.

When someone acts from an effective and primary moral motive, it could well be said that such a person is morally fit. But the nature of this fitness includes more than the presence of a moral motive sufficient to produce a dutiful action. It expresses a kind of independence from circumstances and need, such that in acting from the motive of duty, we are, as Kant saw it, free.

2

Integrity and Impartiality

MOST OF US were brought up on the idea that moral theories divide as they are, at the root, either deontological or consequentialist.[1] A new point of division has been emerging that places deontological (mainly Kantian) and consequentialist (mainly utilitarian) theories together against theories of virtue,[2] or a conception of morality constrained at the outset by the requirements of the "personal."[3] In a series of important essays Bernard Williams has offered striking arguments for the significance of the personal in moral thought based on the role of integrity in human activity and character.[4] His criticisms of both Kantian and utilitarian theories for their deep-seated tendencies to undermine the integrity of persons brings to a new level of seriousness and subtlety long-standing complaints against these theories—the invasive do-gooding of utilitarianism, the coldness and severity toward normal human concerns of Kantian theory. Although Williams is inclined to find the sources of the attack on integrity in these different features of the two traditional theories, in the end his complaint against

---

1. This chapter differs from the earlier published version primarily in the inclusion of the central argument of "Rules, Motives, and Helping Actions," *Philosophical Studies* 45 (1984), 369–377, as section I.

2. See, for example, G. E. M. Anscombe, "Modern Moral Philosophy," *Philosophy* 33 (1958), 1–19; Philippa Foot, "Virtues and Vices," in *Virtues and Vices* (Berkeley: University of California Press, 1978).

3. See, for example, Peter Winch, "Moral Integrity," in *Ethics and Action* (London: Routledge and Kegan Paul, 1972); Michael Stocker, "The Schizophrenia of Modern Ethical Theories," *Journal of Philosophy* 73 (1976), 453–466; John Kekes, "Morality and Impartiality," *American Philosophical Quarterly* 18 (1981), 295–303.

4. "A Critique of Utilitarianism," in J. J. C. Smart and Bernard Williams, *Utilitarianism: For and Against* (Cambridge: Cambridge University Press, 1973); "Morality and the Emotions," in *Problems of the Self* (Cambridge: Cambridge University Press, 1973); "Persons, Character and Morality," "Moral Luck," and "Utilitarianism and Moral Self-indulgence," collected in *Moral Luck* (Cambridge: Cambridge University Press, 1981).

both of them turns on their demand that the moral agent submit himself to the authority of impartial value.

For example, Williams argues that the basic utilitarian requirement—that the sum of utilities in a particular course of events (including other people's actual and proposed actions) should determine what the moral agent is to do—constitutes an attack on the agent's integrity "because it undermines the way his actions and his decisions have to be seen as flowing from the projects and attitudes with which he is most closely identified."[5] But if the requirement of integrity is that agents be able to treat their own projects and actions as (morally) special, the problem Williams finds with utilitarianism should occur within any moral theory that gives the central place in determining how the moral agent should act to the realizing of impartial value.[6]

In this chapter I will be concerned not at all with Williams' criticism of utilitarianism and very little with his positive account of integrity. I want instead to examine the use he makes of the connection between integrity and the personal to criticize Kantian moral theory. Williams sees Kantian theory as impinging on integrity in three main ways: (1) Kantian morality often demands that we care about the wrong thing—about morality—and not about the object of our action and natural concern; (2) it leads to an estrangement from and devaluation of our emotions, especially in the rejection of emotions as morally valued motives; and (3) it insists on dominion over even our most basic projects and intimate commitments, demanding a degree of attachment to morality that alienates us from ourselves and what we value.

I

The first line of argument goes this way. In Kantian ethics, impartial value is represented by an abstract moral principle, the Categorical Imperative. The moral agent—one who acts from the motive of duty—strives to act as the Categorical Imperative requires.[7] The inadequacy of action so motivated is perspicuous in morally motivated helping actions. Because the Kantian agent acts to bring about what moral principle requires, he is concerned in helping only indirectly with the welfare of others. His helping is a means to satisfying moral principle. In acting *from* the motive of duty, the Kantian

5. "A Critique of Utilitarianism," pp. 116–117.

6. That agent-impartiality, and not utilitarianism's treating states of affairs as the ultimate bearers of all value, is at the root of Williams' dissatisfaction with utilitarianism is also argued by Nancy Davis in "Utilitarianism and Responsibility," *Ratio* 22 (1980), 24–25.

7. See Williams, "Persons, Character and Morality," p. 2. The position I discuss in this section is developed more by those who associate themselves with Williams (such as Michael Stocker and Lawrence Blum) than it is in Williams' own work. I believe it represents a key assumption behind the critical arguments that Williams develops.

agent acts *for* the wrong thing. Kantian theory is thus unable to register the plain moral structure of caring about others, and the Kantian motive of duty is shown to be morally inappropriate in at least some cases of moral action. It would be better—morally better—to act on a motive of direct concern for the welfare of another.

This argument gets it wrong about what it is to act from principle or on a motive that gives an agent concern for the conformity of his action to principle. Consider how we describe acting from nonmoral practical principles. Suppose I alter certain eating habits because I am concerned about my future health. I do this because I accept and act from principles of prudence. I do not fail to be concerned with the object of my action (my future health) because I act from prudential principles. Indeed, prudence is not the object of my action at all. I *am* interested in my future health because prudential considerations move me. What motivates me explains my interest in my future health; it does not stand in the place of my future health as the object of my action. It is the requirements of health I must attend to, and not prudence, if I am to determine the appropriate means to future health. Principles of prudence regulate and guide my actions; they do not stand between me and the natural object of my concern.

Errors about these matters can come from thinking that "motive" and "end" (the object of action) are merely reciprocal concepts. They can be, but they are not always so. The end is that state of affairs the agent intends his action to bring about. The motive of an action, what moves the agent to act for a certain object, is the way he takes the object of his action to be good, and hence reason-giving. The motive explains his interest in the end. Thus a given end of action—helping a friend—can be the object of various motives: compassion, prudence, fear of rejection, and so on. The different motives affect my conception of what I am doing, its value and point for me; they give sense or meaning to the state of affairs I bring about. And the same motive can prompt the choice of different objects of action, given variations in circumstances as well as other interests an agent has. A full account of what an agent is doing must therefore include both motive and end (the union, in action, of fact and value).

In this light, let us look at the way a moral principle enters an account of morally motivated action. Consider a case of acting from the motive of duty according to the principle, "Keep the promises you make." (Call this principle *P*.) The motive of duty prompts me to act as morality (or *P*) requires: to do what is right. What the motive of duty prompts me to do, then, is to keep my promise. The object of my *action* in following *P* is to do whatever it is I promised to do. I am moved to do this thing because *P* requires it; that is my reason for doing it, the nature of my interest in it. I am not trying to bring about "kept promises" or even "my kept promises." (I will not have made the world a morally better place if I make and keep more promises than I now have reason to do.) I am trying to do what I promised because I promised to do it: that is, I act from the motive of duty.

Moreover, the motive of duty is the appropriate motive to act from in such a case. Suppose I kept my promise out of concern for the pain my breaking it would cause. This is not only *not* morally better than keeping my promise from the motive of duty (although someone acting this way would still satisfy *P*); it is not a *keeping* of a promise at all. The function of the promise in such a case is merely as a background fact that explains why someone will suffer if I do not do what he expects me to do.

One important reason why moral rules have been thought to be the object of dutiful action is that there has been a failure to see *how* rules enter a moral agent's motivational commitments. There is a tendency to think of moral rules introducing moral content into action by identifying right and wrong actions. Thus the role of moral rules is seen to be in the agent's determination of what he ought to do: rules structure deliberation. The attachment of a motive to a rule understood in this way suggests that in acting from such a motive, what I want to do is to act as the rule dictates (to instantiate it, as it were). We might call this an "externalist" view of moral rules. The agent is seen as attached to the rules as a source of authoritative guidance. But moral rules do not characteristically guide action in the way that someone in authority gives orders. And we are not characteristically moved simply to ensure that rules are not disobeyed.

Ignored in this externalist picture is the fact (and the way) that moral rules are learned. We acquire knowledge of how, morally speaking, things work, and we employ our knowledge in determining what we should do. Moral rules are internalized; when learned in the right way, they are a constitutive part of the agent's conception of himself as a person. They are neither memorized rules (as Ryle pointed out, they are not the sort of thing that can be forgotten), nor are they present as mere habits of response. In knowing such rules, we know how to go on. It is not appropriate here to consider how such rules are learned. But if they have the status in the life of a moral agent that I suggest, the relation of motives to moral rules will not take the form of trying to obey them (or bringing about the condition of their satisfaction). Moral action can be an arena for self-expression.

Consider various ways one might satisfy a rule (or a duty) to help others. Suppose in each case that someone is in danger and I recognize he needs help that I could easily give.

1. The dutiful case. The object of the action is to save this person; the motive is to provide morally called-for help.
2. The emotion-based case. The object of the action is to save this person; the motive is compassion: I am moved to help by this person's plight.

3. The rule-fetishism case. The object of the action is to do what moral principle (or the duty to help) requires; the motive is to act in conformity with duty.
4. The personal-relation case. The object of the action is to save George; the motive is to save my friend George.

Case 4 is of interest because it is the only one of the four ways of helping that includes truly personal concern for the person saved. When the person saved is my friend, concern for his safety involves a concern for him and failure to save him will involve real loss for me. In this respect, the emotion-based act is just as impersonal as the dutiful act. For there to be loss and personal concern there must be attachment. Compassion involves affective connection with others; this is not itself a ground of, though it may lead to, attachment. (Because compassion is not an emotion that involves prior attachment to individuals, it, unlike motives of friendship, allows a degree of substitution.)

The critical comparisons are between cases 1 and 3, and 1 and 2. It seems to me clear that many who find fault with the motive of duty see the helping action and its motive on the model of the rule-fetishism case. There we do have the sense of a person ticking off his dutiful actions from a list of moral requirements, viewing the case of saving a life as just another item (perhaps differing in gravity) of the same kind as keeping a promise, refraining from lying, and so on. Those who benefit from the rule-fetishist's help do so as circumstantial beneficiaries: their need becomes an occasion for rule satisfaction.

But rule-fetishism, as we have seen, is not an appropriate model for acting from the motive of duty. It is in the dutiful case (2) that the agent acts from his moral concern to help as he can (the help being something he acknowledges he has a duty to provide). He does not act to save this person in order to fulfill (fill) his duty, nor does he act to avoid failing to do what he ought to do. He acts to provide help: this is what he ought to do. Moral rules describe what our duties are; they are not the objects of dutiful actions. The rules direct that, in certain circumstances, actions of a certain sort are to be done. A moral rule that requires us to help will direct us to provide help, not to follow rules.

In helping from a motive of duty, my interest in helping is a moral interest. This means that I will take some things and not others as sufficient reasons for helping and for refraining from giving help. When the motive for helping is compassion, a different set of reasons and excusing conditions is relevant. The motive involved makes you think about your action in a different way. On an "internalist" view, moral rules give shape to the agent's desire to be a moral person. Here it is worth noting that the role of the motive of duty is more like that of compassion than one might think. A compassionate person (one to whom it is a good that he is moved by feelings of compassion) does not act in order to be compassionate or to do the compassionate thing. His actions are expressions of his compassion. In a similar way, when Kant describes the actions of the moral person, they are presented as expressions of his "respect for duty."

This structural similarity does not answer the objection that there may be something that emotion-based helping allows or provides that dutiful helping omits or prohibits (cases 1 and 2). For example: when helping is prompted by feeling for the person's plight, that feeling persists beyond the attempt to give help, coloring the response to both success and failure. So the engagement of my emotions leads me to feel joy when the person is saved (joy for him, for the end of his difficulty), since it leads me to feel sorrow or sadness if he cannot be saved. Is the person acting from the motive of duty untouched by these things? Can he care about what happens once he has done what duty requires?[8] There are two issues here: one about right feeling, the other about continuity of motivation. If the motive of duty cannot meet these additional concerns, it would be deficient as a human moral motive.

Let us suppose the moral agent feels nothing beyond satisfaction when things go well and distress at not being able to succeed if they go badly. Is there some fault in this? Should he feel more or differently? If he fails to save a person in need, his distress is directed at *what* he has been unable to do: save this person. Since the object of his action has importance, his distress will have intensity and content appropriate to that object. (Here compare the frustration at not being able to find your keys.) Similarly, his pleasure if he succeeds will be pleasure at having saved this person—not pleasure at his having saved someone (in the sense of anyone), but pleasure that this person had been saved. These are different feelings from the feelings of sorrow and joy that the person who acts from emotion-based motives might feel, but they seem to me neither inappropriate nor wanting. Even in the extreme case, where there is need but nothing can be done, the motive of duty would not leave the agent unmoved. The motive of duty leads the agent to acknowledge the claim of need, and requires that he do what he can to help. Being unable to help while acknowledging the claim of need, it will be natural to feel regret at being unable to satisfy the need. (We do not fault the emergency-room physician or the triage nurse for not experiencing extreme sorrow when they cannot help someone, though there is surely regret at the limits of what they can do.)

If an attempt to save someone fails, one may not have done all that is possible and so may need to continue or renew efforts. Can the motive of duty provide this continuity of motivation? (Having an end for which you

8. The question is asked and answered in the negative by Lawrence Blum, in *Friendship, Altruism, and Morality* (London: Routledge and Kegan Paul, 1980), chaps. 2 and 7.

make but one attempt would be quite special—"I'll give it one shot"—or circumstances might be such that no more than one attempt was possible.) Insofar as one makes the attempt to save out of acknowledgment of a morally valid claim on one's help, one *must* continue to act so long as the claim remains valid or there are no counterweighing reasons to desist (say, a threat to one's life). Again, one does not help in order to satisfy a moral rule; the rule requires that you take the need of another as a reason to help. So, in this dimension, the motive of duty functions at least as well as the emotion-based motive in maintaining the agent's attachment to the goal of saving someone through unsuccessful attempts.

There are two distinct points here: both kinds of motives can give the agent a continuing interest in saving the person's life; they do not do so in the same way. In acting from the motive of duty, it is the moral claim on available resources that "attaches" the agent to the end. Nonmoral motives identify different aspects of the circumstances of need as reason-giving, and thus construct the attachment differently. We understand neither the agent nor the action when we ignore the way motives introduce reasons that determine the agent's conception of his action and end.

II

It is this fact—that motives construct the attachment to ends—that is the key to understanding the larger disputes between Bernard Williams and the Kantians about emotions and moral motives. As Williams sees it, Kant dismissed emotions as moral motives (suitable to give an action moral worth) on the grounds that they are not reliable. Indeed, if emotions are capricious they would not be suitable moral motives: one could not expect consistency of response in morally similar cases, or that the emotion as motive will always be available (given that emotions cannot be summoned when needed), or that the emotions will be invariable in the right way (they can be affected by morally irrelevant factors). By contrast, because in acting on the motive of duty one is acting on principle, morally similar cases will be treated consistently; attachment to a principle is not emotional, and therefore stable; and, given the moral content of the principle, morally irrelevant elements are excluded from the start.

Williams has a strong, straightforward response: emotions are not capricious—at least, not necessarily. The Kantian objection

> posits a crude view of the emotions themselves; it suggests that there is no way of adjusting one's emotional response in the light of other considerations, of applying some sense of proportion without abandoning emotional motivation altogether.[9]

9. "Morality and the Emotions," p. 226.

Moreover, we often take emotional capriciousness to be a *moral* (and correctable) fault. Someone whose feelings of sympathy were capricious—characteristically here today and gone tomorrow—would not only fail to possess the virtue of sympathy, but would be criticized for not having his emotions under control.

Focus on reliability, however, mistakes the issue the Kantian should want to raise (and the issue I believe Kant had in mind). Williams is right in rejecting the capriciousness argument. What he misses is the difference in structure that emotions as motives impart to actions. Imagine a set of emotions cured of both capriciousness and narrowness: we might suppose the relevant emotions inculcated as habits of response and broadened in scope so that we do not respond only to those we already care for. A judicious Kantian would still not be satisfied, for even with an agent who habitually had reliable and available emotional responses, actions from such emotions would "hit on something right and beneficial" (Kant's phrase, G398) in the wrong way: that what is done is morally right is a contingent fact about the way the agent acts.

In acting from a motive attached to a moral principle, the moral rightness of the action gives the agent reason for action. In action from emotion (say, responding to someone's need for help from feelings of sympathy or compassion), this is not so. It is not that someone who acted from emotion would frequently fail to act rightly: he might and he might not. The connection between sympathy and helping someone is not fortuitous; the connection between helping someone and doing what is right is. The person we are moved to help may be doing something we should (morally) oppose and not promote; someone may be better off, even morally better off, for not being helped. Emotion-based motives fail to support the necessary internal connection between the motive and the rightness of a proposed action. This is why Kant holds that maxims of action based on the motive of sympathy have no "moral content."

Williams might accept this account of why Kant held that emotions could not do the same job as the motive of duty.[10] But I think he would then want to say that even if the motive of duty secures a special connection to the performance of morally correct actions, the exclusion of the emotions as motives can stand in the way of an agent's acting in a natural and humanly appropriate way. Say someone helps a friend out of the motive of duty, where failure to help would be a moral failure. What seems lacking is the appropriate attitude and reason for action. The help is offered because of a commitment to morality and not from a feeling of care and concern

---

10. Since I am introducing detail into arguments that Williams has only sketched, I am not sure he would develop the arguments in just these ways.

for a friend.[11] "You don't care about *me*," we can imagine the friend complaining, "you are here only out of a sense of duty."

The worry is that if the Kantian agent is required to act from the motive of duty, then when morality is at issue, his responses to others will be less personal, less an expression of his feelings for them. The motivational structure of Kantian morality might then be thought to undermine an agent's integrity by requiring that he dissociate himself from natural and appropriate responses to others. This would be especially grave in relations of love and friendship which call for such personal response.

What seems to be assumed in this argument is an either-or structure to Kantian moral motivation: that is, *either* the agent acts from the motive of duty and so impersonally, *or* he acts from an emotion-based motive and in so doing is morally deficient. We need to look further at what is involved in acting from the motive of duty to see why this is not the case.

First of all, it is not the function of the motive of duty to bring about moral states of affairs. Some kinds of motives do lead us to try to realize states of affairs (hunger: eating); others direct us to act from one motive rather than another (these are sometimes called higher order motives); still others may best be described as "limiting condition" motives. These last permit us to act as we will on the condition that our action satisfies some additional requirement (that we stay within our budget, not break some rule, and so on).

In the wide range of cases, the role of the Kantian motive of duty is as such a limiting condition: it expresses the agent's commitment that he will not act (on whatever motive, to whatever end), unless his action is morally permitted. Thus, in the case of bringing aid to someone in need, it would be quite ordinary for the action of the normal moral agent to be overdetermined: he might act from the emotion-based desire to help (meeting the other's need would then be the direct object of his action), *and* he would act from the motive of duty (the permissibility of what he was doing would be a necessary condition of his acting to help). The helping action is not thereby made the means to some further object of the agent's concern. Refusing in advance to act in ways that are morally impermissible is not the same as taking the object in acting to be the bringing about of morally permissible states of affairs.

If the claim against the motive of duty was that whenever it is present and effective in controlling the way someone acts it excludes the influence of emotions as motives, or makes the agent unable to respond directly to the need of another, when the motive of duty functions as a limiting

---

11. The fault here is not necessarily one of moral self-indulgence. The agent can want to do the right thing without also being concerned with his own moral display: that *he* is the one doing something right.

condition, neither of these claims against it are valid. As a limiting condition, the motive of duty in fact requires the effective presence of some other motive. Its role is to prevent the agent from embarking on impermissible acts the agent has an independent interest in pursuing. So one could well be prompted by feelings of sympathy to give help, while committed (in advance, by the motive of duty) not to do this if it turned out to be morally wrong (what the other needed aid in doing was impermissible; the agent himself had more serious obligations that would be neglected if he followed his feelings here, and so on). Likewise, since the motive of duty as a limiting condition does not direct the agent to act for any end, insofar as in acting from emotions as motives the agent is able to respond "directly" to the other, the regulative presence of the motive of duty cannot alter the direction of response.

More serious problems emerge where the motive of duty functions as a primary motive, one sufficient by itself to bring the agent to do what is morally required.[12] It is, after all, possible to give help from the motive of duty alone—and surely morally worthy action requires more than commitment to permissibility. Now, while the Kantian holds that it is better to act out of principle with no other motive present than it is to act out of feeling or emotion with no attention to principle, it does not follow that acting in the absence of emotions is desirable. There is reason to encourage the complementary influence of emotions even when the motive of duty is sufficient to bring about the required action. An agent whose emotions cooperate with the motive of duty has a desirable kind of internal unity; it is a good thing, from the agent's point of view, that internal struggle over doing what is right is diminished. Struggle with recalcitrant inclination is no special mark of moral virtue. Indeed, Kant thinks we are required to engage our natural sympathetic feelings, to place their special sensitivity to others at the service of beneficence, in order to increase the range of cases where we may be of help (DV456).

The Kantian claim is rather that the complementing of the motive of duty by nonmoral emotions cannot be morally necessary. That is, the motive of duty must be by itself sufficient to bring about whatever is morally required. Nonmoral incentives may add to the action (sweeten it, as it were),[13] but

---

12. The motive of duty cannot, as a primary motive, direct the agent to merely permissible actions, for it is a matter of moral indifference whether such actions are performed. In cases of dutiful action, the motive of duty can be the primary motive (with other motives present); something else can be the primary motive and the motive of duty functions as a limiting condition only; or a nonmoral motive can lead to the performance of a dutiful action without any involvement of the motive of duty (or knowledge that the action is required).

13. Kant does not hold that morality is the *sole* source of value. The Highest Good, after all, requires happiness as well as moral goodness.

if they are not present, nothing that could be morally required is thereby out of reach for the agent acting from the motive of duty.

Williams objects to this aspect of the fundamental Kantian claim on the grounds that what a person may need is the benefit of some "human gesture": a helping act that is of value to the recipient *because* it is "the product of an emotional response."[14] The problem is not that without the presence of emotion no help will be offered, but that the kind of help that can come from the motive of duty is not the kind of help that is needed. If a person can need the support of the human gesture, then it seems we might need something that cannot be had through the motive of duty alone. This leads Williams to argue that since it may be rational to prefer an emotion-based to a morally motivated action, it may be rational (sometimes) to place higher value on nonmoral than on moral conduct. And if this preference for nonmoral value is rational, "the value of moral men becomes an open question."

Is this argument compelling? Does the value of morality (of the moral man) depend on our preferring to have as much of it as we can? Must a Kantian set morality the task of providing satisfaction for all human needs? I do not think a Kantian must view morality as pervasive in this way. Ubiquitous, yes. But that is the matter of requiring that in the pursuit of what we value we do not act in morally prohibited ways.

Rather than consider what refinements might be introduced to improve Williams' argument, let us see whether the deep intuition behind it can be accommodated in a Kantian view of moral motivation. We should start by reviewing the conditions for assigning moral worth in a case of a helping action done by someone with *both* moral and emotion-based incentives.[15] Mistakes about this may be responsible for the tension Williams marks between moral demands and Kantian moral requirements.

The necessary condition for a dutiful action having moral worth is that the action be done from the motive of duty. When the action is overdetermined (both incentives would be sufficient by themselves as motives to produce the dutiful action), it must be the motive of duty itself on which the agent acted for the action to have moral worth. That is, we would not say the helping action had moral worth unless it was the idea that it was morally required that led to the giving of help. If the moral incentive is present but does not produce the action—that the action is morally required is not what brings the agent to act—there is no reason to credit the action

14. "Morality and the Emotions," p. 227.

15. An incentive is a motivational potential. An agent will act from the motive of duty when he has a sufficient moral incentive *and* accepts that moral reasons determine what to do in his circumstances. The review of moral worth is a summary of the argument of Chapter 1, section II.

with moral worth. (Kant would say that the maxim the agent in fact acted on, since it was adopted for nonmoral reasons, had no moral content.)

Now, if the agent who is to help has both sorts of incentive available *and* acts in a morally worthy way, Williams would say the recipient of the needed help might still have grounds for complaint. The mere presence of emotions and feelings will not eliminate the sense of inappropriateness when someone who cares for him comes to his aid out of a sense that it is the morally required thing to do. The feelings seem to be secondary; the concern for *him* second to the moral desire to bring aid to a needy person (who he happens to be). Such a sense of being treated badly seems to me in order. But if it is rational to prefer the emotion-based action over the dutiful one (even where emotions are present), then we would have to conclude that it is not always desirable to do a dutiful action in a morally worthy way.

Can a Kantian accept that it is better, in some cases, that a morally worthy act not be done? Can he allow that there are occasions when we could act from the motive of duty but it would be better if we did not? One is inclined to say no because of the place in Kantian theory assigned to the good will. It is of supreme intrinsic value, it is the sole thing ("in this world or out of it") that is unqualifiedly good, and it is good willing that morally worthy actions done from the motive of duty express.

This negative answer assumes that good willing is present only in actions done from the motive of duty. But not all things required of the Kantian agent are required *actions*. For example, the duty of beneficence requires that the agent adopt a general maxim expressing a willingness (a commitment) to help others sometimes. Let us suppose, without argument, that what this amounts to is that we commit ourselves to help those in real need or distress, when we can and when the help given does not involve great cost to ourselves.[16] A helping act is a beneficent act only if the agent offers help from the motive of duty—if the agent conceives of what he is doing as an instance of what any moral agent is required to do when he can relieve another's distress, and acts to help for that reason. Only such helping acts have moral worth. But we are also required to adopt a general policy: to be willing to help when the need is there. As we adopt this policy, we conform to moral requirements and do so from the motive of duty. It seems right to say that when we commit ourselves to a policy of beneficence from the motive of duty, our will is good. But this good willing is not necessarily expressed in action.[17]   Moral worth is the mark of

16. There is usually good reason to think that if someone never offers help, he could not sincerely be committed to beneficence. But it is possible that a combination of unlikely circumstances, lack of resources, or a person's own great need would make his never helping anyone compatible with a strong commitment to beneficence.

17. One might argue that a general policy commitment involves a continuing act of the will, and so it is the act of willing that has moral worth. I would resist this idea, since it is more

good willing in the sphere of action. It is not the only expression of the good will.

What I am suggesting is that the good will is as much present in the settled and sure commitment to beneficence as it is in the helping action done from the motive of duty. Thus in a case where one is unable to act beneficently (you do not have the necessary resources; someone else provides the needed help), one's will is not less good, so long as the general commitment to beneficence remains. It follows, then, that if the circumstances are such that one can aid, and one does, one does not have a better will just for being able to act effectively. We probably will perform more acts with moral worth the better our will is. The number of morally worthy acts performed, however, is not proportional to the will's goodness. (Making many promises and keeping them all from the motive of duty would surely increase the number of morally worthy acts performed. It would not indicate the presence of a spectacularly good will. Moral worth is an expression of good will in our actions. It is not a quantitative measure of good will.)

The problem that initiated this discussion of moral worth and the good will was that it seemed difficult for a Kantian to allow that a helping action that might be done from the motive of duty (in a morally worthy way) would be better if done from some other motive. If the relationship between moral worth and good willing is as I have suggested, it is no longer obvious that the Kantian must prefer the beneficent (morally worthy) action to the helping action done from a nonmoral motive.

Imagine a case where X needs help and both A and B can help him. A's help will be prompted by the motive of duty, B's will be emotion-based. X prefers being helped by B, because B's help is an expression of his feelings for X. On what grounds might one suppose the Kantian had to think either that X ought to prefer A's help, or that it would be better (morally) that A help? Only, it seems to me, if the Kantian holds that it is always morally preferable that when an action that would have moral worth is available, it should be done. This thought makes sense only if the choice not to do the action that would have moral worth made someone's will less good. But as A is prepared to act beneficently, he has a good will. It will not be improved if he acts, nor will it be diminished if, in a case like this, he refrains from action, deferring to B, whose help will bring X greater satisfaction. The duty of beneficence directs us to take the need of others as a reason for acting. If X is helped by B, A knows that X's need is met. Beneficence requires that A be concerned with X's good; it does not require that A be the one who brings it about that X has what is good for him. So if X's need would be

---

natural to describe such moral commitments in the language of virtue. I take this to be the view Kant adopts in the *Doctrine of Virtue*.

met by the actions of either A or B, and X would prefer the help of B, the duty of beneficence does not prevent A from deferring to B.

If there is no loss of good will when a person willing to act beneficently defers to someone whose helping action is in other ways more appropriate, the same conclusion should be possible in the case of a single person. Suppose C's friend Y needs help. C has a settled and sure commitment to helping others, and his personal feelings for Y also move him to help. There is no moral reason why C would have to help Y beneficently: that is, help him with the sense of doing what any moral agent is required to do for any person with such need. He would be acting no less well in deferring to his feelings than A was in the earlier case when he deferred to B. As C was ready to help without regard to his feelings, and so from the motive of duty, he fully satisfied the moral requirement of beneficence. We might say: given his feeling for Y, C had no need to act out of a sense of duty.[18]

This suggests a reason why we should seek to produce "moral men." I may prefer that my friends help me out of their feelings for me, but it is rational to prefer that they be morally prepared to help as well, so that in the absence or distraction or exhaustion of such feelings they will still be there for me. It would only be if such moral preparedness stood in the way of acting from feelings that we might feel we had to choose between people with fully developed moral sensibilities and people of feeling. I do not think it does, although the issues involved are too complex to argue the matter here. What I have hoped to show is that there is nothing in the Kantian conception of good willing that requires an absolute preference for actions done from the motive of duty as a primary motive. What Kantian theory does require is that the motive of duty always be present and effective in its limiting condition function. The Kantian moral agent is one who is motivationally prepared not to act in ways that are wrong. This is the routine expression of his autonomy.

We can now answer the challenge that the motive of duty in Kantian ethics undermines integrity by devaluing the direct emotional responses we have toward others (especially those with whom we have strong ties of affection). If, as we have seen, it is not morally required that we always set

---

18. It is not different when the moral element in the case involves a perfect duty: an obligation to do something. While no one can keep my promises for me (though someone can be my delegate), if what I have promised to do is done by someone else first, there is no moral deficit so long as I was fully intending to do what I promised to do. Similarly, it is not necessarily deficient to do what one promised for some other reason. A promise is given when there is need to secure commitment to future performance. If conditions change such that there is no longer need for the promise—I promised then to do something that I would now do as an act of friendship—there is no fault if my act is motivated by friendship, so long as I remain aware of the fact and ready to act as I promised.

the motive of duty between our feelings and our response to others, Kantian theory seems able to respect this aspect of our integrity as persons.

III

In taking seriously the ubiquity and authority of the motive of duty in its limiting condition function, we engage with the third line of Williams' criticism of Kantian ethics. He argues that our integrity as persons is essentially connected with our having and acting on a set of projects that partially constitutes our character. Such projects and commitments make us the person we are: we identify ourselves with them; they mark us out from others. The importance of these projects to our identity is not in their uniqueness, but rather in the deep way they are ours: in acting from them we express ourselves in the world. How is all this threatened by Kantian moral principles that require us to regard ourselves and others impartially?

The argument seems to be this. In order to have reason to live at all, a person must have what Williams calls "categorical desires."[19] These are the desires that project a person into his own future, that provide him with a basis for caring that he exist rather than not. When these categorical desires support "ground projects" (so called because acting on them is basic to life's having meaning for the person whose projects they are), the possibility of conflict with the requirements of impartial morality has radical implications. The problem is that "impartial morality, if the conflict really does arise, must be required to win; and that cannot necessarily be a reasonable demand on the agent." This is so because "there can come a point at which it is quite unreasonable for a man to give up, in the name of the impartial good ordering of the world of moral agents, something which is a condition of his having any interest in being around in that world at all."[20] Thus the demands of impartial morality cannot respect, or make room for, the necessary and deeply personal conditions of individual character and integrity.

There is surely something true in the thought that our basic commitments and loves may be such that they make us morally vulnerable: in order to sustain our ground projects, we may find ourselves wanting to do something that impartial morality condemns. And knowing that what we would do is wrong may not, in these cases, seem sufficient reason for us to desist. But Williams wants to claim something stronger. Suppose our ground projects are what give us a reason to go on with our lives at all. Then if impartial morality can interfere with the pursuit of a person's ground project, there will be cases where an agent *could not* have reason to act as morality

19. "Persons, Character and Morality," p. 11.
20. Ibid., p. 14.

requires, for the *only* reasons he will have for acting are those that direct him to the impermissible pursuit of his ground project. It is not just that some projects that give meaning to lives are immoral; *any* basic project, even the selfless concern for justice, may lead one into conflict with other moral commitments. So the Kantian idea that a rational agent will always have reason to act as morality requires is false. Since having ground projects is a condition of character (of having a character), the demands of impartial morality and those of character may conflict in deep ways.

This sketch of the relations between the conditions of character and morality places morality *outside* the projects that give meaning to a life, even when the projects the agent identifies with have moral content. But an attachment to impartial morality can itself be a project that gives a life meaning. It is a defining feature of Kantian morality that one basic attachment, one self-defining project, is morality itself.[21] (Kant describes the moral agent as someone who has a conception of himself as a self-legislating member of a kingdom of ends.) As one can define oneself in part through a variety of impersonally described roles (American, feminist, university professor), so living a moral life can be partially constitutive of character.

Williams could accept this much. The threat to character remains because being *one* among a set of ground projects does not capture the authoritative claim that Kantian morality makes. It is not the usual sort of project. Its nature and purpose are to judge and regulate all of a person's activity. That is why it may conflict with what a person most wants to do (being moral is not, in a certain sense, a doing at all), even when a person has no more than a reasonable attachment to morality.

In his essay "Moral Luck" Williams sets before us a hypothetical Gauguin figure whose basic project is to be a certain sort of painter: in order for his life to have meaning, for him to want to go on living, he has to paint. And in order for him to paint the way he must, he cannot fulfill his (acknowledged) obligations to his family. Let us take it that under these conditions impartial morality says no to his pursuit of his life's work. (It does not matter whether it would in this case; we can always imagine another where the moral transgression is more grave.) An attachment to morality (in the way impartial morality would have it) then stands in the way of Gauguin's acting on those desires with which he is most deeply identified. If I understand Williams, it is at this point that he wants to say such a demand cannot be reasonable: this is where you cannot ask a person to give up the activity constitutive of his being the person he is.

21. See John Rawls, "Kantian Constructivism in Moral Theory: The Dewey Lectures, 1980," *Journal of Philosophy* 78 (1980), for a contemporary elaboration of this feature of Kantianism.

Williams is not misreading Kantian morality here. It does involve a requirement that one be prepared to set aside one's deepest projects if they require impermissible actions. The question is whether a moral agent committed to morality in this way would have his integrity as a person threatened. Utilitarianism is thought by Williams to threaten integrity because it demands that a person give up what his ground project requires in a given case "just if that conflicts with what he is required to do as an impersonal utility maximizer when all the causally relevant considerations are in."[22] Even when he can act as he would, the utilitarian agent must accept as the justifying reason for his action that it turned out to be the impartially preferred path. So he must not only be prepared to interrupt his projects when utility calls, but he must also pursue his projects without the sense that what makes them worth pursuing is connected to the fact that they are his.

The Kantian idea of morality as a limiting condition on the pursuit of ends does not have this result. Whereas utilitarianism places a moral requirement on all actions (that they maximize value relative to the available options), Kantian morality imposes a regulative ideal: some of the actions and goals one may choose will be judged impermissible. Those actions and projects that are judged permissible are not distanced from the agent's primary interest in them by that fact. He is not allowed to act only on condition that his action will realize some impartial value in the world.

For morality to respect the conditions of character (one's integrity as a person), it must respect the agent's attachments to his projects in a way that permits his actions to be the expression of those attachments. Kantian morality, understood as a morality of limits, can do this. What it cannot do is honor *unconditional attachments*. The moral agent knows in advance that neither his identification of himself with a project nor the (true) fact that if he is unable to act as he wants his life will be emptied of meaning for him is sufficient to justify his acting against (serious) moral requirements. Indeed, given the possibility of grossly immoral projects or vile actions taken for the sake of morally neutral projects, it does not seem rational to want it otherwise.

While it is (psychologically) true that attachments to projects can be unconditional, it is not a requirement of the conditions of having a character that they be so. Unconditional attachments can be as much at odds with one's loves, one's other interests, even with the physical limitations on action, as they may be in conflict with limits imposed by morality. One who shapes or modifies his projects in light of physical and material limitations is attached, but not unconditionally, to his projects. That demands of a child may limit the possible scope of the parent's work does not prevent

22. "Persons, Character and Morality," p. 14.

success at work from being a character-defining ground project. The Kantian argument is that at the limit, where conflict with morality is serious and unavoidable, morality must win. The "victory" of morality does not diminish the value of the project (unless it is the project itself that is judged immoral), and so does not constitute an attack on the agent's integrity. It is rather an indication that in this world, or in these circumstances, there is no permissible way to continue the project.

The attachment to morality *is* supposed to be unconditional. But this is compatible with the conditions of character: the moral agent is to be one who has a conception of himself as someone who will not pursue his projects in ways that are morally impermissible. Such restraint is, in our ordinary way of speaking, a matter of integrity. For Kant, or for a Kantian like Rawls, commitment to impartial morality acknowledges the respect owed other persons. In his willingness to shape and limit his projects so that they do not conflict with principles of respect for others, the moral person expresses his conception of himself as a member of a community of equally moral persons.

This is not an argument that explains *why* a person should have a moral sense of himself. What I am arguing is that Kantian morality can be (and is meant to be taken as) defining of a sense of self and that, in having a moral character, a person will not have given up something in the way of integrity that standing aside from impartial morality would allow. In the light of this, it seems reasonable to think of ground projects as having more than one kind of structure. Some will direct us to goal-oriented courses of action; others will have us act with respect to the needs of another. But pursuits and commitments are not the only basic attachments. We can have an idea of the whole: a project whose point is to shape and limit other projects so that they are compatible with an ideal sense of how a person ought to live. This is the kind of place that Kantian morality is supposed to have.

In fact the appeals that Williams makes which would tell against this conclusion do not seem convincing. Two of these can be dealt with somewhat briefly. He argues that we do not condemn Gauguin because we value his painting. "The moral spectator has to consider the fact that he has reason to be glad that Gauguin succeeded, and hence that he tried."[23] If we are glad that he tried, then we must be glad that morality is not always victorious. This would make it seem (intuitively, at least) that we are sometimes ready to reject the idea that the proper place for morality is as a basic limit on actions. This argument involves a confusion. Given that Gauguin's paintings exist, that they are objects in our world, we value and enjoy them. It does not follow from this that we are committed to valuing whatever led to their production. Nor even that we have to think a world with Gauguin's paintings is preferable to one without them. While valuing

23. "Moral Luck," p. 37.

the work, it would not be irrational to judge that the moral cost of the paintings had been too high.

Williams also makes much out of the fact that his Gauguin could not rationally regret his choice to abandon his family and pursue his art. As Gauguin took success at painting to be the project of his life, the achievement of success gives his life its deepest significance to him, and so constitutes the only standpoint from which he can assess previous choices. But couldn't this just mean that Gauguin is deeply satisfied with how his life turned out? Why must the moral spectator agree? The Kantian need not deny the possibility of deeply satisfying lives that have been built on morally impermissible actions. Likewise, he need not deny that in altering his hierarchy of values, Gauguin put his action beyond the reach of moral criticism. What the Kantian must hold is that, despite all of this, it is possible that Gauguin was wrong in acting as he did.

A third appeal fastens on the *procedures* of impartial judgment on the grounds that they lead an agent to make practical decisions in ways that compromise his integrity. In developing this idea Williams borrows an example from Charles Fried designed to show the role of deep personal attachments in moral deliberation. There is a shipwreck and a number of people are drowning, including the agent's wife. A moral agent following procedures of impartial judgment may determine that when there is more than one person in danger, it is morally permissible for him to save his wife if only one person can be saved. Williams does not object to the conclusion, but balks at the idea that morality would require judging *first* that it is permissible, making the decision to save a loved one's life conditional on its perceived permissibility: "this construction provides the agent with one thought too many: it might have been hoped (for instance, by his wife) that his motivating thought, fully spelled out, would be the thought that it was his wife, not that it was his wife and that in situations of this kind it is permissible to save one's wife."[24] There are things his wife might have hoped that I do not think we need to take very seriously. She might have hoped his love for her was such that he would save her, without a second thought, at no matter what cost to whom. Or she might have thought that being *his* wife made her special, and therefore he would not need to think of anyone else. What fits with Williams' argument is the idea that she might have hoped his saving her would be an expression of his love. The thought that he acts on the condition that it is permissible to save someone you are attached to signals a willingness not to save her if that were morally necessary. This willingness makes his saving her something other than an expression of his attachment. Williams concludes: "somewhere (and if not in this case, where?) one reaches the necessity that such things as deep

---

24. "Persons, Character and Morality," p. 18.

attachments to other persons will express themselves in the world in ways which cannot at the same time embody the impartial view."

The issue here is the nature of the space that Kantian morality leaves for nonmoral reasons, given the ultimate authority of moral over nonmoral considerations. Williams is quite right in thinking that the moralization of personal relations involves "righteous absurdity." To preserve the domain of the personal, however, it is not necessary to divorce it from the moral. A Kantian might hold the following sort of view. While it is true that moral reasons are always relevant (and authoritative where they apply), part of being a moral person involves the recognition of the limits of the moral: when moral reasons are not the appropriate reasons to act on. On the other hand, although nonmoral reasons are often in order, their authority is limited, or conditioned, by morality. A moral person knows that he cannot only appeal to his love for another as a justifying reason in all circumstances: its fittingness as a justifying reason is itself a moral matter (although that does not make it a moral reason when it is appropriate).

Let us return to the "saving the spouse" case with the above in mind. Suppose we asked, after the fact, "Why did you save *her?*" We would get the answer, "Because I love her" or "Because she's my wife." These are the reasons on which one acts, and the actions they support express the relationships they refer to. Moreover, it is morally appropriate (not in any way inappropriate) in these circumstances to act on these reasons.[25] None of this is undermined by the agent's awareness (he need hardly be thinking of it) that in *some* circumstances the reason would not be sufficient to justify his action. (Suppose he would have to throw a child overboard to reach her.) It is in this sense that "the thought that it was his wife" is not separate from moral considerations. It would be one thing if the husband paused to weigh the claims of his wife against those of others he might save; that would speak against his having the kind of attachment that might be hoped for by his wife. What the Kantian requires is only that he not view his desire to save his wife as an *unconditionally* valid reason. This does not stand in the way of the direct expression of attachments in action.

IV

Something more needs to be said in defense of the claim that Kantian morality can attend to the elements of individual character and circumstance necessary to the maintenance of personal integrity. Generations of

25. We do not want to forget that a normal moral agent knows things: he does not have to figure out whether it is permissible to save his wife. He knows it is, and that partly explains why he can act spontaneously, from feeling, and yet according to principle. No less a non-Kantian authority than Aristotle made this the charge of a moral education.

critics, after all, have begun from the sense that it is obvious that the particular and the personal were what was abstracted from in Kantian moral judgments. The flavor of this criticism of Kantian "abstract" morality is nicely expressed by Stuart Hampshire: "An abstract morality places a prepared grid upon conduct and upon a person's activities and interests, and thereafter one only tends to see the pieces of his conduct and life as they are divided by lines on the grid." And again, contrasting Aristotelian and Kantian conceptions of morality: "The contrast can be represented as that between noticing a great number and variety of independently variable features of particular situations on the one hand, and on the other hand, bringing a few, wholly explicit principles to bear upon situations, which have to be subsumed under the principles, as in some kinds of legal reasoning."[26]

This is not a complaint that the moral point of view is removed from the agent's point of view; the concern is that in directing the moral agent or spectator to abstract from the particular context and personal texture of an action prior to assessment, something of *moral* relevance is eliminated. The consequence of this could be that abstractly similar cases judged in the same way in fact ought to be judged differently because of features lost in the abstraction; or, even when the final assessment of an action is unaffected, the way of reaching the conclusion ought to acknowledge particulars of context and person. To put this in Williams' terms: if to have a certain character is to have specific loves, projects, and such, then procedures of moral assessment that involve the impartial employment of abstract rules cannot register the importance of considerations of character in our moral thought.

This criticism of Kantian ethics depends upon a failure to distinguish rules of duty from the Categorical Imperative as a moral principle. Rules of duty are, by their nature, general. They may be useful as prima facie requirements, or appropriate in circumstances where there is a need to introduce uniformity in action. Rules of duty are designed to ignore detail and to focus on "relevant" similarities in cases: they must include general descriptions of persons and states of affairs to perform their sortal functions. Such rules *are* abstract, impartial, and impersonal. But rules of duty do not provide the normal standard of action and deliberation in Kantian ethics.

The tradition notwithstanding, the procedures of moral judgment in Kant's ethics do not call for the impartial application of such general moral rules. The Categorical Imperative is a regulative moral principle to which actions (actually, maxims of actions) are to conform. It is a higher-order deliberative principle, not an abstract and general rule. Instead of including

---

26. "Public and Private Morality," in *Public and Private Morality,* ed. Stuart Hampshire (Cambridge: Cambridge University Press, 1978), pp. 40, 28.

very general descriptions of actions under which the particular is to be subsumed, it provides a procedure for structuring the particular in a moral way. That is, since the CI is used to assess maxims, and maxims are the subjective principles on which agents in fact act, when an agent constructs his maxim he is to include in it just that detail of person and circumstance necessary to describe *his* action.[27] The outcome of the CI procedure is to tell the agent whether the conditions he has taken as relevant in determining his course of action in fact give moral warrant to what he would do.

The moment of employment of the CI as a principle of judgment is characteristically when the agent is drawn to make an exception for himself to an acknowledged moral rule or precept.[28] That is, he knows his action is one that is normally proscribed, yet he is inclined to believe that he is, in his circumstances, justified. For the procedure to be effective, the maxim he brings to the test must include whatever makes the agent (sincerely) think his case is exceptional. The CI test procedure will, in effect, impose a moral analysis on an agent's projects—assaying the relevant particulars to see if they have the justificatory significance the agent believes they do.

It is Kant's conviction that the usual use of the particulars of character and circumstance is to support "special pleading" for moral exemptions. And I think it is true that he supposes the Categorical Imperative will show that most of these, when sincere, show the force of moral temptation more than any great variety in the judgment of moral permissibility. How such judgments would work out is beside the point. The central acknowledgment that the particulars of person and place need to be examined (and not merely abstracted from) leaves it open for them to make a moral difference.

27. To forestall the objection that there is no evidence for this sort of account of maxims in Kant's writing, let me offer the following example from his *Doctrine of Virtue*. It comes in a note where Kant is objecting to the "superficial wisdom" in moral formulas such as "happy are those who keep the mean": "What distinguishes avarice (as a vice) from thrift (as a virtue) is not that *avarice* carries thrift *too far* but that avarice has an entirely *different principle* (maxim): that of economizing, not for the sake of enjoying one's wealth, but merely for the sake of possessing it, while denying oneself any enjoyment from it. In the same way, the vice of prodigality is not to be sought in the excessive enjoyment of one's wealth but in the bad maxim which makes the use of wealth the sole end, without regard for maintaining the wealth" (DV403n). For the purposes of this argument, what we need to attend to is the fact that maxims are meant by Kant to describe a particular agent's *willings;* in order to know just what a particular agent has willed in a given case, you would need to know more than what could be abstractly and impersonally described.

28. The moment of employment of the CI is clearly described in each of the four well-known examples in Kant's *Groundwork*.

3

Mutual Aid and Respect for Persons

> Yet a fourth is himself flourishing, but he sees others who have to struggle with great hardships (and who he could easily help); and he thinks: What does it matter to me? Let every one be as happy as Heaven wills or as he can make himself; I won't deprive him of anything; I won't even envy him; only I have no wish to contribute anything to his well-being or to his support in distress! Now admittedly if such an attitude were a universal law of nature, mankind could get on perfectly well—better no doubt than if everybody prates about sympathy and good will, and even takes pain, on occasions to practice them, but on the other hand cheats where he can, traffics in human rights, or violates them in other ways. But although it is possible that a universal law of nature could subsist in harmony with this maxim, yet it is impossible to will that such a principle should hold everywhere as a law of nature. For a will which decided in this way would be in conflict with itself, since many a situation might arise in which the man needed love and sympathy from others, and in which, by such a law of nature sprung from his own will, he would rob himself of all hope of the help he wants for himself. (G423)

IT IS surely no crude mistake of reading to interpret this passage as making some kind of prudential appeal in arguing for a duty of beneficence and as depending in its conclusion on the contingent, empirical fact about human agents that they may encounter situations in which they need the help of others. Such reading underlies the belief of some of Kant's most serious critics (Schopenhauer and Sidgwick, for example) that this argument is peculiarly well suited to reveal deep inconsistencies in Kant's claims about morality. It is, after all, a central claim of the *Groundwork* that no categorical imperative can have a prudential foundation (or else it could not be a principle of duty); and it is our rational, rather than our empirical, nature that is to be the ground of moral duty. I do not think the accounts of these critics (and those of many friendly commentators as well) have taken seriously enough the idea that the sense in which Kant holds that impermissible acts are irrational is not to be captured by considerations of a prudential nature.

In offering another interpretation of the *Groundwork* argument for beneficence, I hope to make some progress in describing the sense of rationality that Kant conceives to be connected with morality. The reconstruction of the argument is guided by two methodological constraints. Since the argument takes place within a procedure for moral judgment, and procedures of moral judgment provide moral instruction to agents using them beyond their rulings of permissibility, there are grounds for rejecting an interpretation of the argument for beneficence if the way in which the argument proceeds teaches a moral lesson alien to the spirit of Kant's project. Second, the Categorical Imperative procedure is used to establish moral requirements. It also is to guide sincere moral agents in assessing actions and policies whose moral permissibility is uncertain. Given this double function, it is reasonable to expect that the casuistry of beneficence (how we determine what we must do in particular cases) will be informed by those considerations used to establish that there is a duty of beneficence. Casuistry should not be separated from the main line of moral argument.

Let me turn now to the argument for beneficence, as it is presented in the *Groundwork,* as the fourth example of the employment of the Categorical Imperative.

I

It will help to begin by recalling the role the examples play in the argument of the *Groundwork.*[1] At the point of their introduction, Kant has just produced the formula of the CI: "Act only on that maxim through which you can at the same time will that it should become a universal law" (G421). What he then must demonstrate is that the CI is a moral principle: the CI must be able to judge an appropriate range of test cases correctly. This will show that it correlates well with our considered moral judgments. But Kant also believes that the CI is the principle embedded in ordinary moral judgment, and correlation is not enough to show that it is. For this we must look to the detail of the examples—what is revealed by the CI procedure to be at work in the logic or rationale of impermissible maxims.

There is now fairly general agreement about the formal mechanics of the CI procedure of judgment.[2] The agent is to cast his maxim of action in

---

1. The argument showing the impermissibility of nonbeneficence is one example; the others argue against suicide, deceitful promising, and neglect of talents.

2. Here I do not explicitly challenge the agreement. But the method of argument I use—especially in sections II and III—suggests that moral judgment is not best understood as an iterated sequence of passes through the CI procedure. In Chapter 7 I argue for the shift in understanding of the role of the CI procedure in moral judgment that is implicit in this chapter.

universal form and then to examine what would follow if that universalized maxim were to become a law of human nature. That is, the agent constructs a hypothetical world that has all the features of the world as it is except for the addition of the universalized maxim as a law of its nature. An action is judged impermissible either if its maxim cannot be conceived as a law of nature without contradiction or if it is impossible for an agent to will that his maxim should become a law of nature without his will contradicting itself (see G424).

The *Groundwork* argument for a duty of beneficence takes the case of a man "himself flourishing" who is aware both that there are others who have "great hardships" and that "he could easily help." Only he would be indifferent: whatever he may feel,[3] he wishes to live so that "every one be as happy as Heaven wills or as he can make himself." He has no wish to contribute to the well-being of others or to their support in distress. Kant's comment that "if such an attitude were a universal law of nature, mankind could get on perfectly well," irony aside, implies that there is no difficulty (contradiction) in conceiving the maxim of non-beneficence ("to never help anyone") as a law of nature. A world just like this one except for the addition of a law of nonbeneficence would be a possible world; universal nonbeneficence is a possible natural law. (Something is not a possible natural law if it is impossible for everything subject to it to act according to it. It is possible for everyone to act nonbeneficently.)

It is not possible, however, "to *will* that such a principle should hold everywhere as a law of nature." This is so because "a will which decided in this way would be in conflict with itself, since many a situation might arise in which the man needed love and sympathy from others, and in which, by such a law of nature sprung from his own will, he would rob himself of all hope of the help he wants for himself" (G423). The most obvious reading of this places the supposed contradiction in will in a self-produced (if hypothetical) failure of prudential reasoning. The procedure requires the agent to imagine that his maxim of nonbeneficence has become a universal law of (human) nature through his willing of it (for himself). He would thereby have created a world in which no one could help anyone. Yet in the hypothetical world, as in this world, he might come to need help and want to be aided. Then he would have willed a world in which he was the cause of his being unable to get the help he wanted. Here is the supposed contradiction in will: he would be will-

---

3. It is not a necessary feature of the example that the man be cold—only that he wants to refrain from any involvement in the well-being of others. The "any" here is quite thorough, for he also wishes not to envy others when they are well-off.

ing both that the world be such that no one could help anyone and that he be helped.[4]

There is no specifically moral element in this demonstration of a contradiction in will. Suppose I adopt a policy of never saving any money. And suppose I also know that many situations may arise in which I will want something that (as a matter of contingent fact) will require my having saved money. When this comes to pass, my general policy of not saving will then stand in the way of my getting what I want. This is often enough to ground a charge of imprudence, and, to the extent that I could foresee this state of affairs, I have acted irrationally. As both the general policy and the want that requires savings are expressions of my will, it is not implausible to describe my will as in conflict with itself.[5]

I escape such ordinary conflict in two different ways. Knowing that I will want something I can have only if I save, either I may give up my general policy of never saving, or I may adopt the attitude toward future wants that require savings that it is tolerable for them to be unfulfilled. Other things equal, I will have acted rationally if I adopt either course.

So, similarly, we might expect the conflict of will in the nonbeneficence example to be resolvable either by abandoning the general policy of never helping anyone or by adopting the attitude toward needed help that it is a tolerable unfulfilled desire.[6] Of course, if the general policy is abandoned, the argument is over: the agent will have rejected nonbeneficence. But so long as it is open to the agent to maintain his nonbeneficent policy on condition that he give up the possibility of help, it is not necessary to reject nonbeneficence. The problem then appears to be: can the argument in the example be construed in a way that makes it impossible for a rational agent to adopt the strategy of being willing to forgo help in order to keep his maxim of nonbeneficence?

---

4. Throughout Kant's argument there is the (reasonable) assumption that, if you want something, then, other things equal, it is irrational to act in ways that prevent your getting what you want. On the connection between needing help, wanting it, and willing that one be helped, I will have more to say later.

5. The "contradiction" arises in the ordinary case from the effects, over time, of holding to a general policy of not saving. Under the CI procedure, these conditions are simulated by the supposition that the intended maxim becomes a universal law of action. In the first case, I place irrational constraints on my future actions through commitment to a general policy. In the beneficence example, the constraints are there through the inaction of others, imagined to come about through my willing of a policy of nonbeneficence.

6. In Kant's terminology we would describe the resolution of the conflict as either abandoning the policy or giving up the end of wanting help. To adopt x as an end is to set oneself to bring about x. To give up x as an end is to forgo x (not to act to bring about x or, when necessary, to act to prevent x from coming about). It does not follow from giving up x as an end that one no longer has a desire for x. Adopting the attitude toward x that it is a tolerable unfulfilled desire is a way of giving up x as an end.

So, we might think, the agent needs to be reminded of his vulnerability. (He is, we are told, a flourishing individual, not someone struggling with great hardships or routinely needing assistance; such an individual might not find it difficult to be convinced that he is self-sufficient.) We let the examples turn a bit melodramatic: we ask him to imagine himself lying in the road about to be run over by a truck. Someone could easily help him escape certain horrible death. How could he not want help? Thinking of this, can he now decide that such a desire for help will not be satisfied? Surely he would want to live more than he wants to abide by a policy of never helping anyone. That, after all, was a policy based on no more than the desire not to be bothered by the needs of others. So, if he would want help in that case (and would be unwilling to forgo help for the sake of his policy of nonbeneficence) and since in the hypothetical world of universal nonbeneficence he would be robbed of that help by an act of his own will, he is then forced, insofar as he is rational, to resolve the conflict by abandoning the maxim of nonbeneficence. Prudence seems to require it.

But if the reasoning is prudential, then it would also be appropriate to consider the likelihood of situations arising when he would prefer help more than he prefers the benefits of his policy of nonbeneficence. This is Sidgwick's argument: "Even granting that everyone, in the actual moment of distress, must necessarily wish for the assistance of others: still a strong man, after balancing the chances of life, may easily think that he and such as he have more to gain, on the whole, by the general adoption of the egoistic maxim; benevolence being likely to bring more trouble than profit."[7] Indeed, any person well situated in life and of a sufficiently self-disciplined temper might have good reason to feel that the price of increased security in having the help of others available (in this world or in the hypothetical world of the CI procedure) is too high. The risk of accident with no one helping is one he can bear. Everyone must die sometime, and so on. To salvage the argument for beneficence then, it must be possible to show that such considerations cannot legitimately be introduced. As we have so far interpreted the argument, there seems to be no way to exclude them and so no way to show that people willing to tolerate risk have a duty to help others, if they would prefer not to help.

Moreover, this line of reasoning would show that not all who have a duty of beneficence are obliged to the same degree. Since attitudes toward security and the felt onerousness of beneficence will vary from person to person, this argument will yield a strong duty of beneficence for some (low-risk tolerators) and a decreasingly stringent duty of beneficence for those who have greater tolerance for risks. (And what of those who find risks not only tolerable but desirable or exciting?)

7. Henry Sidgwick, *The Methods of Ethics* (New York: Dover Publications, 1966), p. 389n.

It is not just these consequences that are disturbing. The form of the argument urges our thinking about the duty of beneficence as a kind of (hypothetical) insurance policy. In the hypothetical world, prudence indicates rejection of the maxim of nonbeneficence in order to secure aid for oneself, as needed, in the future. The moral question seems to turn on the "premium"—how much protection you would lose if you do not want to pay in the currency of beneficence. (There is no obligation to do everything necessary to save one's life.) But how one comes to understand why we have the duties we do is part of how one learns what morality is about. The CI procedure tells an agent that what would happen were his maxim to be a universal law of nature matters in a way that will make a moral difference. So if the salient question in the procedure is, "Would this harm or benefit you? Would it put you at risk or enhance your chances for the satisfaction of desires?" it would then be reasonable for an agent to conclude that it is his well-being that turns the moral argument—albeit his well-being in hypothetical circumstances. And since use of the procedure contributes to an agent's understanding of his place in a moral scheme, the role of the prudential elements must lead him to think that the satisfaction of his desires is significant in deriving duties. To center moral deliberation on a strategy for even hypothetical self-protection provides a lesson one would not have expected Kant to endorse.

One way out of this impasse is to use an interpretive strategy suggested by John Rawls.[8] He locates the difficulty in the argument for beneficence in the use made by the judging agent of those contingent facts of his life (his strength, fortune, health, and so on) that support the rationality of his risking a world of nonbeneficence. As Rawls holds, on what he argues are Kantian grounds, that such facts about persons are morally irrelevant in determining duties, he would amend the CI procedure by introducing a veil of ignorance, to eliminate differences in judgment produced by different risks and attitudes toward risk. By putting constraints on information, the veil of ignorance allows one to use the form of ordinary prudential reasoning to get moral results from the CI procedure.[9] Without the information necessary to assess one's chances of needing the help of others, it is no longer rational to risk the frustration of such need for the sake of the benefits to be had in not having to help others. Supplementing the Kantian

8. This account is drawn from Rawls's lectures on Kant's ethics at Harvard in 1977 and from a written version of those lectures that he generously made available to his students. Since at some points I introduce elements based on interpretive conjecture, Rawls might not endorse the views that I attribute to him. Yet the account I give seems to me "Rawlsian" in spirit and, in any case, worthy of examination since it provides such a tempting amendment to Kant's argument.

9. Rawls finds a textual support for such a move in the "Typic of Pure Practical Judgment" (*Critique of Practical Reason* 68–72).

procedure with the veil of ignorance has the effect of making everyone conservative about risk taking. The duty of beneficence would then apply to all persons and apply to them all equally. So Sidgwick's strong man would be answered.

The Rawlsian strategy produces the desired moral results because the veil of ignorance excludes distinctive personal information in a way that makes each person function (as he judges) as a kind of representative person. What the Rawlsian strategy fails to capture is a critical element in the Kantian conception of moral judgment. For Kant, the embeddedness of the person in the particular is the natural and necessary starting point of moral judgment. Rawls's strategy is drawn from the context of the "original position," where agents have no moral knowledge (apart from strictly formal matters) and are to decide together on the duties, obligations, and principles by which they will live. The Kantian moral agent, if the standard examples can be taken as a guide, comes to need a procedure for moral judgment when he is tempted to make an exception for himself from known moral precepts. It is because he believes that his particular circumstances are special that he concludes that he is morally entitled to act in ways others may not.[10] He will not be shown that he is wrong by being told that all features distinguishing him from others are morally irrelevant. If, as Kant suggests, those who are not evil are drawn to moral error through the sincere conviction that they may make an exception to the moral law for themselves to the advantage of inclination—he says we pretend the exceptions are "inconsiderable or apparently forced on us" (G424)—then a procedure of moral judgment will be more effective to the degree that it allows agents to bring their sense of their distinctiveness in and then shows them that it is not enough to justify excepting themselves.[11]

There is confirmation for this view in the fact that the CI procedure does not assess actions directly but, rather, assesses them through their maxims: actions *as they are willed* by the agent. As it expresses his conception of what he is doing and why, his maxim must be based on the kind of information the Rawlsian restriction is designed to eliminate. In the case at

10. See G424. Moreover, given the structure of the CI procedure for moral judgment, unless the agent is able to formulate his maxim in a way that includes the relevant moral precept—in a way that uses his moral knowledge—it would be remarkable if the proposed action were described in a way that captured its morally problematic features.

11. It does not follow from the fact that the agent needs to see that his particular circumstances do not warrant an exception from a rule of duty that the assessment of his maxim must be through a procedure allowing him to take his point of view. An impartial procedure could show that as well. I am arguing only that a procedure that does allow him to maintain his point of view would be more effective (a practical argument) and that such a procedure provides a more natural reading of the passages in which Kant sets out the procedures of judgment of the first formulation of the CI.

hand, the choice of a policy of nonbeneficence follows from the agent's assessment of his fortunate situation. In asking whether this choice is permissible, he wants, in a sense, to know why his special circumstances should not give him moral title to refrain from involvement in the welfare of others. That, to him, is the morally relevant background to his adoption of his maxim. Given his reasons for adopting this maxim, we may fairly conclude that he would not choose nonbeneficence if he were someone likely to need the help of others. He is not without feeling for consistency and reciprocity. The CI procedure amended in a Rawlsian way does not explain (within the Kantian framework) the moral error in his reasoning.

Still the difficulty with allowing this information in remains, compromising the generality of results yielded by the CI procedure.

II

If the problem is not to be dealt with by restricting the information allowed into the procedure, the remaining aspect of the argument that bears reexamination is the appeal to prudence. We have been assuming that Kant's idea of a contradiction in will is accurately represented by errors in prudential reasoning, translated into conflicting willings by the device of the CI procedure. Here I want to argue that, although a contradiction in will is an expression of irrational willing, it is not in virtue of prudential considerations that it is so.

Let me begin by suggesting an alternative reading of the last sentence of the opening quotation, taking its point to be the ubiquity (inescapability) of the possibility of needing help. That is, for any end, it is not possible for an agent to guarantee in advance that he can pursue his end successfully without the help of others. I will argue that this is enough to demonstrate a contradiction in will (supposing one has already willed a law of universal nonbeneficence) if either of two conditions holds: (1) that there are ends that the agent wants to realize more than he could hope to benefit from nonbeneficence and that he cannot bring about unaided or (2) that there are ends that it is not possible for any rational agent to forgo (ends that are in some sense necessary ends).

I view the CI procedure as being designed to draw our attention to those features of our condition—as rational agents in this world and as members of a community of persons—that serve as the conditions of our willings. In part because we are moved by moral considerations (we may at times be bad; we are not often evil), we are drawn to use the surface logic of moral reasoning (its requirements of impartiality, consistency, and so on) to support the belief that we may on occasion be morally justified in acting as others would not be. It is just this sense of specialness that underlies the belief of the strong man that it would be possible, even reasonable, to live without the help of others. The CI procedure is to show that, for any of us, the availability of the help of others is not something it can be rational to forgo. It is this limit on what it can be rational to will that the strong man needs to be shown.

In willing an end, an agent conceives of himself as "an acting cause"— that is, as using means (G417). The willing of means to an adopted end is not, then, some separate and contingent act of willing. As we will an end we are, in that act of will, committing ourselves to will the necessary means, so long as we do not abandon the end. The things that are means for us are of three kinds: ourselves (as we have abilities and skills), things (both animate and inanimate), and other persons (given their capacities, as end setters, to take our ends as their own). The argument to a contradiction in will asks, in effect, whether it could be rational for a human being to renounce irrevocably the resource (means) of the help of others. That one will need (be unable to act for some particular end without) the help of others is something that may or may not come to pass. It depends on the nature of one's ends, the availability of resources (who has what), one's skill, strength, and so forth. Most important, it depends on how things happen to work out—the nature of the impersonal forces, the actions of others, and the like, that intersect with one's life. (There is a limit to "making one's own luck.") The extent to which one's skills are adequate to one's needs and projects, the extent to which the things one needs are plentiful or ready to hand, and the extent to which the help of others will be necessary for the successful pursuit of any given end—all of these involve contingencies that are not within our power.

Now the question is: why, knowing this, can't the strong man commit himself to abandon any end he discovers he cannot pursue without help? This is a kind of negative stoicism, and such a policy will describe for him a distinctive way of life. He must practice self-discipline, learning to withhold his will from desires, however strong or attractive they may be, that he cannot fulfill by his own unaided efforts. His stoical end serves as a limiting condition on his pursuit of all other ends and is thus acknowledged as of greater value (at the limit) than any other end. But with all this, a stoical strong man cannot escape the logic of his agency. It is always possible, however strong his commitment to living without the help of others is, that he will be tempted to abandon that end—tempted to reassess the priority he has given to his independence. First, there is room for temptation where there is need for discipline and strength. We have to imagine no more than an attachment to some other end strong enough to allow for the possibility that he will be tempted to forgo his stoical end and accept help for its sake. Second, whether the conditions of life he encounters are gentle or overwhelm his strength of will is not itself something he can control. It is also then possible that he will need help in resisting that temptation (perhaps someone just to distract him for a moment, to get his mind off the question, so that he will be able to regroup and sustain his discipline). If he rejects the possibility of help here, he will no longer be able to guarantee that he will abandon any end that he discovers he cannot pursue without help. So long as temptation is an open possibility for him, the stoical man cannot (rationally, given his commitment to a stoical end) withdraw from all possibility of help from others.[12] The point of the stoic example is to dramatize a very general fact: even with the focus of one's life directed at independence from others, at the limit, this may not be a goal one can pursue unaided.[13]

The stoic succumbs to the argument against his maxim of nonbeneficence because he has an end he is committed to—his independence. But what of a "wanton" with respect to ends: someone who does not care whether any of his particular ends are realized and so seems to be attached to nothing that would require him to accept the help of others? The argument against him will go through only if there are ends that he (and so we) cannot forgo for which the help of others may be needed.

---

12. It seems to me a strength of Kant's argument that we are pushed to the edge of what we can imagine to find a potential exception to the CI procedure. To force the stoic example further, to deny that the stoic will form attachments or pursue projects in a way that will make him vulnerable (only) to temptation is to save his independence by sacrificing the idea of his having a life. Bernard Williams uses this sort of strategy in his Humean counter to the possibility of a complete egoism. See his "Egoism and Altruism," in *Problems of the Self* (Cambridge: Cambridge University Press, 1973). I can imagine someone forgoing ends for the sake of some project or commitment. Then it seems to me that I can imagine someone being prepared to forgo all ends for the sake of stoical independence. But from the fact that I can imagine someone lifting something I am not strong enough to lift, it does not follow that I can imagine someone lifting my house, although I can picture it (form an image).

13. Stephen Engstrom, in "Herman on Mutual Aid," *Ethics* 96:2 (1986), 346–349, has argued that this analysis mistakes the nature of the stoic's end. He suggests that the end belongs to a class of ends that are "personal in the sense that the possibility of assistance from others is ruled out by the nature of the end itself." If someone wants to solve a difficult geometry problem, his "chances of doing so will be ruined by someone who, say, gives [him] hints that makes the problem easy to solve." There appears to be nothing irrational in refusing help for such personal ends. This misses the strangeness of the stoic's end. There is nothing irrational in accepting all kinds of support while working on the geometry problem: a glass of juice, some quiet, a pad of paper. Having a personal end does not remove one from the normal network of social support. Yet it is from just this network that the stoic seeks independence. This fact, and not the fact that the end is personal, accounts for his double bind. Further, personal ends fit within a framework of other ends and projects. Part of the structure of a personal end will (typically, not necessarily) include provision for failure: it may make sense, given other ends, to get help if the problem proves to be too hard (though it can also make sense, given other ends, to hold that if *this* problem resists one's efforts, one should abandon the project). Because the stoic's end is regulative with respect to all his other ends, he cannot accept help, but he can have no *reason* to reject help if he thereby abandons his stoical end.

We are not like the wanton since there are ends that we may be unwilling to forgo because of their value to us—because of the sense or meaning their pursuit gives to our lives. (The stoic represents an extreme form of attachment to a single end.) We are like the wanton since even ends that we may be unwilling to give up can be given up nonetheless. Ends, however, that are necessary to sustain oneself as a rational being cannot (on rational grounds) be given up. Insofar as one has ends at all, one has already willed the continued exercise of one's agency as a rational being. The ends that must be realized if a person is to function (or continue to function) as a rational, end-setting agent come from what Kant calls the "true needs" of human agents.[14] They are the conditions of our "power to set an end" that is the "characteristic of humanity" (DV51). The ends set to meet our true needs are like all other ends—we cannot guarantee that we can realize them unaided. But in contrast to all other ends, we cannot on rational grounds forgo them for the sake of other contingent ends. Willing universal non-beneficence conflicts with what, as dependent rational beings, we must will, if we will anything at all.[15]

If we are asked to imagine a life independent of things (objects) to be used as means, we cannot do so, for our existence depends on them straightforwardly. The adequacy of our skills to our needs is a contingent state of affairs. The very bounty of nature and ease of life that might make us feel we will never have to place new demands on ourselves are not of our making or within our control. Thus it would not be rational to "freeze" our skills if we could not also control our circumstances.[16] This is parallel to the idea that I mean to capture in saying that, unless one could guarantee in advance that one will not require the help of others as means to ends one could not forgo, it would not be rational to will universal nonbeneficence. It is a fact of our nature as rational beings that we cannot guarantee that we shall always be capable of realizing our ends unaided, as it is a fact of our nature that we need things and skills to pursue our ends. If what we lack is some thing, we cannot call on that object to serve our need; nor can we obtain new skills and abilities at will. But we can call on the skills and resources of others to supplement our own.

The willing of a world of nonbeneficence thus conflicts with the practical consequences of the conditions of human rationality: the natural limitations of our powers as agents. This does not involve questions of risk and thus

14. This term is introduced in DV53. Rawls also appeals to "true needs" to explain which ends a person, behind a veil of ignorance, would agree to have covered by a duty of beneficence.

15. It does not follow from this that we may never will self-sacrificially or choose to forgo help (suppose the only help available involved impermissible action). It is only within the fiction of the CI procedure that forgoing all help produces a contradiction in will.

16. This is of course the ground of the argument against neglect of talents in the third *Groundwork* example.

of prudence. The natural limits of our powers as agents set the conditions of rational willing within which prudential calculations are made. It is because these limits are not transcended by good fortune that considerations of risk and likelihood are not relevant.[17] Because we are dependent rational beings with true needs, we are constrained to act in certain ways (toward ourselves and toward others). Thus the argument to defeat the maxim of nonbeneficence goes through: the world of universal nonbeneficence is not a world that it is rational for any human agent to choose. And since differences among persons with regard to their neediness, strength, and so on, do not affect the argument, the duty of beneficence that emerges is of the same degree or stringency for all persons.

One might worry that the reasoning used to defeat the maxim of nonbeneficence could be employed to show that we have an implausibly strong duty of beneficence: a duty to sacrifice ourselves when that is necessary to help another in need. Suppose I consider adopting a maxim of nonsacrificial beneficence (I will help others, but not when that requires great sacrifice). I imagine a world where no one can put himself at great risk or endure great cost in order to help. Can I guarantee that I will never need help that requires sacrifice? Obviously not. Then the CI test seems to require that I reject my maxim of nonsacrificial beneficence and accept a duty of helping others at all costs.[18] Quite apart from ordinary moral objections to such a duty, it is one Kant says we do not, and morally could not, have (DV122).

But we need to go carefully here. The response to the nonbeneficent person turned on the claim that no human being can guarantee his never needing help that it would be irrational of him to forgo. To arrive at a duty of sacrificial beneficence, it must be that I cannot guarantee that I will not need help that requires sacrifice. And of course I cannot make that guarantee. But in the first case it is the willing of a law of universal nonbeneficence that deprives one of what one needs. In the case of nonsacrificial beneficence, it is not what is willed but the contingent unavailability of resources that raises the issue of sacrifice. When I need help that requires sacrifice, I do not need a sacrifice. (It is quite a separate issue whether, if what I need is a sacrifice, I have any claim on help at all.)

---

17. This seems to me a significantly different acknowledgment from the realization, behind a veil of ignorance, that without knowledge of one's personal strengths and fortune it is not rational to risk nonbeneficence.

18. A better way of evaluating the maxim of nonsacrificial beneficence is through the agent's justifying reasons. An argument that shows the impermissibility of a maxim of nonbeneficence tout court sets a moral presumption the more restricted maxim must rebut. We then ask whether the exclusion of sacrificial acts is out of respect for the conditions of our agency or instead expresses a desire not to give when it hurts. This method of judgment and deliberation is argued for in Chapter 7; it also explains the practice of section III of this chapter.

Suppose I needed a complete set of new organs to stay alive: that could require the sacrifice of a life for my needs. In the imagined world of universal nonbeneficence I would be denied help. But were technology different, there might be artificial organs, and my need might be met easily. Someone may starve unless he is given food. In circumstances of plenty, his need can be met with no sacrifice. In times of famine, to feed one might require the sacrifice of another. So whether I can get the help I need (in this world or in the imagined world of nonsacrificial beneficence) depends on the accidents of circumstances (resources) which make it the case that the satisfaction of my need requires sacrifice. This is not a function of my willing. The maxim of nonsacrificial beneficence therefore does not generate a contradiction in will.

But couldn't the same argument be made about needed help? When one has a need he is not able to meet, it is not help that he needs but whatever it is that he lacks. If I am hungry and unable to get food that another could bring me, his help is just the contingently available means to what I need—which is food. So there is a sense in which needing the help of others is as much a contingent feature of my circumstances of need as needing help that requires sacrifice. (I do not have control over whether I will have needs I cannot meet or over whether help can provide what I lack.) Looked at this way, the help of another is a resource for me, as a long stick might be if what separated me from food was the limit of my reach. What makes the help of others more than just a contingently available resource is the fact that only another person (or rational being) can act for me, in response to my need, in answer to my call for help. Objects and animals cannot respond to need as such, nor can they take my ends as their own. It is the potential of others to act for my needs that it is irrational to forgo: it can stand in the place of my agency.

Now it may seem that willing any maxim to be a universal law creates the possibility of conflict with other ends or maxims, and thus the risk of not being able to satisfy ends that are true needs. Someone could reasonably adopt the maxim, "To set aside 10 percent of my income for my children's education." But this maxim, considered as a universal law, might deprive the agent of just those resources required to meet his true needs at some future time. Would it therefore be impermissible to adopt such a maxim of saving? Worse still, suppose a rich person adopts, as a positive maxim of beneficence, "To help others with true needs when doing so does not threaten my own true needs." As before, willing as a universal law a maxim that calls for the expenditure of resources creates a potential risk to one's own true needs. (Suppose he thinks: if I give resources to others, then I might not be able to afford some expensive medical treatment necessary to save my life in the future. Since I cannot now guarantee that I will never need such treatment to meet my true needs, it cannot be rational to will universal beneficence!) Would the rich person then have no duty of beneficence?

The maxims of saving and of positive beneficence do not generate any such contradiction in will. In the case of the rich man, it is not his willing of positive beneficence that causes trouble in the hypothetical world but the contingent possibility that his beneficence will absorb resources he could conceivably require later to meet true needs. With the stoic or the wanton, it is a function of what each wills (given life in a community of rational persons) that, within the hypothetical world, he will be denied help. But the rich man will not be denied help as a function of what he wills when he wills positive beneficence. What he may come to need is some sort of medical treatment; his giving away resources to meet the true needs of others does not interfere with his getting that. What may interfere is the costliness of the treatment. But costliness is a contingent fact of circumstances, on a par with the unavailability of a spare kidney machine. The stoic, as a result of his willing, cannot get help. The rich man may or may not get his medical treatment: that will depend on its cost, his resources, and the helpfulness of others. The maxim of saving poses no additional difficulties.

Only if we were required to do everything possible to minimize risks to our true needs would the maxims of saving and positive beneficence generate contradictions in will. But we cannot be required to do that. Suppose we were. Then the rich man could do nothing that involved true-need-independent expenditure of resources—including the most ordinary use of his resources for pleasure. The maxims of the rich man and saver involve use of resources. The use of any resource creates the risk that some future need may not be met. That is why questions of tradeoffs are appropriate. The stoic and the wanton would permanently alienate one of the three general categories of resources available to persons to meet their needs. This is not irrational because the risk involved in the loss of all possible help is greater than any possible benefits. That is a matter of circumstantial prudential reasoning. It is irrational because a person cannot both forgo any of the general conditions of successful agency and guarantee no contradiction in will insofar as he wills other ends: a condition of rationality set by the CI procedure.

The reasoning that showed why we do not have to adopt a maxim of sacrificial beneficence can also be used to explain why a maxim of exclusively self-interested helping will be rejected (as will any such restricted maxim of the form "To help only those with characteristic *c* or in conditions *d*" where the restrictions mark preferences, prejudices, and the like). Since one cannot control whether one has needs that may require help, so, the argument of the CI procedure will show, it is not consistent with one's rationality to restrict in advance the nature of the help available. One may be lucky and never need help that is not also in the interests of others to give. But the moral status of this possible state of affairs is just the same as that of needing any kind of help at all. Its coming to pass or not is not a possible object of human willing. I cannot make it that the help I may require satisfies some condition decided on earlier. This does not mean that it is impermissible to provide self-interested help. What is rejected is a policy of never helping unless doing so is in one's interest.

Something needs to be said now about the central place in this construal of Kant's argument of contingent, empirical facts about human beings: their dependency and their true needs. When Kant speaks of excluding empirical considerations from morality, he has two related things in mind. First, the foundation of morality is to be nonempirical. This involves a thesis about the nonempirical status of reason and an argument that it is only if morality is a function of reason that its unconditional claim on us is valid. Second, each of us is subject to moral requirements independent of any contingent, empirical ends we may happen to have. (This is the thesis that morality is not a system of hypothetical imperatives.) Kant does not need to argue (nor does he) that the content of morality is to be determined without regard to the empirical nature of things.[19]

Nonetheless one may feel, for moral reasons, that the role of dependency in the argument introduces a disturbing element. It was an important result of the argument for beneficence that among dependent, vulnerable rational beings capable of mutual aid, variations in such things as risk tolerance, or resources, do not affect the application or stringency of the duty of beneficence. But suppose there are rational beings who are not vulnerable and dependent (call them angels); the argument for beneficence could not require them to reject a maxim of nonbeneficence toward human beings. (We suppose that they are in a position to intervene in human affairs.) Angels could will a world in which no one is able to help since they cannot need help. Would they then have no duty of beneficence toward human beings? Should not all rational beings have the same duties?

All rational beings are subject to the same fundamental practical principle—the Categorical Imperative. This is all that follows merely from the fact of their rationality.[20] Not all rational beings will have the same duties. The duties they have (that is, what follows if they apply the CI to their maxims) vary as their natures vary. For example, human beings are said to have no duty to promote their own well-being (happiness) because each of

19. A clear argument for this can be found in Allen Buchanan, "Categorical Imperatives and Moral Principles," *Philosophical Studies* 31 (1977), 249–260.

20. Being subject to the CI does not even entail obligation. Only imperfectly rational beings are under moral constraint.

us naturally desires his own happiness (DV46). Suppose that there were rational beings who had no such natural desire, say, natural self-sacrificers. Such beings might have to be enjoined (morally) to care for themselves, perhaps on grounds suggested by Kant's argument against the neglect of one's talents. (This reasoning would also apply to human beings bent on self-neglect or servility.) So the mere fact that angels might not have the same duty of beneficence that we do should not in itself pose a problem.

What is troubling about the possibility that angels would not have a duty to help us is that their not having such a duty seems to stem from the fact that they do not need our help. This looks to be just the sort of consideration that the new interpretation of the beneficence example was to block. But for angels it is not a contingent fact about them (there is no appeal to strength, wealth, and such) that leads them not to need help. They can guarantee that they will never be compelled to want help in the pursuit of ends that they rationally cannot abandon. That is defining of their species of rational being. So we might say that the dependency interpretation of the argument for beneficence makes use of species-relative constraints on reasoning: if you are such and such a kind of rational being, you cannot rationally will a world in which beings like yourself act (as a function of natural law) as you propose. The procedure of moral judgment shows something about what a certain sort of rational being can rationally will.[21]

The dependency argument against a policy of indifference, then, does not simply yield a duty to help others. It defines a *community* of mutual aid for dependent beings.[22] Membership in the community is established as much by vulnerability (and the possibility of being helped) as by rationality (and the capacity to help).[23] It may well be that this is not the sole

21. One might argue in a slightly different way here. The contradiction-in-will test depends on an agent's appreciating what he must will, given his nature, under the assumption that his maxim is to become a universal law of nature. A rational being with a different nature might require a different kind of test to show it its duties. That is, from the fact that a course of reasoning does not generate a duty for angels, it might not follow that angels have no such duty. The CI procedure might not represent an exhaustive procedure of judgment for all rational beings. Its usefulness, and its validity, might be tied to the nature of the being using it. Kant discusses the constraints imposed on the procedure of moral judgment by features of the human imagination in the *Second Critique*'s "Typic of Pure Practical Judgment."

22. In DV121 Kant concludes that the argument for beneficence compels us to regard one another as "fellow-men—that is, rational beings with needs, united by nature in one dwelling place for the purpose of helping one another."

23. Schopenhauer argued (1) that Kant's argument for beneficence has an egoistic foundation because we are moved to reject nonbeneficence in order to ensure the satisfaction of our natural inclinations and needs, and (2) that the CI procedure itself therefore depends on conditions derived from our inclinations, which Kant holds that we, as rational beings, must want to overcome. See *On the Basis of Ethics* (1840), trans. E. F. J. Payne (New York: Liberal Arts Press, 1965), pt. 2, no. 7, pp. 89–92. The dependency interpretation, however, works from

duty to help others that we have. Other arguments might yield duties with different requirements, different scope (some of which might apply to angels as well). In this case it is the fact of dependency—that we are, equally, dependent (again, not that we are equally dependent)—that is the ground of the duty to help. I may not be indifferent to others not because I would thereby risk the loss of needed help (this is not a duty of fairness or reciprocity) but because I cannot escape our shared condition of dependency. The claim of each of us on the resources of the others is equal. The argument that defeats the maxim of nonbeneficence leads, positively, to a duty of mutual aid.

Membership in the community of mutual aid is more inclusive than it may first appear. Those we are unable to help can still belong to our community of mutual aid and so be obliged to help us. Imagine a race of rational dependent beings, capable of helping us, yet outside the reach of any help we have to offer. Perhaps they live too far away; perhaps we do not possess food that would nourish them; and so on. But that someone may be unable (as it happens) to be helped is the way things are among us as well. Our need for help is no guarantee that the help we need will be available or possible. Membership in the community of mutual aid gives one's need a valid *claim* on the resources of the community. The claim does not (necessarily) fail to be acknowledged when left unmet. So long as there is no ultimately unbridgeable barrier to mutual help between us and this other race—so long as it is not true that nothing we could ever do, in any possible circumstances, could be of help to them, while they continue to be able to help us[24]—their inclusion in the community will stand.

Likewise, a rational being with needs counts as a possible provider of help even though, at any given time, he is not able to provide help. Membership does not depend on one's usefulness. All that is necessary is that one be the sort of being who could—given the desire, the opportunity, and so on—provide help. So a normal adult who through illness

---

the practical conditions of human rationality, which are a function not of inclination but of the natural limitations of our powers as agents. There need be nothing egoistic in the content of the maxims which generate a contradiction in will. A rational, perfectly altruistic human being would be equally subject to the duty of mutual aid for the same reason, and in response to the same facts about his human nature, that apply in the ordinary case.

24. If there were in principle no way one could help, it is not clear to me in what sense the need of the other could establish a claim. When as a matter of fact one cannot help, there is a sense of how things could be otherwise. If the help can in principle go only one way, we might have to imagine something like one-way causality. I suppose this is the nature of a relation to God. His acts are, of course, miracles. There is nothing in principle we could do that could be of help. (None of our actions could reach God: he is not within the realm of our effects; but then he is also not a dependent being.) It may be a feature of God's goodness that he will acknowledge human need, but his doing so would not follow from any acknowledgment of shared dependency.

or other disability is not able to provide help has an undiminished claim on the community's helping resources. We do not pass in and out of the community in cycles of sleep; nor are we exiled when lack of skill or resources or knowledge make us unable to help. Membership in the community is strictly a matter of one's status as a dependent rational being.

It is tempting to wonder whether a parallel line of reasoning could be used to extend the scope of the argument to include babies and future generations. The idea would be to treat the fact of being contemporaries as arbitrary with respect to membership in the community of mutual aid. Since it is not the possibility of another's being of use to me that is the ground of his claim on my help, but our both being dependent beings, capable in principle of providing help, we might regard an infant as one whose present inability to help will be overcome in the passage of time. In time, he will come to have the necessary resources to provide help, as his now "dormant" physical and rational capacities come into use. Of course, problems with this sort of argument abound and are familiar in questions of the moral status of the fetus. Still, given Kant's deep silence on the question of the moral status of children, it is of interest to follow out elements in his argument that might bear on the question.[25]

That future generations might have a claim of mutual aid (despite the fact that they will never be able to provide help for those who look to their needs) would not mean that they have an equal claim on current resources. As we shall see when we investigate the casuistry of mutual aid, a valid claim requires that one's needs be considered, not that they be met.

No parallel considerations emerge for animal-human mutual aid. We may have duties of kindness to all sentient beings, but if we do it will be for reasons different from those appealed to in the argument for mutual aid. Animals are not, strictly speaking, capable of providing help, although they may of course do things that are helpful to us. This seems to be recognized in the fact that, apart from considerations of training and discipline, we do not believe that we have any claim on an animal's help. This is not because animals are privileged or selfish or dumb. Rather, I think we suppose they are not capable of recognizing human needs as such or of conceiving of themselves as agents of help. It is these capacities that are called on by the duty of mutual aid. (Those rational capacities necessary to be able to act under the conception of meeting another's need are, in Kant's view, just those that make one a moral agent, subject to moral requirements.)

25. Considerations extending the argument to infants would not take account of defective rational beings. In those cases, the inability to help cannot be seen as a function of naturally transient circumstances. Perhaps the model here should be innocent loss of resources.

III

If the CI procedure shows that it is impermissible to adopt the maxim, "To never help anyone," it follows that we must adopt its contradictory, "To help some others sometimes."[26] This is the maxim that describes our positive duty of mutual aid. But this maxim, as it stands, is not much of a guide to action. It does not tell us whom to help, or in what circumstances, or when we may permissibly refrain from helping. Nor does it offer a way of determining when our efforts fall short of what mutual aid requires.[27]

By contrast, when the maxim of the deceitful promise is rejected (see G422), we know exactly what we may not do: we may not make a deceitful promise when that is necessary to extricate ourselves from financial difficulties.[28] But we do not thereby get a positive duty based on this maxim's rejection. One would get a duty to truth in promising ("Never make a deceitful promise") only if no maxim that involves not telling the truth in a promise can pass through the CI procedure. What maxims we may (permissibly) act on, in the circumstances prompting the deceitful promise maxim, are not indicated by the procedure. And it is appropriate that it be unclear what one is to do on discovering that a proposed course of action is

26. That is, it would not be permissible to fail to adopt this maxim. That would not prevent one from having a more extensive maxim of mutual aid: the rejection of "Never help anyone" sets a minimal maxim of mutual aid.

27. There are always such issues for duties of wide obligation, as Kant calls them: they leave room for choice. The question is of what sort. In this section, I sketch a casuistry for mutual aid based on the fact that the argument for the duty establishes a claim of need.

Kant offers two suggestions about imperfect duties worth noting. The first relies on the *Groundwork* division of duties: perfect duties differ from imperfect duties in that the former allow "no exception for the sake of inclination" (G421n). This seems very un-Kantian. Why should any sort of duty allow exceptions for inclination? Could one refrain from helping A because of fondness for B? May one withhold help because one is inclined to do something else? It does not follow from the fact that I may make exception for *some* inclination that the grounds for excepting an inclination are arbitrary; but the *Groundwork* division of duties gives no guidance. A second interpretation of the choice that attends duties of wide obligation marks the fact that they are duties to adopt an end: "if the law can prescribe only the maxims of actions, not actions themselves, this indicates that it leaves a play-room *(latitudo)* for free choice in following (observing) the law, i.e. that the law cannot specify what and how much one's actions should do toward the obligatory end. —But a wide duty is not to be taken as a permission to make exceptions to the maxim of actions, but only as a permission to limit one maxim of duty by another (e.g. love of one's neighbor in general by love of one's parents)—a permission that actually widens the field for the practice of virtue" (DV389). That is, "latitude of duty" allows exception for inclinations (love of parents) only when they are taken up into a more restricted maxim of duty. There is room for judgment, but judgment constrained by a complex array of moral requirements.

28. Or, if we follow Allen Wood's interpretation, the argument for the second example yields the more general result that we may not use deceitful promises as means in promoting our self-interest. See "Kant on False Promises," in *Proceedings of the Third International Kant Congress,* ed. L. W. Beck (Dordrecht: D. Reidel, 1972), pp. 614–619.

blocked by considerations of duty. Other courses of reasoning, other proposals for action, need to be introduced and in turn examined by the CI procedure.

Part of the difficulty with the maxim of mutual aid is that it is not directly a maxim of action at all. There is no action properly described as "sometimes helping someone." One might call such a maxim a general policy maxim, in that it expresses an agent's intention to act, in general, in a certain sort of way.[29] General policy maxims stand toward specific maxims of action as their principle. So when someone fails to help because he does not, as a matter of principle, want to help those in need, we conclude that he is acting on (or out of) a maxim of nonbeneficence (a maxim contrary to mutual aid) and therefore impermissibly. This gives us enough to begin the casuistry of mutual aid.

Suppose someone acts on the maxim, "To ignore requests for charitable donations." The no-donations maxim (as stated) would not fail the CI procedures. One can will a world in which no one does (because no one can) make charitable donations without a contradiction in will, for there is nothing we must will that is not possible in a world with no charitable institutions. Is this policy then permissible?

For the purposes of moral assessment, the no-donations maxim is incomplete. Compare the following:

1. To refuse requests for charitable donations because charitable institutions are likely to be corrupt and wasteful. (Something one disapproves of.)
2. To refuse requests for charitable donations because it is better to help as one can in a more personal way. (Something one wants to do.)
3. To refuse requests for charitable donations because making such donations leads to helping those in need. (Something one does not want to do.)

The relevant differences involve the ends that bring the agent to refuse to make charitable donations. Though people acting on the three maxims behave in the same way (none gives charitable donations), there is good sense in saying they are not doing the same thing. They act on or from different principles, and the moral quality of their actions is judged differently in light of the different principles their actions instantiate. A maxim like 3 above will be judged impermissible because it is an instance of the general policy maxim, "To never help anyone." Maxims 1 and 2 raise no similar moral difficulty because their general policy maxims are permissible (let us suppose). Knowing what is be-

29. Although all maxims are general in form ("To do x, in circumstances y, in order to z"), a maxim of action need involve no commitment or intention to act in similar ways in similar circumstances.

hind a maxim's adoption is therefore essential to its assessment by the CI procedure. It is through the general policy maxim that the morally distinctive aspect of each is revealed. It is not the refusal to give but the purpose or principle of indifference it serves that is impermissible.

How, in general, to determine a maxim's principle is a technical matter in the theory of maxims that we cannot investigate now. What I want to argue here is that, for the purpose of practical judgment, attending to elements in the argument which defeat the maxim of general indifference can help determine if nonbeneficence is the principle behind particular maxims of not giving help.

Although the duty of mutual aid allows one not to help sometimes, in the normal course of things someone who acknowledges the duty will in fact give help. One cannot have the opportunity and the ability to help, never help, and yet claim to have (to live by) a policy of sometimes helping others. We call this hypocrisy.

Now suppose someone is in a position to give life-saving help with little cost to himself. He is just a passerby, with no special relation to the person in need. He knows it is wrong never to help anyone, and so he does, sometimes, help. This time he would rather not. But from the fact that the duty of mutual aid does not require us to promote the well-being of others on every occasion, it should not follow that we are free to refuse help to a person in distress on such grounds. The action we are considering seems to epitomize the spirit of indifference to others. How can an understanding of the argument for mutual aid help us here?

Suppose someone passes by a serious request for aid with the thought, "I helped someone yesterday." The agent acknowledges that the duty of mutual aid applies when he registers that help is needed, his would serve, and that some excuse, or excusing idea, needs to be brought forward to justify his passing by. We want to say that someone who passes by with such an excuse cannot have adopted the required maxim of mutual aid (as the principle of his maxims of action), even though he seems to accept the idea of sometimes helping someone.

Someone who monitors the frequency of his beneficent acts perhaps holds the belief that the satisfaction of the duty of mutual aid involves taking a (fair?) share of the burden of helping others; that the "sometimes" in the principle of the duty is a numerical notion—like a quota. The argument of the CI procedure shows where this belief mistakes what mutual aid requires. In requiring that we recognize one another as equal members of a community of mutual aid, we are brought to acknowledge the claim on us of others' needs. The rejection of the maxim of nonbeneficence is a rejection of indifference to others. We may not be required to help in all cases, but we may not be indifferent to the claim of need.

The fact of having done a good deed yesterday cannot weigh against that claim. If the cost of giving aid in this case is negligible,[30] there is nothing in the agent's excuse that legitimately stands between the need of the other and the help he can give. To acknowledge the claim of the other's need is just to take his need as a reason to offer help. So unless one has a morally relevant reason why one need not help, the valid claim is sufficient. Someone who rejects the claim on his help because he believes his beneficence quota has been met has failed to take the duty of mutual aid as the principle of his helping maxims.

There is a striking consequence of this. It may be my lot that people needing help are frequently in my path. If it turns out that I am often in a convenient position to help, then I must. I do exactly what I ought to do, and so no special moral merit is earned. I am no more virtuous than someone genuinely prepared to help whose encounters with those needing help are less frequent.[31] What counts, morally, is the willingness to take need as a reason to give aid. There is a parallel feature of mutual aid on the receiving side. If it is someone's misfortune to need help frequently (suppose through no fault but through bad luck and the like), he does not use up his stock of mutual aid and has a claim on the help of others that is undiminished by his past withdrawals.[32]

Morally relevant reasons for refraining from help will be those that have weight when placed against the claim of need on one's help. Suppose helping is something one would rather not (in a given case) do; or suppose it poses a minor but real inconvenience. Do these count as legitimate reasons to refrain from helping someone in distress? One way to proceed is to look further at what I have called "the claim of need." There are two issues here. First, what are the sorts of needs that are relevant to the duty of mutual aid? Surely I may not claim aid for every end I have that I cannot pursue without help. Second, when are the costs of giving aid sufficient to justify a refusal of help? When we know what the argument for the relevant class of needs is, we will know why some reasons for refraining from help do not have moral weight.

---

30. As we shall see later, it does matter if helping turns out to be costly, disrupting one's life and basic projects; but that is not relevant to the case at hand.

31. There is a fuller argument for this nonquantitative model of virtue in Chapter 2, section II.

32. This sort of case is complicated when the needy person requires constant help from the same source. Then we are inclined to think that a relationship of dependency has formed, which might well alter what each might legitimately expect from the other. How such cases are to be understood will figure importantly in the full casuistry of mutual aid, but they must not be taken up at the outset, when the relevant reasons in deliberations about mutual aid are being laid out.

The duty of mutual aid has its ground in the facts that we are dependent beings and beings with ends that it is not rational for us to forgo: ends set by "true needs" whose satisfaction is a necessary condition for the exercise of rationality. As we are rational agents, we set ends. We are able to formulate and act from a conception of the good. If to set ends is to put oneself to the realization of more or less complex goals and projects, one respects one's humanity in oneself by developing those capacities needed to realize a wide variety of ends (DV51). Thus an imperfect rational being must acknowledge the obligatoriness of developing his powers and talents: they are necessary conditions of the possible expression of his rationality. As a person's true needs are those that must be met if he is to function (or continue to function) as a rational, end-setting agent, respecting the humanity of others involves acknowledging the duty of mutual aid: one must be prepared to support the conditions of the rationality of others (their capacity to set and act for ends) when they are unable to do so without help. The duty to develop (not neglect) one's talents and the duty of mutual aid are thus duties of respect for persons.

The ground of the duty of mutual aid then reveals its moral point. The good it looks to is the preservation and support of persons in their activity as rational agents. The needs for which a person may make a claim under the duty of mutual aid are those that cannot be left unmet if he is to continue in his activity as a rational agent.[33] Thus we may refrain from helping only if such action would place our own rational activity in jeopardy. Excuses that look to the ordinary difficulties encountered when help is given or that look to other helping actions recently done to get the agent off the hook therefore provide good evidence that the principle of the agent's particular maxims in the circumstances where help is needed is not that of mutual aid.

We are not obliged to help everyone, or everyone we can, because the point of the duty of mutual aid is to sustain dependent beings in the (permissible) activity of their lives. If giving aid undermines the life activity of the giver, the point of mutual aid is not achieved. (It is a duty of mutual aid, not sacrifice.) The requirements of beneficence do not interfere with what is necessary for one to continue to live a human life; they also do not protect all that one may find necessary to live as one wants. We are required to acknowledge both the claim of true need on our aid and the moral weight of that need against the claims of our own interested desires.

---

33. It might seem that the stoic had grounds drawn from the argument against his maxim of nonbeneficence to claim aid for his end of independence. But that argument showed he could not guarantee that he could act unaided for any end, even his end of independence from aid. It establishes the inescapability of the condition of dependency. The duty of mutual aid follows as there are ends that cannot be abandoned (true needs). The stoic remains free to abandon his stoical end.

It is possible that a person will be called on frequently to give aid and that each time his help is needed no serious sacrifice is required. Yet the cumulative effect on his life may be such that the frequency does undermine his pursuit of his life. It is not clear to me that this affects what he is to do when help is needed again. For although his well-being is compromised over time, what he is being asked to do in a given case is not the cause. I think it is appropriate to look at such a scenario as one of moral misfortune—in much the same sense of misfortune that one would find in a series of physical accidents hindering one's legitimate pursuit of happiness. As there are historical and physical limitations on what one may expect to be able to do, so there may be moral ones—undeserved, compassion-provoking, but not changing what one is morally required to do. We might hope that the cumulative effects of past helpings would have moral weight in determining who among several possible helpers should be the one to give help, but the argument for mutual aid does not show that this is so.

In general, looking to the point of a duty lays the ground for explicating intuitions about relative stringency, setting the framework for a casuistry of excuses. Compare the Kantian arguments against deception. Kant takes the point of fidelity or nondeception to be centrally involved with sustaining what he calls "the dignity of man as a rational being" (DV93–94). The argument against deception is that it subverts the natural function of one's rational faculties. Therefore, excusing one's proposed deception on the grounds that honesty will jeopardize one's projects or goals (that one "needs to" deceive) will be judged impermissible because the loss of well-being is less grave than the subversion of one's rationality. What is at stake is respect for oneself as a rational being.[34] This manner of argument seems to fit well with Kant's belief that apparent conflicts of duties are to be resolved by looking to the stronger "ground" of obligation (DV23).

IV

If each person, in adopting the general policy maxim of mutual aid, is to be prepared to help those in need except when the degree of sacrifice is

---

34. This suggests an interesting contrast with the duty of promise keeping. I would think that this duty would be less stringent in the face of serious misfortune. Let us conjecture that the good this duty looks to is the security of mutual expectations. If keeping a promise would endanger one's life (or the conditions for the exercise of one's rationality), it would be reasonable to see that fact as sufficient to excuse breaking it. Moreover, if keeping the promise would involve such loss, one might suppose the duty of mutual aid would require the promisee to release the promisor from his obligation. (It is, after all, a duty to help where we can.) Of course it might be relevant to consider whether the promisee was the only one in a position to help and the release from the promise the only way to avert the loss. However this worked out, the purpose here in pursuing these speculations is to emphasize the role the point of a duty plays in determining the duty's scope and stringency.

too great, this will generate a lack of uniformity in what is required of different people in similar situations of meeting need: the cost of helping will not be the same for all persons. But in fulfillment of the duty of mutual aid, the difficulties of one's own situation are relevant in determining what one must do. This is not true for all duties. Such difficulties are irrelevant in determining whether one may deceive for self-interest, betray a trust, and so on. The facts of one's situation that are relevant differ for different kinds of duties. In a given set of circumstances it is morally appropriate that the duty of mutual aid should oblige only some people to give aid.

But different people will put different value on the cost of their helping act. And different people will decide differently about which of their needs cannot be sacrificed. How is this to be dealt with? The duty of mutual aid does require some sacrifice. We are not to help only when it costs us little or nothing. On the other hand, we do not need to help when the cost undermines our lives, and each person must judge when that is so. There can be no simple rule that will guarantee correct judgments. This is why training in casuistry is an essential part of a moral education, for when it is not taught we are more likely to require simple principles that cannot do justice to particular cases. But if we suppose that knowing how to assess one's needs is something that can be taught (to know what one may permissibly ask for as well as what one may legitimately protect), then we may expect sincere and reasonable people, with a proper attachment to their own lives and a commitment to doing what is right, to weigh fairly the cost of the helping act against the gravity of the need it will meet.

Differences in circumstances and needs do not weigh at all in the argument for the duty of mutual aid. Since we are all dependent rational beings, we are all equally obliged by the duty of mutual aid. One should not confuse the uniformity of obligation (where all of a kind of rational being must have the same obligations) with the uniformity of what one is obliged to do (which will vary with the kind of circumstances picked out as morally relevant by the duty).

If true needs set the content of the duty of mutual aid, not all (not even many) of our normal helping actions fall within the scope of mutual aid. We loan money so that pleasures do not need to be postponed; we stop and give directions; we lend a hand. These are all helping acts that (normally) are not responses to true needs. Are they actions we have a duty to do? Surely it is a good thing that people help each other. But since not everything that would be good to do is something that we are morally obliged to do, it may be that most helping actions are not matters of duty. Given the argument for the duty of mutual aid, there are two possibilities here. Either, on most occasions where we are asked for (or are in a position to) help, it is permissible not to help, or there is some other argument to a duty of aid that would cover these cases.

There are passages in the *Groundwork* and in the *Doctrine of Virtue* that suggest this stronger version of a duty of beneficence. We are to take the ends of others as our ends, to further them as we can (G430). We are to take the happiness of others as an obligatory end (DV47). It would then seem that we may limit our helping activity only when it would put us in the position of needing help ourselves, or when helping would prevent our doing something else we had a duty to do, or when we disapprove of the pursuits we are to lend a hand in promoting (DV47, 122). Otherwise, wherever we can help we must.

There are considerable grounds for skepticism about such a duty. It involves a radical conception of a community of need and action in which it does not seem to matter whose end an end is. All one would need to know is that a person has an end, that he is unable to realize it unaided, and that one is in a position to help. Although it is hard to avoid seeing Kant's words as implying such a duty, it is implausible in its own right and at odds with deeper features of Kantian ethics.

First, it makes no distinction between ends that an agent could easily give up on discovering that he could not realize them without aid (going to a movie on a day I am short of cash) and ends that an agent cannot rationally abandon (true needs). Both sorts of ends would have an equal claim on others. Second, the duty neglects the way in which it matters how a desire is satisfied: from what source, by whose agency. That is, the radical community of aid that such a duty describes would not be supportive of the expression of rational agency in one's life. The duty would thus be at odds with a moral conception that stressed the development of capacities for responsible choice and effective action: the practical expressions of autonomy.

There is a way of making good sense of what Kant says. One might view the idea of taking another's ends as my own not in the sense that I should be prepared to act in his place (I act for him; I get for him what he wants when he cannot) but, rather, in the sense that I support his status as a pursuer of ends, so that I am prepared to do what is necessary to help him maintain that status. We might say "I help him pursue-his-ends" and not "I help him in the pursuit of his ends." This interpretation acknowledges the other as a rational, autonomous agent in a way that the "community of ends" interpretation does not. It leads me to view the well-being of another as something more than the (passive) satisfaction of his desires. What I support is the other's active and successful pursuit of his self-defined goals. I promote another's well-being or happiness by supporting the conditions for his pursuit of ends. That is, what I have a duty to do is to contribute to the meeting of his true needs when that is not within his power. On this interpretation, then, in taking another's ends as my own or his happiness as an obligatory end, I acknowledge him as a member of the community of mutual aid.

If, within the Kantian system, the duty of mutual aid is the only duty directing us to help others, there remain reasons to offer help for less than true needs and moral reasons to encourage an attitude of helpfulness in oneself and others. Although general helpfulness (or kindness) shares with the duty of mutual aid a willingness to take the need of another as a reason for action, it is the expression of a distinct attitude toward other persons. The helpful person is willing to set aside or delay his own pursuits to ease the way for someone else. He views the other as, in a sense, a fellow pursuer of happiness. In that, they are equals. Yet it is appropriate for him to weigh costs. While it matters to him that others succeed in their (permissible) endeavors, the demands of his own pursuits need to be met. The helpful person has an interest in the well-being of others. It is this interest that makes the need of another an occasion for his acting. This is unlike the circumstances of mutual aid where the true need of another has a claim, independent of interest, on one's help.

So, if someone needs help changing a tire, a helpful person, in the absence of pressing demands of his own, will help. There is no moral requirement that he do so: it is not impermissible not to help. If, however, the person who needs this help is in great distress (someone on the way to the hospital, an elderly person who cannot tolerate exposure to bad weather), it is no longer an act of kindness but a duty to help. When if help is not given, a life will be in jeopardy or gravely diminished, then changing a tire is addressing someone's true need. It is not the action (its strenuousness, and so on) but the nature of the need to be met that determines whether it is an occasion where helping is required of us.

I am not saying that kindness and benevolence are without moral structure or content (they are not "mere inclinations"). The claim is rather that they have a different moral structure, one that parallels the difference between interests and true needs. The difference is most readily seen in the nature of the excusing conditions each allows for refraining from giving help. According to the casuistry of mutual aid, when the true needs of another constitute a claim on one's help, it does not count as a reason to justify not responding that one gave yesterday or that the price in terms of sacrificed interests (not sacrificed true needs) is high. The casuistry of benevolence accepts these as excusing considerations. When someone's life is at stake, benevolence might have us see that the cost of helping is outweighed by the gravity of the need. Mutual aid, by contrast, instructs that, if one's own true needs are not at risk, one is simply to help as one can. The needs of the other do not outweigh the losses that will be involved in giving help. The losses have no moral weight in such cases. Consequently, one might expect the casuistry of gratitude and indebtedness to be significantly different for help required by the duty of mutual aid from that called for by benevolence. This is part of what is involved in distinguishing a duty of mutual aid from benevolence. They are different moral requirements, fulfilling different moral roles. A complete Kantian account of the morality of helping should contain them both.

Nothing is required of a helpful or kind person as such. But what it is to be such a person involves a readiness to take someone's need as a reason for helping. It is an active attitude, leading one to be engaged with the lives and projects of others. We call this sort of attitude a virtue and praise (value) those who become truly helpful persons. Although the duty of mutual aid and the virtue of kindness present different moral requirements, it may be that both need to be present for the exemplary exercise of either. Although true needs usually speak for themselves, one may turn away or become preoccupied with activities insulated from encounters with others who have such needs. A kind person maintains a sense of connectedness with others, an a priori acknowledgment, as it were, that he may be of use. Kant says: "Thus it is our duty: not to avoid places where we shall find the poor who lack the most basic essentials, but rather to seek them out; not to shun the sick-rooms or debtor's prisons in order to avoid the painful sympathetic feelings that we cannot guard against" (DV126). Kindness, on the other hand, may need to be supplemented by the clarity about what the moral point of helpfulness is that can be derived from attention to the duty of mutual aid. Our good-heartedness is to be tempered by the moral need for self-development and struggle in others. So we should not meddle and we should be wary of impulses to paternalism, not because they may bring more harm than good (as they may) but because they go against the grain of the respectful help we are morally required to give.

There should be no suggestion here that these remarks complete the casuistry of mutual aid. I take it as barely begun. What I have hoped to demonstrate is the power of the argument for the duty of mutual aid to guide reflections on fundamental casuistical questions.

4

The Practice of Moral Judgment

THE ROLE of moral rules in Kant's account of moral judgment has been the focus of severe and trenchant criticism of the Kantian enterprise in ethics. It bears much of the weight of criticisms of the theory for its narrow rigorism, its abstraction from the particular, its inability to accommodate moral change, and the absence of an account of moral sensitivity or perception. These are all legitimate concerns. In response I want to offer a new account of how moral rules are used within a Kantian theory of moral judgment.[1] I think this account not only shows that the criticisms are misplaced, but also generates a set of moral insights that one might have thought foreign to Kantian theory.

It is my intention in offering this account to be faithful to Kant. But much of what I introduce as essential to his theory will seem alien to what is familiar from both friendly and critical discussions of Kant's ethics. This is to some extent natural with any new interpretation of familiar theories or texts. In this case it also has a deeper cause. Kantian ethics has not been as fully explored and developed in contemporary moral writing as it has been criticized, and on many issues the critics have had decisive say as to what the theory involves. I think the theory as Kant presented it is stronger and more interesting than our tradition would have it. And this is what I argue, though I cannot always prove that it is so. Since my interest here is more in moral theory than in the historical Kant, however, I am not too much troubled by this. We might think of this project as a normative reconstruction of Kantian ethics: the ultimate object is to present a plausible moral theory that is clearly and distinctively Kantian.

---

1. That is, how moral rules are used in *making* moral judgments. Their role in moral action is another matter.

I

Let us get our bearings by looking at some specific standard criticisms of the role of moral rules in Kantian theory. Moral rules are seen as a central feature of Kantian ethics either in the form of the Categorical Imperative or as rules of duty. In either case they are thought to distort moral judgment. In employing moral rules, the critic argues, we are forced to discard those particular features of texture and detail which give actions their moral significance to agents. Rules, by their nature, must be coarse-grained. Their purpose is to achieve regularity by enabling similar cases to be judged in similar ways. To accomplish this, they must direct us to pick out only some features of an action or set of circumstances as the features relevant from the rule's point of view. The uniqueness of our actions, each one being a product of "a great number and variety of independently variable features of particular situations," must be ignored.[2]

In short, the difficulty with a conception of morality that ties moral judgment to rules is that it ignores details (particular facts about individuals and cases) that are morally relevant. This would be significant even if the judgments rendered by a more context-attentive theory were the same as those derived from moral rules. People draw meaning and value from the particular. Even if they acknowledge the role of morality as a limiting condition on their actions and projects, *how* it sets its limits must affect the way people think about their own and others' activities. The thought is that, if moral rules function as some kind of externally imposed grid,[3] the intersection of moral rules with the particulars of action may leave what is significant to an agent in his action (perhaps even in an explanatory or justificatory way) unnoticed or, from his point of view, incorrectly described. He will be regarded (or find himself regarding himself) impartially and impersonally. And although impartiality may be a moral ideal, it is desirable for it to be realized without requiring from the outset that agents ignore what is personal and important to them.

There is an important distinction to be made between moral rules and moral principle in Kantian theory which, I think, defuses this sort of criticism and suggests a quite different role for moral rules than as the gridlines for a system of uniform impartial moral judgment. The first thing to be noticed is that the Categorical Imperative is not itself a moral rule—it

---

2. Stuart Hampshire, "Public and Private Morality," in *Public and Private Morality* (New York: Cambridge University Press, 1978), p. 28. Similar criticisms are made by Bernard Williams, "Persons, Character and Morality" and "Moral Luck," in *Moral Luck* (New York: Cambridge University Press, 1981), and by Peter Winch, "The Universalizability of Moral Judgments," in *Ethics and Action* (London: Routledge and Kegan Paul, 1972).

3. Hampshire, "Public and Private Morality," p. 40.

is an abstract formal principle. It does not set duties directly, but assesses agents' maxims of action (the subjective principles on which they act). Indeed, when in the *Groundwork* Kant speaks of deriving duties from the CI as their principle (G421), this is the introduction to four examples that are to show the procedure by which the CI is used to reject (as impermissible) particular maxims of action. (Agents have duties in the usual sense of the term only when an entire range of maxims—say, all those pertaining to lying—is judged impermissible.)

Now in order to use the CI as a principle of judgment or assessment, the agent must first produce his maxim. That is, he must formulate a (subjective) principle that correctly describes what he is intending to do and why (for what end and in response to what motive).[4] Since a maxim is a subjective principle of action, it contains as much of the particulars of person and circumstance as the agent judges are necessary to describe and account for his proposed action. Rules of relevance will be necessary to determine which facts it is legitimate to include in a maxim, but these are not themselves moral rules. They will require, for example, that the agent include in his action description only those features of the circumstances of action that are conditions of his acting as he proposes. So the fact that an action is to be performed on a Tuesday is rarely a condition of anyone's acting, and so will rarely have a legitimate place in any maxim.

But if actions are to be assessed (directly) by the CI through their maxims, there is a need in the Kantian system for some kind of independent moral knowledge. An agent who came to the CI procedure with no knowledge of the moral characteristics of actions would be very unlikely to describe his action in a morally appropriate way. Kant's moral agents are not morally naive. In the examples Kant gives of the employment of the CI procedure (G422–423), the agents know the features of their proposed actions that raise moral questions *before* they use the CI to determine their permissibility. It is because they already realize that the actions they want to do are morally questionable that they test their permissibility. It is hard to see how any system of moral judgment that assessed maxims of action could work with morally naive or ignorant agents.

We might think of the problem this way. Indefinitely many descriptions of an action are possible, most of which omit the aspects of the action that raise moral questions. Suppose you wanted to construct a machine capable of rendering the most primitive moral judgments using a system that re-

---

4. For the standard view of maxim construction, see Onora (Nell) O'Neill, *Acting on Principle* (New York: Columbia University Press, 1975), chap. 3. A different account of maxims and their content can be found in Chapter 10, section III. The differences between these two accounts are not relevant to the argument here.

quired maxims as the objects of assessment. Let us suppose the machine already has a natural descriptive language. Just to recognize that it should present the event "A punching B in the nose" for moral judgment, the machine would also have to know that such actions involve injuries and that injuries are morally salient features of human events. (Imagine how much more complex its information would have to be to pick up the harm of an insult or demeaning remark.) So we must imagine the machine equipped with a list of morally salient characteristics and some kind of mapping instructions that indicate appropriate correlations between moral features and the terms of natural descriptions. In general, judgment is possible only when the material to be judged is presented in a manner that fits the form of judgment. Moral judgment is not the first step in moral deliberation.

But even if the machine were given a full set of moral categories, it could still not judge in the manner of a Kantian moral agent. Not just any moral categories that "fit" are those by which a Kantian agent is to judge his action. An action is not shown to be impermissible because *some* maxim containing a possible description of it is rejected by the CI procedure. The point of using maxims as the object of moral assessment is to have actions judged as they are willed by the agent. (It does follow from this that an action might be permissible if willed under some descriptions but not under others. I take up some of these difficulties in the last section of the chapter.) The moral agent must not only know a set of morally appropriate categories (or else he might have no way to notice that what he was doing required moral scrutiny); he must also intend his action under an appropriate moral description (or else his maxim might have no moral content). What then is to prevent an agent from thinking of (and so describing) his action in morally idiosyncratic ways?

The danger here is not a gridlike view of agents' actions. The use of maxims as the object of moral assessment seems to threaten the objectivity of the CI procedure with too much detail and insufficient uniformity of (morally relevant) description.[5] We can find a response to this in Kant's view of moral judgment as an activity with a customary context of occurrence. Normal moral agents do not question the permissibility of everything they propose to do (having lunch, going to the movies, and so on). We expect moral agents to have acquired knowledge of the sorts of actions that it is generally not permissible to do and of the sorts of actions that, in the normal course of things, have no moral import. And we do not imagine normal moral agents bringing maxims of grossly immoral acts to the CI procedure routinely, only to discover (to their surprise?) that these acts are forbidden.

5. It bears considering how the parallel problem is solved to guarantee uniformity of so-called natural description.

Kant's analysis of his own examples in the *Groundwork* (G424) suggests that the need for judgment characteristically arises when an agent has what he takes to be good or compelling reason to act to satisfy some interest or need and yet realizes that what he would do violates a known moral precept. The issue that brings the agent to the CI is his feeling that the need or interest involved may justify making an exception to the moral rule in his case. The agent who proposes a deceitful promise to extricate himself from financial difficulties knows, without appeal to the CI, that what he proposes *may* be impermissible. He knows in advance that deceit is the sort of thing marked for moral review (because, presumably, he also knows it is the sort of thing that is normally impermissible). But, he may think, as with all things usually proscribed, there are cases, particular circumstances, and so on, in which what one may not ordinarily do is permitted. The question for this agent is whether his is such a case. We may think of the judgment rendered by the CI as showing whether the moral weight the agent is inclined to give his particular circumstances (in order to justify deception in his case) is warranted.[6]

In short, what I have argued here is that, because the CI procedure assesses maxims of action and because maxims contain only those descriptive elements that belong to an agent's conception of his action and circumstances, the CI cannot be an effective practical principle of judgment unless agents have some moral understanding of their actions before they use the CI procedure. I believe there is support for this view in Kant's own examples and in his account of moral education (DV152–156). But the claim that such prior moral knowledge is necessary follows from the structure of the CI as a practical principle of judgment and not from the correctness of my textual interpretation.

It is useful to think of the moral knowledge needed by Kantian agents (prior to making moral judgments) as knowledge of a kind of moral rule. Let us call them "rules of moral salience." Acquired as elements in a moral education, they structure an agent's perception of his situation so that what he perceives is a world with moral features. They enable him to pick out those elements of his circumstances or of his proposed actions that require moral attention.

The rules of moral salience do not themselves have moral weight—or not in the way that rules of prima facie duties do. The rules of prima facie duties pick out certain aspects of circumstances or actions and assign them moral weight, as they conform to or conflict with the relevant duties. What an agent is to do is determined by a "balance" of weights. The

---

6. I follow tradition here in taking moral judgment to involve the application of the CI procedure to maxims. Although I offer a different account of moral judgment in Chapter 7, I do not want my argument here to depend on accepting that view.

rules of moral salience pick out certain aspects, too, but with the point of letting the agent see where moral judgment is necessary. Typically they are acquired in childhood as part of socialization; they provide a practical framework within which people act. When the rules of moral salience are well internalized, they cause the agent to be aware of and attentive to the significance of "moral danger." They are not learned as bits of information about the world, and not as rules of guidance to use when engaged in particular sorts of activities (moral ones). The rules of moral salience constitute the structure of moral sensitivity. They may indicate when certain sorts of actions should not be taken without moral justification, or they may prevent certain kinds of actions from occurring to the agent as real options for him (functioning here as a kind of moral taboo).

In addition to picking out the morally significant features of actions, then, the rules of moral salience (RMS) indicate a burden of justification. The agent in the deceitful-promise example understands that normal prudential or instrumental justifications of actions will not do in the case of deceit. This is the mark of his "conscience." It seems he already knows that deceit in the pursuit of mere self-interest is usually not permissible. (He asks, "Is it not unlawful and contrary to duty to get out of difficulties in this way?" [G422].) So he comes to the CI knowing that, unless his situation is morally exceptional, it will not be judged permissible. Issues of excuse and justification do not enter moral thought only *after* an action has been done; they are part of the way a normal moral agent explains the permissibility of his actions to himself.

An action can be judged through the CI procedure without the agent's being aware that it has moral import (by someone other than the agent, for example). And an agent could bring a maxim to the CI without any sense that it posed moral difficulties and only subsequently discover its impermissibility. So the CI procedure can function without RMS—they are not part of the formal system of judgment. But I do not think these are the routine uses of the CI as a practical procedure of moral judgment. For those, agents have to know when to bring maxims to the CI and, to know that, they have to know the moral marks of their actions and circumstances.

If the function of the RMS is to guide the normal moral agent to the perception and description of the morally relevant features of his circumstances of action, the rules cannot be very complex. That is, they will not include the range of exceptions, limitations, and so on, that one would require of rules of judgment. The activity of moral judgment proceeds through the use of the CI; it is there that exceptions and limitations are introduced, as a case is judged to warrant them. The relevant RMS are not then qualified; they are not expected to be exceptionless (because they are not rules of moral judgment).

II

The value of introducing RMS is not just as a necessary practical device in the Kantian system of moral judgment. Their inclusion provides a means of approach to some of the issues that critics have felt Kantian ethics simply cannot deal with adequately. I want to say a few things here about two of them: conflicts of duty and the problems of moral perception and sensitivity.[7]

First, conflicts of duty. Rules of moral salience enable an agent to appreciate what is at issue in hard cases by making perspicuous the morally significant features that make them hard. In circumstances of apparent conflict of duty, the RMS do not resolve the conflict, but bring the conflict out into the open. The first moral requirement in such cases is that the agent see his situation as involving conflict (or just incompatibility) between plain moral features of the case. Failure to recognize the presence of an element of conflict in such a case is not a failure of moral judgment, but a failure of moral awareness or sensitivity. For the practice of moral judgment to go well, more than the ability to apply rules or work a principle of judgment is necessary. Knowing that more than one RMS may govern any case, the possibility of conflict is admitted from the outset. Principles of judgment are assigned the role of resolving conflict when it is clearly perceived. There is no reason to think there is something at fault in a conception of morality or in the RMS because they can reveal conflict at this level.

Conflict of duties is thought to threaten the consistency of moral systems because it precludes the possibility of agents fully satisfying valid moral requirements. This view of duty conflict is connected with a view of moral rules as obligation- or duty-generating (such rules give reasons for acting in the form "In circumstances Y you ought to do X"). When there are circumstances where more than one rule applies and the agent cannot instantiate both, the agent is left with something undone. And since it would have been better had he been able to do what he of necessity left undone, the unsatisfied rule is thought sometimes to leave a moral residue: something still owed.

But to know that something is a morally salient feature of a situation is not to know what one ought to do: rules of moral salience do not themselves generate duties. The agent is not to instantiate an RMS but to acknowledge, when an RMS applies, that the feature it picks out must be included when moral judgment is made. Thus when two RMS apply, they do not pick out two things an agent ought to do; they reveal the presence of two morally salient features of the situation which must be acknowledged. The rule-as-duty model for resolution of conflicts of duty requires the determination of

---

7. I have more to say about conflicts of duty in Chapter 8 and more about moral perception and sensitivity in Chapter 9.

which of the duties (or which in this situation) has the greater weight and which, therefore, ought to be acted on. When the model of judgment involves RMS and principles of judgment, one feature does not outweigh another—they do not present themselves as matters of independent moral weight. Both are seen as present in the circumstances of action. When more than one feature is seen as present, each is to be included in the description of the action and its circumstances which belongs in the agent's maxim. The agent's proposed action, as presented in his maxim, is then what is judged as a suitable (permissible) response to this configuration of moral features.

In circumstances of conflict, and before the CI can render judgment, the Kantian agent must contemplate a course of action. His determination is made in light of what he takes to be the moral features of his circumstances (as a function of the RMS), and represents his idea of how it is best to proceed in such circumstances. The agent's choice may well represent his sense of the relative weight of the different moral features present, but the judgment of what is right to do is not arrived at by balancing these weights. That judgment is made by bringing to the CI procedure a maxim that expresses the relative weights.

Two further differences with the rule-as-duty model should be noted. First: if we ask of each account, "What produces the conflict in conflicts of duty?" we get different answers. In the rule-as-duty model, conflict occurs when circumstances fit more than one duty, and to satisfy either of them involves the neglect or violation of the other. So conflict occurs because of a failure of one-to-one fit between circumstances and rules. In the Kantian model there are different moral features that require attention, and there is a presumption of a correct moral response to the complex of moral features present in the agent's circumstances of action. There is no lack of "fit" because there is no thought that dutiful actions are to instantiate moral rules or duties. The agent recognizes that, were his circumstances of action characterized by only one of the moral features present, he might act differently than he may have to when the other feature is present as well. This may produce a feeling of moral tension or difficulty (moral features affect a moral agent). But in a straightforward sense, there is no "conflict" at all. Understanding these cases of apparent conflict through the role of RMS can give us some purchase on Kant's claim that there cannot be conflicts of duties, only conflicting grounds of obligation (DV23).

The second difference involves the idea of a "moral residue." If there is no duty that is not complied with when a case with multiple moral features is resolved, there is no moral residue. But it does not follow from the absence of moral residue that if, say, a moral feature of a situation is not "picked up" in the action judged appropriate by the CI, nothing further needs to be done. If the moral feature remains, it may still require attention—not as residue but as a moral feature of the circumstances in which the agent now stands. So if I cannot at once help and tell the truth, a judgment that truthtelling is required does not free me from a requirement to help, if it is still possible to do that, or to do something else (explain myself, say) if the time for help is past. Or, if after I have made a promise other moral considerations make it impossible for me to keep it, the fact of the broken promise remains in my subsequent circumstances of action, and maxims of response to that fact will be assessed by the CI.

Introducing RMS into Kantian ethics changes the way we view conflicts of duty because RMS alter our idea of how an agent perceives situations that require moral judgment. Let us turn now to the question of the supposed moral insensitivity of the Kantian moral agent. If RMS shape perception, we may expect their presence to alter our ideas on this question as well.

The problematic picture is this: a Kantian moral agent is described as one who is attentive to what he sees as falling under principles of duty (say, of beneficence). So if he is not attending to questions of duty, he might see nothing at all. Or he may be attentive to duty, but not very perceptive, and so not see that his circumstances fall under a principle of duty. (He fails to recognize some situation as one calling for help.) A contrast is often drawn with someone whose perception is informed by compassion or sympathetic concern. Such a person simply and directly sees need: he is open to it. This contrast is morally significant if, for example, the Kantian agent really is less likely than the sympathetic person to see distress (or to see it as clearly, with the same degree of insight). The scope of beneficent actions (how much good is done) will be greater for persons who can more readily perceive the distress of others.

There is no doubt that moral principle alone cannot make you sensitive to need. So if you do not see that another is in pain (know what pain looks like) and appreciate what pain signifies (know why and when pain is to be avoided), you will not be an effective helping agent, however correct your principles of action may be.

The suggestion that the Kantian agent might do everything that the morality of principle requires and yet be insensitive seems to me connected to a mistaken view of what is involved in possessing and being attached to moral principle. First of all, if the ability to recognize distress is necessary if one is to act beneficently, then the Kantian moral agent will have failed to do what beneficence requires if he cannot recognize distress. Helping others is an obligatory end,[8] one we are required to adopt or will. Since in willing an end an agent is to will the necessary means (in his power), a Kantian agent *must* do what he can to recognize distress, and so do what

8. Obligatory ends emerge when no maxim of neglect of a (kind of) end is permissible.

he can to develop his ability to recognize distress. But perhaps the thought is that the sensitivity required to act effectively for the good of others is not something a moral agent can will himself to have. If you are a cold and unsympathetic sort of person, you cannot make yourself (will yourself to) see what a sympathetic person does. Such a person is not open or attentive to the same sorts of things.

In all of this we tend to imagine a person of fully formed character (a character formed independently of morality) adopting moral principles as an adult, and then possibly being hampered in his moral activities by his insensitivities. If, however, we focus on the RMS and their place in the development of a normal moral agent, the picture is different. The RMS provide the substantive core in a moral upbringing. When they are well learned, a person is able to identify morally significant elements in the situations he encounters. Small children do not know the range of things that cause pain, and need to be instructed that such and such a behavior is hurtful and that what is hurtful and unnecessary must (morally) be avoided. (I suspect that knowing how and when to avoid hurting is necessarily prior to being able to give aid, and involves knowledge and constraint that do not require compassion.) The rules of moral salience relative to beneficence must be learned in the same way. The point in learning these rules is not to get one to help when one has recognized distress (so that recognition would have to precede application of the rule), but to enable the agent to recognize distress *as* something morally significant, so that he may judge whether his help is morally appropriate or called for. To learn the rules of moral salience is not to learn that x or y is a moral mark, but to learn to recognize *and* respond to x and y as moral marks.

But might not the ability to discern distress require the development of affective capacities of response? I do not know the answer to this. Let us suppose that it does. Then we will have found a Kantian argument for the development of the affective capacities, and Kantian grounds for valuing them—not, of course, valuing them for themselves but as morally necessary means. Thus the affects would be valued as among the human powers whose development makes possible the realization of moral intention in action. If, on the other hand, the affects are not necessary for full attentiveness to and perception of distress, then whatever sets of abilities are necessary (or sufficient) will be encouraged in the acquisition of the rules of salience, and valued instrumentally as powers of effective moral agency.

Those who have emphasized the importance of perception relative to matters of principle and moral decision making have been right to do so. I think they have not seen the place of moral perception in Kantian ethics because they have assumed that all of the Kantian agent's moral knowledge resides in rules of duty or in the CI. Of such an agent it does seem in order to ask whether he is morally perceptive and, even when he is, to question whether there can be any requirement of perceptiveness within the theory of judgment. What I have argued here is that the Kantian moral agent *must* have a characteristic way of seeing if he is to judge at all. To be a moral agent one must be trained to perceive situations in terms of their morally significant features (as described by the RMS). As those features are difficult to discern, or need to be perceived with insight and accuracy to be correctly described, the Kantian moral agent can be as well equipped to do this as anyone can be brought up to be. His perceptiveness will be a mark of his virtue. Gross failures of perception—such as the inability to realize that unprovoked injury is morally significant—would be counted as marks of moral pathology. A person will be less than a *normal* moral agent unless he achieves a certain minimal level of moral sensitivity.

What distinguishes the Kantian agent's moral sensibility from plain emotional sensitivity (say, to the suffering of others) is the fact that the Kantian agent's responsiveness is shaped by moral knowledge (from the RMS), and his attendant motivation includes a higher-order (or regulative) concern for the permissibility of his actions and projects. So even if moral concern is achieved by means of heightened emotional sensitivity, the sensibility of a Kantian agent requires more than the development of emotional traits (such as sympathy).

III

In this last section I want to look at two connected issues. The first concerns the *content* of the RMS: its source, its subject matter, the possible standards a given set of RMS must meet to be valid. The second concerns the implications of this solution to the content problem of the RMS for the objectivity moral judgment. This discussion will take us, albeit in a preliminary and speculative way, into areas not usually illuminated by the insights of Kantian theory.

If moral judgment depends on moral perception and if the content of moral perception is determined by RMS, then changes in the RMS could affect the moral judgments made by sincere moral agents. There would be no question of change in judgment if the RMS were eternally fixed. But if we think of the RMS as a vehicle for moral education, then they will, in practice, represent the moral understanding that in part defines a "moral community." Nor does it seem likely that there is an ideal set of RMS: what has to be taught and with what sense of importance will be a function of a community's particular circumstances (the way social or economic conditions shape moral temptation, for example). On the other hand, not just any set of rules a culture might teach would count as rules of *moral* salience. There is, in G. J. Warnock's phrase, an "object of morality." Certain aspects of human action and interaction call for the sort of consideration we call "moral": for example, actions that hurt or deceive; practices that include some but not all within the circle of equal consideration; who has what and under what conditions; responses to unmet human need and want. These matters are the appropriate content of the RMS, but the form of their presentation could not, I think, be once and for all fixed.

Three lines of inquiry start here. (1) Where do the RMS come from? Do they represent some source of moral value independent of the CI? (2) What can count as valid RMS? (3) What is involved in change in RMS? How does the need for change emerge and make itself known? Is there any way of determining a direction of moral progress? (Kant certainly thought there was.)

In considering the first question—where do the RMS come from?—it is important not to confuse this with the historical problem of how and in what circumstances and for whose sake actual moral rules develop. The question at issue is the relation of the RMS to the CI. This relation looks problematic because the role of the RMS in moral judgment is to provide the descriptive moral categories that permit the formulation of maxims suitable for assessment by the CI procedure of judgment. The RMS may then seem to have—must have—an independent source. The CI procedure can show whether maxims are permissible or contrary to duty. The RMS are not maxims, and they do not describe anything appropriately permitted or forbidden. Thus it does not seem possible for the RMS to be generated by the CI procedure. But if they are independent of the CI, the unity of the Kantian system is compromised, consisting partly of formal procedure and partly of something like preprocedural intuition or convention.

Independence from the CI procedure, however, does not entail independence from the Moral Law. The CI *procedure* is a principle of judgment; it represents only one aspect of the Categorical Imperative. The Categorical Imperative itself is a formula that expresses the Moral Law: a principle (or law) of pure practical reason that determines the will a priori. The CI procedure interprets the formula in a manner suited to the limits of the human understanding and the conditions of human judgment.[9] But if the CI procedure represents an aspect or interpretation of the Moral Law for certain purposes, other aspects or interpretations may serve other roles.

Readers of the *Groundwork* know that there are three main formulations of the CI.[10] Each is said to be a way of "representing the principle of morality," different from the others in ways that are "subjectively rather than objectively practical" (G436). For example, Kant suggests that the

9. *Critique of Practical Reason* (hereafter cited KpV) 68–72, "Of the Typic of Pure Practical Judgment."

10. Each formula has two versions: one is an expression of the Moral Law, the other is a principle of application.

practical use of the Formula of the End-in-Itself and the Formula of the Kingdom of Ends is to bring the Moral Law "nearer to intuition" in order to "secure acceptance for the moral law" (G437). This is essential to Kant's purposes because any solution to the "motivation problem"—describing the nature of the agent's attachment to the Moral Law—must not compromise the autonomy of the moral agent. Kant argues that what draws the agent to acceptance of the Moral Law is a way of regarding himself and others which is compelling to a rational agent and which is itself an interpretation of the Moral Law. Kant's strategy here suggests a model for solving the "foundation problem" for the RMS.

What I will try to show for the RMS is that, by making further practical use of the key concepts of the CI formulas, we can see how the RMS can have a foundation or source in the Moral Law. We want to be in a position to say that although the RMS are not and cannot be derived from the CI procedure, they are neither arbitrary nor conventional, for they express the same fundamental concept (the Moral Law) that the CI procedure represents for purposes of judgment.

In the *Critique of Practical Reason* the Moral Law is presented as a Fact of Reason.[11] "It is the moral law . . . of which we become immediately conscious as soon as we construct maxims for the will . . . reason exhibits it as a ground of determination not to be outweighed by any sensuous condition" (KpV30). This "fact" explains how it can be possible for the awareness of the moral law as supremely authoritative for us as rational beings to be immanent in our everyday moral consciousness. I want to focus on two related aspects of this claim. First, it asserts our susceptibility to moral experience. That is, we can perceive things under moral categories and, when we do, we cannot be wholly indifferent to what they require. Second, it presents us with a conception of ourselves as moral agents. We know we can act as morality requires even against strong inclination: we know that we are free. We do not, through the Fact of Reason, discover that we are free to do anything. What we see is that in the face of *moral* opposition to our will we are not bound to work out the causal urgings of any set of desires or sensuous impulses. As end-setting beings, we will be moved to act to satisfy this or that desire, inclination, and the like. We are capable of having and acting from a conception of the good. As moral agents, however, we know we can and ought to act only as the Moral Law permits. The object of moral requirements and the task of

---

11. KpV31. The *Critique of Practical Reason* is a useful starting point for this sort of inquiry because its purpose is to provide a critical analysis of the concept of the CI as a principle of pure practical reason. The purpose of the more familiar *Groundwork* is to prove that the concepts embedded in our ordinary moral consciousness require such a critique of practical reason.

moral judgment is to bring our will into conformity with the Moral Law: all willings are to express our natures as free and rational beings.

It is part of the condition of human agency to be in a community of persons, each of whom is regarded as free on the same grounds as we regard ourselves as free: each is seen as capable of forming and acting from a conception of the good, constrained by the Moral Law. The community of agents is in this sense a community of equals. Since to act at all requires some space free from interference, the fact that each has desires, interests, and projects places each in a position to make some claim on the others (at least the minimal claim for some degree of noninterference for permissible projects) and to recognize the point of like claims made by others. To be a moral agent in a community of equals is to know that you may claim (some) space for your (permissible) pursuits *and* that you may have to leave space for others'. This is not a result of any Hobbesian bargaining; it comes in a Kantian account with the Fact of Reason—that is, with a conception of oneself as a moral agent among others. It is therefore the conditions of human agency and not the satisfaction of desire that set the object of moral requirement.

The conception of self and others that comes from the Moral Law provides the rudiments of the conception of a person as an end in himself: a being who may not be treated in certain ways because there is something in the nature of what he is—a moral agent—that compels restraint. This conception of persons as moral agents provides no substantive moral guidance. It rather sets the question that moral judgment is to answer: what are the activities we may perform as moral agents whose actions affect other moral agents? It is this conception of oneself as a moral agent among others that is the aspect of the Moral Law, present to everyday moral consciousness, which, I believe, provides the foundation for preprocedural moral rules (RMS).

I think of the RMS as an interpretation, in rule form, of the respect for persons (as ends-in-themselves) which is the object of the Moral Law. Their function is to guide in the recognition of those areas where the fact that persons are moral persons ought to instruct agents' deliberations and actions. They must therefore instruct agents on at least three sorts of issues *before* questions of permissibility can be taken to a procedure of judgment. (1) Who is a moral agent or end-in-himself? All humans? adults? rational adults? What are the marks that distinguish ends-in-themselves from other entities? (2) What are the conditions of agency for ends-in-themselves? In what ways are such agents vulnerable? Are agents self-sufficient or dependent on others (and in what ways) for sustaining themselves as agents? What forms of action interfere with the exercise of agency? What counts as force? deception? (3) What are the marks of reasonable claims and restraints? What are the areas of activity where they are likely to be present? These are matters an agent must know something about in order to formulate suitable maxims for assessment by the CI procedure. The answers appear as RMS—rules that then make up the substantive core of the agent's conception of himself as a moral agent. The *ground* of the RMS is in the conception of a person as moral agent (or end-in-himself) that comes from the experience of the Moral Law as a Fact of Reason. So, while the RMS are not a product of the CI procedure, their role and their subject matter are a product of the Moral Law.[12]

This much tells us what kind of rules RMS are to be (and so can explain why some kinds of regulative rules are not moral), but it does not yet provide any way of generating RMS. By itself this does not mark any defect in the conception; for attending to the role of RMS in moral education and the great variety in moral experience gives reason to think that there should be no unique, determinate set of RMS. Still, even without an algorithm, we require standards to judge some rules to be better or more complete than others. Rules that specify adult white males as the only entities who are to be treated as moral agents are surely mistaken; rules that include neonates but not fetuses are presumably (at the least) problematic. But how do we judge these things?

The conception of ourselves and others that is derived from the Moral Law sets the terms of a *practical* task for a community of moral agents. This is the "matter" of moral inquiry. The RMS are to be viewed as a set of rules that encode a *defeasible* solution to questions about the nature of moral agents, the appropriate descriptive terms that capture morally salient features of our situations, our decisions, and so on. Terms of criticism can be drawn from the underlying conception and from canons of judgments governing practical inquiry in general. RMS do not make moral theory and principles redundant.

Consider an elementary example. Any set of RMS will include identifying descriptions of rational and free agents. It follows from the guiding conception that any agent who is rational and free is to be accorded moral respect (that is, his ends can give us reason to refrain from certain actions). So, if the RMS that are used fail to acknowledge the moral status of some group known to possess the relevant capacities, then it will be appropriate to criticize the RMS as faulty on those grounds. The guiding conception can be the ground for a charge of inconsistency, and the RMS revised accordingly.

---

12. I am not arguing that the RMS are derived from the so-called Formula of Humanity (G429). The end-in-itself conception of rational agency that I argue is the source of RMS lies behind all of the formulations of the CI, both as the condition of their possibility *and* as the source of moral content. What can and cannot possibly be willed under the Formula of Universal Law is a function of the nature—as ends-in-themselves—of human rational agents.

Of course, not all faults in RMS will be so easy to detect. The range of error can be different with different issues. When, for example, the task of moral inquiry is to determine who is a moral agent, there can be straight-forward mistakes of fact: what is to count as being rational or free can be erroneously or too narrowly defined. Then the emergence of new facts will simply generate new RMS. But some errors of fact have more complex origins (say, of a political or ideological kind) such that merely pointing to the facts will not by itself generate moral insight. As with any inquiry that has significant practical import, strategies will need to be developed to diminish the likelihood of error. It would be reasonable to attend to claims made by and on behalf of those omitted from equal consideration, to consider who benefits from their exclusion, and so on.

Analogous problems arise in determining the regions of potential imper-missibility, where what needs to be known is what does and what does not undermine or inhibit the exercise of rational agency. Again, some errors will involve plain mistakes of fact, some not.[13] What needs to be emphasized is the idea of a *practical* task for moral judgment: strategies must be adopted for revealing the full effects of actions (for seeing what makes some effects "invisible"), for improving the prevailing understanding of people's true needs, for avoiding parochialism, and so on. As the RMS are necessary for there to be moral judgment at all, the strategies of correction are necessary to make the RMS more accurately reflect moral facts that can be obscured from plain sight. The framework for this practical task is determined by the Moral Law, and the RMS that are the product of moral practice can be criticized and revised by appeal to the grounding framework.

A sketch of a more complex example may be helpful. I do not know (historically) what prompted such notions as "racist" or "sexist" to emerge in contemporary western culture and become moral notions (terms of moral criticism). One way of understanding what happened when they did, when they came to shape a part of our sense of a moral ideal, is to see these categories as having been incorporated in the prevailing RMS. Existing rules of salience bearing on sexual and racial matters were found to be insuffi-cient—to encode concepts that institutionalized inequality. The RMS failed to direct agents' attention to the right things. New rules of salience needed to be formulated and taught, older rules reworked and refined. It was known and accepted that disrespectful and demeaning actions were morally wrong, but *which* actions were disrespectful, or what made an action demeaning, needed to be rethought. Deeply held views about the nature of blacks or women had to be unmasked and corrected, prejudices and fears overcome, so that their full moral status could be acknowledged *and* seen. (These are the sorts of thing I imagine constituting a practical adjustment

---

13. The need for dignity-preserving work has had such a role.

in the concept of "person as an end-in-himself.") The success of such alterations in the RMS (and associated beliefs) is to make agents morally sensitive to features of persons and of situations that were not perspicuous to them before. The terms of criticism are based in the same moral conception of persons that supports the rules and categories needing revision. Thus the moral debate is often carried on in the language of self-criticism, and the alterations are viewed as a development or perfection of already existing concepts.

With such changes in perception, however, there will be different moral judgments made as agents respond to situations with revised RMS. While this opens the theory to moral progress, it raises the specter of relativism. If the RMS that are necessary for moral judgment can be mistaken, and those mistakes taken up into the CI procedure (in agents' maxims), it seems that agents using mistaken RMS may make errors of moral judgment that will not be caught by the CI procedure. This suggests that it can be permissible for agents with mistaken RMS to act in ways that would be judged impermissible if their RMS were correct. If this is so (and I think it is), can we refrain from judging such acts as violations of duty in the strict sense without at the same time embracing relativism?

On a Kantian account, we say that an action is contrary to duty when its maxim cannot be willed to be a universal law. To take seriously the possibility that actions whose maxims have defective RMS may pass through the CI procedure is to claim room in a Kantian system for the idea that not all ways of failing to act as morality requires (in a strict sense) are morally equivalent. But there already is such room. We are not to say what is false because that interferes with another's effective exercise of his agency. But an agent who does not know the truth about something may say what is false without lying: he does not deceive. Someone who fails to understand the nature or seriousness of another's need will fail to help without acting nonbeneficently (he has no desire to refrain from helping acts). We may say about these cases that there is a sense in which, morally speaking, what should be done is not done, but the agents in neither case act from morally defective maxims: there was no intent or interest in deception, no refusal to acknowledge the claim of need on one's help. From the perspective of greater knowledge we can say what maxim a better-informed agent should have adopted. But since omniscience is not a condition of agency, there need be no moral fault where things are not as they might have been.[14] Moral fault (in the strict sense of acting contrary to duty) occurs only when an agent's maxim contains a principle that cannot be willed a universal law.

The sense in which Kantian ethics is a system of objective value does not imply that it must pick out a unique set of judgments as correct for sets of

14. This assumes that the error is reasonable and innocent.

circumstances, independent of agents' maxims. Perhaps it could do this for a system of perfectly rational beings if part of their perfect rationality was perfect knowledge. But for human beings and communities, with their different projects and imperfect understanding, moral theory (of a Kantian sort) must tolerate some degree of difference in moral judgment. What the theory requires of all agents is objective *willing*: agents' maxims should conform to the principle of the CI (they should act from the motive of duty), and their maxims must satisfy the CI procedure (they must not be contrary to duty).

When actions are proposed under the authority of defective RMS, the agent may be unaware that what he would do is even morally problematic. So, for example, he may describe his action as helping or supportive when it is demeaning or manipulative (neither he nor the object of his action may be in a position to see this). There is some kind of moral error in such cases—not just factual error—but it lies at the level of the RMS and not in the agent's willing. Persons working under a given system of RMS may do well, morally, in most cases, but there may be some kinds of cases or circumstances where their RMS are conceptually too weak to generate morally adequate descriptions in their maxims.

Are there any limits, then, to what can count as an acceptable moral judgment? It does not follow from the claim that Kantian ethics tolerates difference in judgment either that it tolerates all differences or that it gives us nothing to say about (no grounds to criticize) judgments that differ, group to group, because they are made using different RMS. If the RMS contain factual error or are conceptually impoverished, that can be discovered. And if error is discovered but not incorporated in agents' maxims, there will be reason to take their resistance as ground for moral criticism. (The CI procedure shows when a volition is contrary to the Moral Law. Other points of moral assessment of maxims need not be drawn from the CI procedure, so long as their source is also the Moral Law.) Furthermore, although agents are not free to describe their actions as they please, they are not wholly constrained by the prevailing RMS. If the RMS are taught with reference to their justifying ground (the conception of the person embedded in the Moral Law)[15] agents will be able to consider whether the moral categories they use are in fact compatible with the respect owed persons. The modes of perception that are part of one's moral upbringing are a proper object of moral criticism. It will be natural to regard the RMS as open to criticism if they are understood to be defeasible interpretations of a more fundamental moral conception.[16]

---

15. According to Kant, a valid moral catechism will always include the authority for moral rules in its formulas (DV153–156).

16. This seems to me to be the right way to respond to Bernard Williams' eschewal of moral

We can go a bit further. It does not follow that the differences in judgment tolerated in a Kantian system of judgment imply that all radically divergent RMS are acceptable. There are checks. (1) Not just any set of rules are moral rules; there is a distinctive content they must have. (2) And not just any set of RMS can be coordinated with the Moral Law as its ground. These suggest standards of validity for RMS (singly and as a system). For example: in Kantian theory, given the moral focus on the conditions of rationality, deception is necessarily a morally salient fact. So a set of RMS that in no way tagged deception as a matter for moral consideration would to that extent be defective. Or: a rule that directed beneficent attention only to members of the dominant social class would be a rule with moral content, but it would not be a valid RMS if maxims making it their principle would be rejected by the CI procedure. If relativism is the view that basic moral judgments are culture-bound because different cultures have different systems of ultimate value, then the account of moral judgment based on RMS is not a relativism.

What do we say of a person who acts under the guidance of faulty RMS and does something obviously (to us) wrong? If moral judgment is tied to maxims, RMS, and the CI procedure, if the agent has willed as he should, we seem compelled to say he has acted permissibly. On the kind of account I have sketched, there seems to be no way to judge actions apart from the way they are willed. Then morally defective RMS may not yield morally defective actions. (It is not the RMS, but the fact that judgment is maxim-based, that introduces this problem: Kantian theory neither describes nor judges actions except as they are willed.) While we do ordinarily feel that there are some sorts of moral criticism we want to withhold from sincere moral agents whose judgments are faulty and yet, for historical or cultural reasons, inevitable, this is usually understood as a division in judgment between the person and the action (the action was wrong but the person did not act wrongly). It is not clear that we can make this distinction here. But it is also not clear that the distinction is necessary.

What is lost if we cannot judge actions apart from the way they are conceived (through RMS) and willed? Can we, for example, condemn Nazis when they might be said to be acting responsibly under defective RMS? I think we can. We will want to distinguish cultures with defective RMS from those whose rules of moral practice are deviant or blatantly invalid. It is not as if individual Nazis were in no position to see (because of impoverishment of culture or upbringing, say) who was and who wasn't a person, or didn't know (because they were moral primitives, perhaps) what kinds of things it was morally permissible to do to persons. To be sure, such

theory in favor of an ethics of thick descriptions. See his *Ethics and the Limits of Philosophy* (Cambridge: Harvard University Press, 1985), pp. 143–145, 200.

extracultural judgments need to be made with care, as will judgments of what another can be expected to see as wrong with a prevailing moral code. But these are matters of limits and caution. They do not extend immunity to agents so long as they remain within culturally given moral rules.

An anthropologist encountering a primitive tribe that takes heads as a rite of manhood or in response to loss and grief might find reason to conclude that the basic rules of conduct of the tribe are not moral rules.[17] If there is reason to believe that people do not act under a conception of themselves and others as moral agents, then there is surely some sense in saying that neither their deeds nor their doings were morally wrong.

Although as many questions are raised as are answered by such quick sketches, I think there is enough in these examples to render at least plausible the claim that, although Kantian theory does not assess actions apart from performances, it enables one to make central judgments associated with that distinction. We can condemn Nazis, even though they act within a given framework of moral rules, and we may at times have grounds to refrain from condemning others when they do things that violate our strongest moral prohibitions.

Let me summarize these conclusions concerning the objective constraints on RMS and the scope and limits of moral judgment across cultural differences:

1. The criteria of validity for RMS make the moral criticism of other cultures and moral practices possible.
2. Agents within a culture are able to criticize their own RMS through the CI procedure itself or by appeal to the basic conceptions associated with the Moral Law.
3. Not all valid RMS will be the same. Different strategies for resolving the task set by the Moral Law ought to be possible, and at times appropriate, given the varied circumstances of human communities.

Relativism is a troubling view because it attacks the idea that morality has foundations in a way that seems to leave us with two equally unwelcome options. Either we take our difference of opinion (and sense of superiority) as grounds for assessing the moral views of others, or we choose an attitude of tolerance. But in the framework of relativism, our opinions have no weight beyond their being ours, and our tolerance is only negative. On the other hand, relativism has whatever appeal it does have because it takes seriously the differences we know there are in the ways that sincere moral communities regulate their lives. What is attractive about introducing RMS

17. See Renato Resaldo, *Ilongot Headhunting* (Stanford: Stanford University Press, 1980), for a useful and morally acute account of a society of Philippine headhunters from 1882 to 1974.

into a Kantian theory of moral judgment is that it would seem to let us have it both ways: while morality has an objective foundation, we have good *positive* reason to tolerate *some* culturally based moral differences.

In many of these remarks I have been going on as if I believed that there are RMS—that *we* use such rules in moral judgment and moral education. And I think we do (though without the full Kantian moral conception of persons behind them). What I have argued for, however, is the need to supplement the Kantian account of moral judgment with RMS. Still, to the extent that thinking in terms of RMS makes moral practice in general more intelligible, that argues, in my opinion, in favor of the Kantian claim to provide the foundations of our most basic moral beliefs and practices. Certainly, when the CI procedure is viewed as a framework for moral deliberation, and agents bring to their deliberations maxims shaped by RMS, the CI does not yield formal or rule-bound or rigid results.

But how much, if any, of this account is actually in Kant? I believe there is evidence to support it in the way Kant sets out his examples, in the use he makes of ordinary moral consciousness in the *Groundwork,* and in a plausible interpretation of the practical import of the Fact of Reason. I do not want to say, however, that this is enough evidence to show the presence of anything like rules of moral salience in any of Kant's texts. I *do* want to say that a Kantian account of moral judgment will not work without rules of moral salience, or something very much like them.

5

What Happens to the Consequences?

KANTIAN ethics is moral theory based on intention or volition. The objects of moral assessment are not events or states of affairs, but willings (or willed actions). Things that happen are not themselves morally good or bad, right or wrong: only willings are. If you take this seriously (and I take it as defining of Kantian ethics) you have, I think, two interpretive options, neither of which seems satisfactory. Either you will come to see Kantian ethics as resembling a virtue-based theory (in assessing willings it looks at agents' underlying intentions and commitments to provide assessments of character or moral worthiness[1]), thereby compromising its claim to provide a real alternative to consequentialist theories of action assessment. Or, if you insist that it provide a means of assessing actions (if not actions as happenings then at least as doings), you appear to get a moral theory of action assessment that does grave violence to important moral intuitions. Since my interest in Kant's ethics depends on its providing, among other things, a method of action assessment, it is the second option I want to explore.

Intention- or volition-based theories have a problem with consequences: actual consequences. Whatever the theoretical justification for taking willings to be the appropriate object of moral assessment, what actually happens when one acts does not seem to make the moral difference it should. Omissions, mishaps, accidents, and the many other ways that well-intentioned actions go awry seem to have no place in such a system of moral assessment. That is, even if there were no question about Kantian ethics' ability to assess volitions—no problems, that is, with the employment of the Categorical Imperative—it appears to lack resources to take account of the events that follow (or fail

1. See Onora O'Neill, "Consistency in Action," in *Constructions of Reason* (Cambridge: Cambridge University Press, 1989).

to follow) an agent's acting. And this goes against the grain. What happens in the world when an agent acts must be able to register in some domain of moral judgment. This is not the consequentialist's worry that Kantian ethics is indifferent to outcomes in the assessment of actions. The Kantian, like the consequentialist, evaluates actions partly in terms of what the agent intends to do, and thus in terms of the outcomes the agent would bring about. The problem is rather that, because states of affairs are not possible bearers of value in Kantian ethics, what actually happens seems to be outside the purview of morality.

There is another, related set of problems that arises from what we might call the subject-relative orientation of action assessment in Kantian ethics. What an agent wills is a function of her grasp of a situation. If it is willings that are the object of moral assessment, judgments of right and wrong will then reflect the perspective of the agent, and so be relative to what she sees or considers relevant in the circumstances in which she acts. If this is the case—as I believe it is—one might well wonder what kind of moral objectivity such a system of judgment could claim.

In this chapter I want to suggest that the resources of Kantian ethics for dealing with these matters are both ample and morally interesting. Although I will attempt only to deal with a limited range of cases, they indicate a strategy for dealing with others. The success of this strategy may alter the way we understand Kantian procedures of moral assessment. I hope to offer some reasons for finding this a welcome result.

A methodological note: In speaking of the resources of Kantian theory for dealing with such problems, I am taking "resources" in a quite literal sense: things you may have to dig for. This is not merely a matter of more finely grained textual interpretation. Part of the power of Kant's ethics lies in the extent of its ability to answer questions that Kant himself did not consider. This enlarges the criteria of interpretive success.

Although this is not the place for a full treatment of Kant's theory of action, it will be useful to highlight a few consequences of the fact that for Kant "willings" are the key to understanding the actions of rational agents. Kantian ethics looks to agents' *maxims* in assessing actions— the expressions in principle form of what an agent wills. Willing is the "kind of causality" unique to rational agents—the capacity to act in accordance with law or principle (G412). Further, in acting from principle, rational agents (insofar as they act rationally) act out of a conception of the appropriateness of what they do or would bring about. Maxims, which describe actions as they are willed, must therefore include a description of what is willed that goes beyond the simple description of what the agent intends to do. To present actions according to the agent's *conception* of her action, maxims must include, in addition to description of the action (as a "doing") and its end, the motive from which the agent acts and which she takes to justify her acting in such a way and for such an end.[2]

Insofar as an agent's pursuit of an end is shaped by the nature of her interest in that end (we might call this the cognitive side of a motive), two agents might intend to act in the same way, to bring about the same effect of action, but on two quite different maxims. Thus, famously, the beneficent person and the sympathetic person both do the same thing to bring aid to someone in need, but only the beneficent person's maxim has moral content, because only the beneficent helping is conceived as the helping that is morally required. The distinction is important in ordinary cases as well, where the same intended action can be the result of various motivating concerns: the need for reliable transportation, the desire to impress my neighbors, boredom, can each move me to buy a new car. The different motives that set up the intended action determine the conception the agent has of what she intends to do. Most important, they shape how the agent proceeds through a course of action, determining which sub-choices she makes, how she responds to untoward or altered circumstances, and so on. Being able to talk about the action as it is conceived will greatly aid our inquiry.

I do not want to worry here about the "action-description" problem for maxims.[3] It is of course a serious problem, but I believe that no general solution to the problem is necessary in order to proceed. If the problems of consequences and subjective bias cannot be independently resolved, it will not matter whether there is a determinate act description for each volition or not. There will be substantive *moral* reasons for rejecting a maxim-based theory of action assessment.

A last preliminary remark. I am evasive, from the outset, about how maxims are assessed—by what procedures, and the like. It may seem obvious how maxims are to be assessed: take them to the Categorical Imperative and see if they can, without contradiction, be willed a universal law. But for reasons that will become clear as we go along, I no longer think that this can be the full story about maxim assessment in Kantian ethics. As an initial working assumption, though, I take it that the CI can produce the sort of results usually expected from its application to maxims of action.

In what follows, I will examine a range of problem cases, offer what seem to me reasonable "Kantian" solutions, and consider some changes in the way we understand Kantian ethics that will be needed to accommodate them.

2. There is a sense, then, for Kant, that a motive is among the things an agent wills. This must be so if rational agents are free. An agent's motives are those of her incentives *(Triebfedern)* she judges give her good reason to act.

3. A fuller treatment of maxims can be found in Chapter 10, section III.

I

Let us consider first the problem of good intentions. Suppose someone fully intends to return a borrowed clock and has a maxim of so acting that is adequate to her intentions. On the occasion of executing the return, however, she trips and the clock breaks. If the moral assessment of actions is based on the assessment of the agent's maxim, the maxim we have to work with in this case is the maxim of good intentions. And if, as in this case, the maxim of good intentions is itself without fault, there appears to be no way for the theory even to register (no less assess) the failure of execution: a failure to bring about what was intended or willed, a failure to return what was owed. Even if we are inclined to say: the failure occurred in circumstances that excuse the agent—releasing her from a charge of wrongdoing—we might still want a way to register the failure of action, to give it moral status, as it were, even if the maxim of action was without defect. Some harm has been suffered, something owed was not (and will not be) returned. And *that* fact appears in no maxim.[4] One might say: it is one thing for a theory to insist that willings (and so good intentions) count; it is quite another for it to be unable to take note of moral phenomena other than what is willed.

On the other hand, why shouldn't good intentions plus adequate care in execution be all we need to know to judge an action? But someone will not get what she is due (or anything else). This is not by itself enough to convict the theory. It does not give reason to conclude that something wrong was done—something that has escaped moral notice. What I think our considered moral intuitions tell us here is simply that something untoward has happened which must have moral significance even if not ramifications. What it is may not be equally intuitive.

Now, given the actual consequences of an action (of acting on a maxim), there is an appropriate moral question raised concerning the agent's *response* to these consequences. If a sincere effort to fulfill an obligation fails, an agent will usually adopt a maxim in response to that failure. This is a maxim that can, in its turn, be evaluated. It is reasonable to think that some maxims (offers to repay or replace, apologies) are morally appropriate, and others not (those that express indifference, an unwillingness to discuss or consider what should be done). Since there are further maxims to be assessed, Kantian theory may have a great deal to say about the

---

4. Since a maxim of good intentions is not a maxim of "intending to return," one might say: if one is acting on a maxim "to return a borrowed clock" the untoward outcome is registered in the failure to act as the maxim indicates. Such a response gets it right about the maxim, but it begs the question about what acting on a maxim involves. One acts on a maxim insofar as the maxim describes the way one wills. If the untoward outcome involves no failure of willing, the problem of locating the morally untoward event remains.

continuation of the moral story. I am not at all sure that "what we think" in such cases is not better captured this way.

It is reasonable to expect that acceptable maxims of response will be sensitive to different causes of failure: accidents, interventions, mistakes, failures of will, or natural disasters may each call for a response that reflects the nature of the failure. This is not just a matter of degrees of responsibility. What I am to do next ought to be determined (in part) by whether it was the post office that lost the clock I was sending back, or whether it was stolen along with other things of mine in my office, or whether I left it in the rain.

The basic idea is that the circumstances of failure *call for* a moral response; the agent does not terminate her relation to a context of action once she has adopted an appropriate maxim and prepared herself to act. In this continuity lies not only a plausible response to the objection about actual consequences, but also a welcome widening of the focus of moral judgment from the isolated action to the more natural interval of intention, action, and response.

There seems to be a thought in the original objection that, unless an untoward *action* can be judged morally faulty, the agent will somehow be let off the hook, or free to go on about her business, leaving the intended recipient empty-handed, both in fact and in moral claim. What is disturbing in this is the assumption that only victims of unsuccessful intentions are concerned with the rectification of undesired and undesirable outcomes. This suggests a picture of moral agents moving through their obligations as if they did not care about the success of their efforts. Normally, agents are concerned that what they will or intend to do should succeed, and when it does not (through accident, mishap, and such), they renew their efforts. It is only in special circumstances that agents look at their actions as one-shot affairs. If we are dealing with agents who care (to a reasonable extent) about morality—that is, they care that what is morally appropriate be done—then the normal agent's ongoing concern for the success of her projects governs the moral case as well.

We can offer a first conclusion: although good intentions plus adequate care *are* enough (whatever the outcome, the agent has done what she ought), they are not the end of the story (the agent may need to respond to what actually happens when she acts). There is room for consequences, actual consequences, to make a moral difference. This is a way of capturing the idea that, even though our powers as agents are limited, our obligations are not just to "try" to do what we ought to do.

The source of the Kantian agent's concern for consequences is either her normal ongoing interest in the realization of ends she sets, or her having a particular kind of end (say, an end of obligation) that requires a commitment of resources beyond any particular attempt to fulfill the obligation. (I will have a good deal more to say about such ends later.) What the Kantian does not have is an independent moral response to the untoward outcome—remorse for loss and distress as such. There is no point of view from which the untoward outcome as such makes the world morally worse. This is not coldheartedness; one may regret that things did not work out. And if a loss is serious, independent considerations of beneficence may come into play.

II

Sometimes the reason we fail to do what we will (say, keep a promise) is that we have failed to do something else. When I am negligent or forgetful, I may not attend to what I ought to do. The maxims I then adopt cannot register aspects of my situation that I do not see, and so it would seem that no correct assessment of what I am doing (or failing to do) is possible. I might be acting on a routinely permissible maxim that expresses my intention to do some ordinary action, while what I am also doing (without then recognizing it) is breaking a promise. There seems to be no way to fault me for breaking the promise, since I am not acting on a promise-breaking maxim. This cannot be right.

In a second kind of case, my failure to do what I ought is a result of my being unprepared. I have been inefficient or lazy or careless. My maxim of action may be quite sincere and morally appropriate. I owe a debt; I cannot pay all that I owe. I act on a maxim of discharging my obligations to the extent that I am able. It is just that I am unable (now) to discharge the debt. There again seems to be no fault that a procedure of moral assessment confined to maxims of action can capture. Yet it seems reasonable to think that I have done something wrong.

In the case of good intentions, when it looked to be impossible even to register the significance of a misfired action, we found that things looked different when we expanded the region of assessment to include the maxims adopted in response to the untoward outcome. The thought was that an obligation can require more than the performance of a particular action at a particular time, and that procedures of maxim assessment can attend to this fact. The strategy is to resist the idea that a moral agent with an obligation stands in some simple relation to a required action. It is when we think that her obligation is to act in such and such a way that failure to act makes us want to locate all moral fault there. But we can just as well think of the agent as standing in a moral relation to a situation with more extended temporal dimensions.

If we widen the focus of assessment in the case of the forgotten obligation as well, we should find that the agent's response to her lapse will involve maxims with moral content, maxims that can be morally assessed. (We can assume for now that she does not forever remain ignorant of her omission;

a more thorough moral amnesia is a problem for later discussion.) Again, what an appropriate response is—acknowledgment of failure, admission of guilt, repayment, responsibility for damages—is (and ought to be) an open question: one that is answered through assessment of proposed maxims of response. If we assume a normal moral agent—one who would have acted rightly had she not forgotten, someone who is concerned to respond to her omission appropriately—then although there can be no judgment of fault directed at the maxim of action, it is possible to assess the maxims arising as a consequence of that fault, including maxims that acknowledge that something untoward happened *at the time* the debt went unrepaid. Once we include responses within the situation or circumstances of assessment, we markedly increase the power of Kantian ethics to register relevant moral facts. It is not silent in the face of omissions. But it should do more.

Assessments of response after the fact do not capture enough. When an agent does not attend to morally relevant features in a situation, we want to say that the agent *ought to have had* a certain kind of maxim (here, one acknowledging an obligation to keep the promise). Our problem is to find a way to count "not having a maxim" as a moral fault, when it seems to follow from the Kantian theory of assessment that all moral fault must be located in maxims we *do* have.[5]

In many such cases, it will be appropriate to widen the scope of moral judgment in *both* directions: to look to maxims of response and to maxims that are adopted *before* the time of action. The requirements of obligation may not begin at the time of the required action. Consider the person who has promised to repay a debt on a certain date, but who then cannot because she has neglected to set aside the necessary funds. Only part of the job of moral assessment can be done when the agent adopts a maxim of nonpayment and maxims of response (we are not now supposing she is unaware of her obligations). But the moral fault in the case is more extensive. The earlier carelessness involves its own moral fault, one caught not in maxims of action or response but in maxims of *preparation*.

When the agent incurred the obligation, she can be said to have adopted "repaying the debt" as her end. She is thereby required to take reasonable steps to ensure that she will be able to repay it, for she must, if she is rational, intend some sufficient means to her end. There are steps one can take (and so maxims one ought to have) to ensure that owed money is available, not spent or lost through carelessness; there are things one can do to diminish the likelihood of forgetting. In short, maxims of sufficient means must be taken for the morally required end. When the agent fails to have such

---

5. A certain sort of rationalist might hold that failures such as forgetting are moral faults, *simpliciter*. But Kant cannot accept this, and we should not want to. Forgetting happens. The task for a moral theory is to be responsive to its conditions of occurrence and excuse.

preparatory maxims, she is morally at fault, even though the effect of the fault (the broken promise to repay) has not yet occurred.[6]

This is what we were looking for. We wanted to see how an agent could be at fault for not having a maxim. Now we argue straightforwardly that, given her end of obligation, she failed to adopt a maxim of sufficient means. So, at the time of the apparent moral failure, it is true that the agent's maxim of action is not faulty or impermissible. Yet we can identify her moral failure in what she did, or did not do, prior to the time of the action, in *maxims* that were not adequate as means.

Moreover, the location of the fault prior to the act supports the most natural explanation of the felt difference in moral responsibility where the agent fails because she has not taken adequate preparatory action and where failure results from accident or some other external intervention. What we have not done should register differently from what we have not accomplished (or successfully brought about). Many matters of moral responsibility will depend on locating the moral wrong in the maxims the agent adopts, before and after the time of action, in response to the array of circumstances that bear on her obligation.

III

In ordinary cases, when someone's maxims of means are not adequate to her end, we might say that she has acted irrationally or inefficiently. But in a moral case that sort of charge is insufficient. There is a kind of transitivity of moral requiredness that makes the means-to-end relation a moral one when the end is either obligatory or an end of obligation. Support for this claim of transitivity is to be found in the fact that Kant's ethics is a normative theory of willing.

We need to explore, then, the kinds of resources available in a moral theory that looks to willings that enable us to explain the special requirements—of maxims of preparation and response—that seem to be necessary for a plausible Kantian account of moral judgment. Since the examples I have considered involve the fulfillment of obligations, we might begin by considering what a Kantian account of obligation should look like.

An obligation is a kind of moral constraint. In Kantian ethical theory, it cannot be the requirement that a certain state of affairs ("the promise being kept") obtain.[7] It can only be a constraint on willing. Yet to have certain obligations is to be held accountable in particular ways for an action or state of affairs. We are to keep our promises. It helps to think of an obligation to keep a promise or to repay a debt as involving, first of all, the

---

6. Quite correctly this implies that there can be moral fault without faulty action.
7. Of course it can be just this sort of requirement in law.

adoption of an end (an end of, say, doing what we promised to do). We know that to act effectively for any but the simplest of ends requires preparation, then efforts, and a somewhat open-textured set of responses to the way well-intentioned efforts may go awry. So if an obligation requires a special commitment of will to an end, it thereby imposes extensive requirements on an agent's willing. This is the practical form of moral agency, the foundation of accountability. To have an obligation is to have (or accept) a particular kind of restraint on one's will—to limit one's freedom. How that freedom is limited follows from the content of the particular obligation.

Much of the structure of willing required by obligations is also present in nonmoral willings. If I have a complex end or project to which I am deeply committed, a great deal follows about what I ought to will which bears on the kinds of constraint that come with having ends of obligation. There is a rich and natural account that can be set out in terms of ordinary willings—one that has been neglected perhaps because Kant so vigorously opposes moral and nonmoral action. The critical opposition, however, is not in the practical structure of willing, but in the nature of the attachment or commitment to an end. So let us look at some of what is involved in our having an important and complex end to see the sorts of general structural features available for ends of obligation.

1. Having an important and complex end has an ongoing effect on other ends and projects, affecting the priority and the timing of their respective claims. Some ends (the welfare of my child, for example) may have absolute priority over other ends; this can require the delay or lengthy postponement or even the abandonment of ends. And some ends, which on their own have relatively low priority (exercise, for me), may gain in value as they are means to a more deeply invested project (one that needs the energy and alertness exercise yields).

2. A serious project of reasonable complexity almost certainly requires the adoption of subprojects, as well as means, and so the adoption of new ends. If we find that adequate or reasonable means, subprojects, and so on, have not been taken, we have grounds for questioning the commitment to the original project.

3. As means (subprojects) are unsuccessful through accident and the like, the agent's commitment and the nature of the project determine what counts as an appropriate response to the particular circumstances of failure. That there is to be a response to failure is a function of commitment.

Thus part of what is involved in having a commitment to a complex end is knowing that acting for it is not a one-shot affair. The agent knows from the outset that she cannot guarantee the success of her efforts and that failed efforts occasion the need for a response: ends don't go away when means fail to reach them. Response may take the form of new efforts, but it may also take the form of attending to the results of failed effort (a failed effort does not leave things where they were before the effort was made). When failure is such that the entire project is undermined, that too is an occasion for response: what can be salvaged, how to take account of the effect of the absence of the project in the future. Having a project introduces elaborate structure into one's willings. With the failure of the project, this skein needs to be unraveled. Otherwise the loss of the project will leave behind a structure to one's willings without a purpose. Intermediate ends whose value was derived from the project need to be reassessed or abandoned. And so on. (Completing projects introduces comparable difficulties.)

When a normal agent adopts an end (sets herself a project), she undertakes actions with a conception of them *as* promoting her end or contributing to her project. Thus an agent pursuing a trivial end will act with a different conception, and so a different maxim, than an agent embarking on a project of much greater significance. An agent pursuing an end of *obligation* will act with a conception (have a maxim) with specific moral content, setting a structure of moral requirement. This is not just a matter of adopting different kinds of means. The maxim or conception appropriate to an obligation will control from the outset a range of responses to untoward events, and so on, that *belong to* the obligation (the effort appropriate to a given end, the cost, the time frame). A normal agent will have a conception of her action adequate to her project. This was the sort of requirement that figured in the earlier discussion of maxims of preparation and response.

Part of the explanation of how obligations can impose complex and temporally extended requirements on an agent is then found in the general structure of normal willing: what follows when we adopt and are attached to complex ends. But obligations (in general) differ from other sources of ends in the conditions or occasion of the attachment and in the conditions for possible abandonment. It is not a matter of preference that we take the ends of obligation to have the weight and priority they do; their abandonment or reassessment is not at our discretion.

Whether there are obligations—and if there are, exactly what requirements each may impose—is not the issue here. The question was: what in the general theory that lies behind the Kantian structure of moral assessment explains how it is that obligations impose complex requirements, extending temporally before and after the time of what we are obliged to do? That question is answered by attention to the fact that obligations impose special requirements on willings: on the adoption of ends. Maxims that contain a conception of the action as promoting obligation will reflect this fact. Agents whose maxims do not contain this conception will be judged not to have accepted or grasped their obligations.

Because the object of moral assessment is a volition (as expressed in a maxim), fault assignment may not always be where or when a morally untoward event takes place. (Such events may be viewed as signs or symptoms of possible wrong willing.) The structure and extended temporal domain of volitions taken under moral requirement (and the different maxims through which what is willed are expressed as an agent acts to realize an end) allow for a different model of action assessment. "There the harm, there the fault" will not always be true. The kind of end required by obligations generates a continuing moral context of assessment. And if there is no fault in what the agent wills (in this wider context of assessment), it is not clear that there is anything that could count as a moral fault in what she does.[8]

IV

When I started thinking about these problems, I included failures from self-deception along with mishaps and forgettings, expecting the relevant moral fault to be located somewhere in the temporally extended cluster of maxims around the untoward action. I am no longer sure that all such cases involve moral failure. Since the upshot of this line of thought suggests a way a "Kantian" might think about certain aspects of character, let me sketch it here.

Consider a case involving self-deception that runs parallel to Kant's deceitful-promise example: a promise to repay is made in order to secure a needed loan. The agent promises sincerely, but her belief that she can repay the loan is based on or in self-deception. I want to suppose that the self-deception involved is incidental to the occasion of the promise—that is, the explanation of the self-deception is not in the agent's need to cover or mask her inability to repay so as to make the promise "all right" with herself. I also want to suppose that the self-deception is effective, blocking the agent's accurate assessment of her true financial status. We will assume that if this promise had been made *with* the knowledge that repayment was not possible (that is, deceitfully), it would be rejected as impermissible. Yet, since the self-deceiver's *maxim* is the same as the maxim of the honest

---

8. This is a suitable place to mark the fact that I have been talking about moral judgment in Kantian ethics in a way that does not depend on iterated applications of the CI procedure to maxims. Even if it is the case that every maxim of morally wrong willing contains a principle that cannot be willed a universal law without contradiction, it does not follow that this can be ascertained only through a universalization test. The sad history of attempts to make the universalization tests do all the work of moral judgment suggests to me both that the role of the CI procedure as such in moral judgment has not been fully understood and that a viable model for moral judgment needs to be developed—as a practice and in its connection to the CI. Some of this work is begun in Chapter 7.

promisor whose maxim is based on an accurate assessment of her future resources, it cannot be rejected. One may well want to object to the idea that there is no moral difference between the self-deceiver's and the honest promisor's actions and maxims.

It is not easy to see what the moral difference could be. It is not simply that deception has taken place. Maxims of deception directed at someone else are impermissible. But the *self*-deceiver's promise is not an act of deception: it is a promise *based on* self-deception, as another promise might be based on mistaken information. A promise based on self-deception is not just a deceitful promise with a different point to the deceit: I deceive myself instead of you. Unless we are to doubt the possibility of what I am calling "incidental" self-deception, it is not clear why self-deception should affect the permissibility of the promising maxim if an honest mistake would not. The result in both cases is the same: the promisee will not get his money back because the promisor has insufficient funds. And in both cases the promise was accepted because of the promisor's mistaken but sincere assumption (expressed in her promise) that she would be able to pay her debt.

There are therefore reasons to think that the self-deceiver's promising maxim *is* all right. It expresses, as it should, an intention to do what is promised. If the fault in the deceitful promise is the manipulation of the will of another (or free riding on the general sincerity of promises), then the self-deceiver's maxim does not contain that fault. At least with respect to the promising maxim, the state of the self-deceiver's will is the same as that of the normal nondeceiver. There is certainly no reason to suppose that she would make the promise if she were consciously aware that she could not repay the debt.

If we widen the temporal scope of assessment, comparing now the maxim of the self-deceived promisor with the maxim of an honest promisor who turns out to be unable to keep her promise, we might think the cases can be distinguished in terms of the *timing* of the event responsible for the default. In most ordinary defaults, we expect the cause of the default to be in the interval between the making of the promise and the debt's coming due. But this is morally arbitrary. Just as "an act of God" would absolve one of much responsibility if it occurred after the promise, so it would if it occurred before, so long as the agent was plausibly and reasonably unaware of its occurrence or import. So the fact that the self-deception occurs before the promise is made does not by itself show that there is a moral difference between the cases.

If there is a moral fault in the case of the self-deceiver's promise, it can only be in the *cause* of the default: in the self-deception itself. But if the self-deception is "incidental," although it may signal a practical fault and lead to morally significant consequences (here an unkept promise), it cannot for those reasons alone be counted as a moral fault. The self-deception need not have been the cause of anything morally untoward: suppose the occasion for the promise had not occurred. After all, money received from an honest promise may be used in impermissible ways, and those subsequent moral faults cast no moral shadow on the original promise. If the maxims involved in the self-deception themselves contain no moral fault, it does not seem right to alter the assessment of them (looking back) as one sees they came to contribute to morally untoward consequences.

I think that part of the difficulty in determining whether there is a moral wrong in the self-deceiver's promise may come from a lack of clarity about the range of wrongs associated with promises. With Kant in the foreground, it is natural to focus on deceitful promises, in part because the *Groundwork* example is so well known but also because deceitful promises exemplify the kind of wrong that Kantian theory is most sensitive to: the manipulation of the will of a rational agent in the service of self-interest. There are other areas where we go wrong with promises—when we do not keep them and when we break them—and they involve different moral faults. We can make use of the structural features of obligations and willings to say what they are. Greater clarity about these matters will help to explain why it may be all right to allow that a promise founded on "incidental" self-deception introduces no special moral problem. Let us look at promise breaking first, for it is (on a Kantian account) the next most serious wrong after deceitful promise making.

To make a promise is to take on an end of obligation that imposes relatively stringent practical requirements: we cannot justify abandoning such an end on grounds of revised preference, and we are required to adjust our other ends so that the necessary means may be taken to fulfill the end of obligation (other things equal). We may represent the fact that an end is an end of obligation by saying that it has greater weight or value than other ends—certainly greater than the ends of "mere" self-interest.[9] In deciding to break a promise on grounds of mere self-interest, we in effect reassign values: deciding (if only for now) to count the end of the obligation as less weighty than some end of self-interest. Since in adopting the end of obligation one accepts an assignment of values that may not be altered for reasons of mere self-interest, maxims of self-interested promise breaking are impermissible. What a full-blooded Kantian will conclude is that the moral fault in this most familiar kind of promise breaking is not in the broken promise (in the fact of it or in the injury to another), but in the

9. There are other and better ways of representing this: exclusionary reasons, weighted orderings, and so on. Treating the value of an obligatory end as a matter of "weight" introduces a metaphor of balancing that is hardly morally neutral. I have used the metaphor here because it allows the point to be made efficiently and its difficulties are not germane.

maxim of the promise breaker which includes (or implies) the prohibited reassignment of values. The self-interested promise breaker abandons an end of obligation on unacceptable grounds.

The wrong involved in a failure to *keep* a promise is not the same. Failure to keep a promise, as I am thinking of it, does not involve an abandonment of the end of obligation. As in most of the cases we have looked at (forgetting, negligence, and the like), there is no reassignment of values setting up the failure to fulfill an obligation. The agent intends to keep her promise. The cause of her failure to act effectively for an end of obligation is elsewhere—when insufficient means were taken, when information pertinent to the possible success of the promise was unavailable or not seen, and so on. At the extreme, such failures may cause us to suspect a reassignment of values: we may want to say of someone who is grossly negligent that she cannot "really" be accepting an end of obligation and acting that way. But that is because as a rational agent her acceptance of an end entails willing to take reasonable means. So when we have no grounds for doubting someone's rationality, the omission of available and obvious means will raise questions about either the sincerity of the promise or the agent's intention to keep it. But the essential point here is that failure to find or take sufficient means is compatible with holding to the end of obligation.

If it is possible for there to be innocent failure, if one can, under stress, just forget (while holding to the end of obligation and willing maxims of appropriate means), then some failures to keep promises may have to be judged innocent. Incidental self-deception would then join with other human faults as part of our various, unavoidable, practical imperfections. The agent must still adopt appropriate maxims of response that, on the one hand, would have to include acknowledgment that she had failed to act as she ought and, on the other, would also reflect the fact that the failure was innocent. (Innocence is thus consistent with responsibility for untoward outcomes.)

We might say more generally: from the fact that character flaws and failures may disable good intentions, it does not follow that an agent has acted in a morally deficient way. We do not, we cannot, attend to everything. We will not always be on top of our tendencies to see only what we want to see or to avoid what we wish not to notice. These are truisms of human agency. Their presence, and even their causal role in unsuccessful willings, is not enough to show moral fault.

We do not hold that, wherever there is a morally untoward outcome, what the agent did should be judged to involve moral fault—particularly when the cause is unforeseen or out of the agent's control. I do not see why the fact that the cause of a failure is "internal" should by itself make a difference. Because something we were under obligation to do was not done, there may be more to say about what must happen next. But the condition requiring maxims of response is in the obligation; we do not need to seek it in any moral failure of or in the agent.

Throughout this discussion I have assumed that the self-deception involved was incidental. Suppose it is not. This need not be nasty. We can imagine a case where the anger I feel toward someone—which I cannot admit I feel—is the cause of untoward actions (and willings). Around this person I am not as effective an agent as I usually am. On my way to return what I have borrowed, I trip; things break; I forget what I have promised; there are accidents. There is always some excusing story I tell (sincerely), and I appear not to have faulty maxims of preparation or response. Yet surely there is a moral fault in this unacknowledged though causally effective anger: a fault of character, perhaps. Can such a fault, such an inaccessible determining ground of the will, register in a maxim-based theory of assessment?

If we could say that the self-deception blocks my seeing what maxim I am acting on—that I am actually acting on a maxim of causing you small injuries I believe you deserve, for example—then I would have a faulty maxim, but not one I am in a position to recognize as mine. We could imagine a role, then, for a Kantian moral therapist, whose task would be to increase the sensitivity of agents to the true determining grounds of their actions. Although one might never be able to know one's deepest motives—the opacity of motives affects more than the motive of duty—there is room for improvement in self-awareness. Where there are unexpected patterns, a careful agent looks for a cause.[10]

On the other hand, to conclude that the problem is in an unacknowledged maxim is to accept a certain account of the way self-deception works. Suppose it were to work through a psychological mechanism that affects beliefs about circumstances or motives. The problem would then not be in an unacknowledged maxim, but in a maxim or action that is in some sense distorted. The options are uncomfortable. Either we must say there is *no* moral fault because such defects of character are not expressions of agency and willing (I would find this hard to accept); or we must widen the scope of the agent's accountability to include matters of character, on the grounds that, given our dependence on desires and beliefs, we must ensure as best we can that the sources of our beliefs are reliable and our desires reasonable.[11] This

10. There are obviously hard problems that come with speaking of unacknowledged maxims (and not just desires or motives shaping action without affecting the maxim). We can at the least admit different levels of self-awareness, so that I may be said to act on a maxim that I cannot admit to myself that I have. Maxims that are in principle inaccessible, or even deeply unconscious, are harder to understand or motivate. Fortunately, we do not need such notions here.

11. To say that willings depend on desires and beliefs is not suddenly to embrace an empiricist theory of action. Because willings give practical expression to an agent's conception

seems to me the better option, and one that is available to a theory of action based on willings.

If we remain inclined to treat self-deception in all its forms with moral suspicion, it should only be because of the central importance of self-knowledge in any Kantian theory of moral judgment. An agent prone to self-deception will be more likely to fail to appreciate morally relevant data that impinge on areas intersecting with this tendency. And where the tendency is general or is easily provoked, its connection with the performance of morally untoward acts is likely not to be accidental or quite honest. That is, among the occasions where self-deception is likely to occur are those where someone is tempted to an impermissible action she cannot squarely perform. Because this is a normal condition of human willing (to some degree), its overcoming will be part of the curriculum of a moral education. If self-deception is pervasive and chronic, it may be an open question whether the agent is normal (from the practical point of view). Though morality cannot demand practical perfection, there are standards to which the normal moral agent is expected to conform.

V

Let us briefly survey the path we have followed. In order to rebut the charge that the Kantian method of assessment through maxims is inadequate because of the volition-based structure of maxims, we had to extend the object of assessment (and so expand the range of the agent's accountability) beyond the maxim of action itself to maxims of preparation and response. This in turn suggested a requirement that a normal agent's maxims contain a sufficiently complex conception of what obligations, and the like, require. Now, to deal with problems like self-deception, we have added requirements on character. Agents must attend to areas of personal susceptibility, temptation, or weakness as part of what it is to be an agent with obligations. Moral education carries a great burden, then, in Kantian ethics. And indeed more than one of Kant's ethical works ends with a discussion of moral education, to the point, in the *Doctrine of Virtue,* of an outline for a moral catechism.

The concern of moral education goes beyond the inculcation of norms and principles and the development of the appropriate (stable, coherent)

---

of what she judges is appropriate (or good) to do in her circumstances of action, willings will reflect not only an agent's character, but also her beliefs and desires. However, desires do not directly determine willings. A rational agent acts on or from motives. Desires are acted *for* if the agent judges she has reason to satisfy them. This leaves room for possible mechanisms whereby desires that are not taken up into motives are yet able to alter the path of action or affect deliberation.

attachment to a life they govern. In a Kantian theory this much simply provides the framework within which what a normal moral agent needs to know will be taught. In Chapter 4 I talked about the need for agents to acquire moral concepts so that their maxims will contain morally salient action descriptions. The upshot of the discussion here is to add further requirements of an analogous kind. To act morally, an agent has to know what an obligation is (that it alters the structure of preferences, that it requires preparation and response), what obligatory ends we have, what will be necessary to satisfy them, including the sorts of responses (maxims of response) that are appropriate to a given obligation and particular conditions of failed outcomes (when are apologies sufficient, when is compensation owed, and so on).

Much of the casuistry attending an obligation is built in, as it were. In promising to meet you at 6:00, I make a promise of a certain sort: its obligation is to carry me to act except in certain sorts of circumstances, and it also carries to a range of responses to outcomes. There is, of course, something quite natural in this. How bizarre it would be if I made a promise, could not keep it (for any justifiable reason you like), and then *wondered* if some sort of response was appropriate (not what kind of response, but whether broken promises called for anything). Or suppose I had, radically, no idea of what sorts of responses went with broken promises of this sort: apologies? money? candy? This is not to diminish the hardness of hard cases. But surely knowing this sort of thing is part of learning what kind of obligation one assumes in promising.

In addition to learning the content of obligations, the agent must be instructed on the general conditions and limitations of human willing: the various ways that actions following from our most rational willings may yet fail to realize our intentions, and the various things that cause our willings to fall short of standards of rationality. Much of this is common-place and part of our education as practical agents: we have imperfect access to the facts on which the rationality of our actions and projects depend; our predictive capacities cannot ensure that we will see how these plans will turn out (the exact effects the actions will produce, how they will interact with other independent sources of effect); we succumb to temptation or weakness. Moral education does not eliminate the limits to human knowing or willing, but it can lead us to appropriate caution as we learn better to apprehend those circumstances where acting in the face of lack of knowledge or weakness of will is likely to make a moral difference.

On this account of Kantian ethics, the character of the moral agent is a first-order component in the structure of moral judgment. We might helpfully refer to these features of character as "the conditions of normal moral agency." And we might say that a maxim is "well formed" only if it contains the background knowledge of a normal moral agent. There will be standards of judgment and volition that a normal moral agent is required to maintain—standards related to but not identical with the requirements of practical agency in general. It may be my business alone whether I am perceptive about the character and integrity of my companions, or whether I see that what I propose to do is bad for me or injurious. But I am morally accountable for knowing that what I propose to do is wrong or will injure someone or will involve breaking a promise—at least when the wrong or injury is in plain sight. Falling short in this is a moral error or a sign of moral pathology.[12]

Since part of the motivation for this way of elaborating Kantian theory was to "save" it as a theory of action assessment, it seems appropriate at this point to ask whether I might have turned the theory away from action assessment to agent assessment, perhaps moving it toward some kind of virtue theory after all. Let me consider the second part of this first.

The reason one might think there has been a shift toward a virtue theory is because of the imposition of requirements on the agent's character. To be a normal moral agent, one must possess certain beliefs, have and act from certain sorts of concepts, possess a certain degree of self-knowledge. This is not normal Kantianism, but it is not virtue theory either. Though it is often those who think about the virtues who remind us of these facts, they are not the property of virtue theory. What I have claimed here is that such facts are the conditions of normal moral agency that provide the background against which moral judgment of actions is possible.

A harder question has to do with the apparent shift from action to agent assessment. Certainly there has been a shift away from the maxim of action to other maxims, whose faults (flaws) do not directly mirror the untowardness of the action in question. There are several things to say about this. First of all, one need not describe the shift as *away* from action assessment. One could say: this is the way to assess maxims of action. There is no particular event and no particular time of action that must bear all of the moral burden. Further, in extending the object of assessment, we do not come to judge the agent as this or that kind of person, or as doing the kind of thing a particular kind of person would do. The focus of judgment remains on willings, and it remains on them in a way that supports an explanation of what the agent *did* that was wrong, or of how the agent's response to failure was appropriate or not, and so on. Of course judgments about willings provide evidence for agent assessment.

If Kantian theory should be developed as I have suggested, some fundamental assumptions about how Kantian ethics works will need to be re-

---

12. Part of what negligence, forgetting, and self-deception do is remove morally relevant features from plain sight. Whether these be matters of fault or pathology or just normal error may be revealed in the maxims of preparation, response, and acknowledgment.

thought. The most obvious casualty is the use of the Categorical Imperative as the sole principle of maxim and action assessment. But since there may be independent reasons for thinking it is not designed for or effective as such a principle, this may be acceptable. In the end, we may not be able to claim this elaborated theory as Kant's, or not all of it; but that seems all right if what we get by proceeding in this way is sufficiently interesting and of some use.

6

Murder and Mayhem

IT IS startling to realize how little is said in Kant's ethics about the more violent forms of immoral action. There are discussions of lying, deception, self-neglect, nonbeneficence—but apart from suicide, a great silence about the darker actions. At the least, this should be an occasion for curiosity. Although the degree of concern with acts of violence in contemporary ethics may be in its own way curious, it does not seem unreasonable to expect a moral theory to provide an account of what is wrong with acts of violence.

Let me begin with a brief survey of several possible but inadequate explanations of this silence.

1. Many acts of violence are spontaneous. Since Kant's ethics assesses actions as the agent's maxim satisfies the Categorical Imperative, a norm of rational willing, such violent actions would not involve maxims of violence—they would not be willed actions—and so could not be judged immoral. While this may be true for some violent actions (jealous rage, perhaps), it is not true of all of them. All too many acts of violence are planned. Surely a moral theory must contain an account of the wrong involved in intentionally harming or taking a life.

2. Perhaps it is just the argument strategy of the *Groundwork* that explains the omissions of violent actions there. The examples Kant chose involve agents who are unsure whether the course of action they entertain is also morally permissible. So perhaps Kant thought: an agent may wonder whether in his circumstances a lying promise might be justified, but he cannot ever suppose that taking the life of another is. This seems implausible. But even if *all* such actions are impermissible (self-defense, killing to save a child from torture), the moral theory of the CI should still be able to show what it is about maxims of violence that violates the canons of rational willing.

3. Is it that violence is directed, for the most part, against the body? Kantian ethics looks to the will as the source and vehicle of moral value. If we thought that Kant held that the relationship between will and

body was radically contingent (one might take the application of the Moral Law to rational beings "as such" to imply this), it might seem reasonable to conclude that what happens to the body is of no, or at most indirect, interest to morality. Although some of Kant's views about the body give one pause, his argument for a duty of mutual aid undermines this explanation of the omission of acts against the body from the forms of moral argument.

4. If we thought (as I have sometimes been tempted) that the four examples of the *Groundwork* represent roughly the basic categories of wrongdoing, perhaps the suicide example is intended to stand for all acts of violence directed against persons. This would reverse the usual order of things: we normally have in place an argument that explains why taking the life of another is wrong, and ask whether the argument applies to taking one's own life. (The alteration in consent conditions is presumably the chief reason for this order.) An argument from the primacy of the prohibition on suicide would conclude, from the fact that taking one's own life is impermissible, that taking any other life must be also, because the life you ought to need least justification for taking is your own. This would not be implausible as a strategy of argument—*if* there is a good argument against suicide and *if* the argument against suicide reaches further than "taking life when its continuance threatens more evil than it promises satisfaction" (where the evil averted is directed at the life to be taken) and *if* there is no deep moral asymmetry between taking one's own life and taking the life of another: that is, taking the life of another is not a less serious action. I would not want to try to argue that the Kantian argument against suicide satisfies any of these requirements. Moreover, it would leave us with no basis for thinking about mayhem, unless we were to try to derive that from a prohibition against self-mutilation.

5. A last and perhaps the most obvious possibility: one might think that violence is not discussed in the *Groundwork* because the wrongness of such acts is dependent on prior principles of justice. If, for example, the prohibition of acts of violence follows from the nature of the rights—to bodily integrity, to life—that individuals have against each other, and since the *Groundwork* arguments cannot establish rights (they only show faults in certain forms of willing), silence on the subject of violence would be fitting. Something like the *Rechtslehre* (Kant's systematic work in political philosophy) is needed to establish such special moral claims. But why would we need to know that persons have a right to life in order to know that the taking of life is impermissible, when we do not need to know that persons have a right to the truth in order to know that deception is impermissible?[1]

---

1. Although the deceitful-promise example is in the terms of a moral institution, it is not the fact of the institution that shows the moral wrongness of the deceitful promise. (If the

Insofar as the *Rechtslehre* completes the ethical program, it addresses two sorts of problems. First, it provides the necessary derivations for institutional rights of property and contract, and second it describes the domain and justification of external constraint. The critical distinction between ethics and justice for Kant looks to the latter to explain why we may compel people to perform or avoid certain sorts of acts, when compulsion in most circumstances is impermissible. But even if acts of violence are in the province of the *Rechtslehre* (though I should note that they are not in fact of much interest to Kant there), it would be troubling if the question of what makes *maxims* of violence wrong were not answerable in the basic moral theory associated with the *Groundwork* formulations of the CI.

I

Given all of this, the next reasonable thing to try is a direct approach to violent actions through the *Groundwork*'s CI procedure. Let us for now accept the view of the CI procedure as consisting of two tests: a maxim is judged morally wrong either if it cannot be conceived as a universal law without contradiction (the "contradiction in conception" or CC test) or if it cannot be willed a universal law without the will contradicting itself (the "contradiction in will" or CW test).[2] I am looking first for answers to two questions. Is the CI procedure able to handle maxims of violent action, that is, reject at least some of them? And are these maxims rejected in a way that accounts for their wrongness?

This second question raises a neglected issue in Kant interpretation. A satisfactory moral theory should offer more than an algorithm for permissibility. It is not enough to get a version of the CI procedure going that can spit out the expected, correct results. This is so for two reasons. First, a procedure of moral judgment ought to be able to challenge our moral intuitions; the adequacy of the algorithm must not, then, be judged by its fit with them. Second, actions (or maxims) should be rejected for reasons that explain what is wrong with them. Being told that we may not act on maxims that we cannot will everyone to act on does not explain enough. Rulings on permissibility need to be completed by an explanation of what it is about the different kinds of impermissible actions that brings them into conflict with the formal requirement. If the attachment of an agent to the Moral Law is expressed in a commitment to the CI procedure *as the*

example were one of promise breaking, this would not be the case.)

2. The standard version of these tests is to be found in Onora (Nell) O'Neill, *Acting on Principle* (New York: Columbia University Press, 1975), chap. 5; a somewhat revised version is to be found in her "Consistency in Action," in *Constructions of Reason* (Cambridge: Cambridge University Press, 1989), pp. 81–104.

procedure of moral deliberation, the workings of the procedure—its internal argument—should engage the agent in some kind of moral reasoning. If moral judgment is to express moral understanding, and guide moral perception, there must be a way of connecting the argument of the CI procedure to a useful account of the "wrongness" of an action. Murder and mayhem are especially useful test cases for exploring the power of the CI procedure's arguments, for we take ourselves to know both that they are wrong and what it is that is the matter with them.

I want to begin by looking at what the CI procedure can do with an extreme and general maxim of violence: to kill if that is necessary to promote my interests. In effect this asks whether killing is a permissible routine means. What makes this the appropriate maxim to use is not any belief that it is the likely maxim behind acts of violence (indeed, even a minimally cautious killer would act on a prudentially more restricted maxim). The maxim is of interest because, first of all, if any maxim of violence ought to be rejected it is a maxim of convenience killing. But the more significant reason for starting with this extreme and general maxim is methodological. It is only in addressing general maxims that the CI procedure's tests are effective and useful for deliberation.[3]

This claim may seem immediately implausible given well-known objections to assessing general maxims. Bringing very general maxims to the CI procedure is said to yield unacceptably rigorous duties and prohibitions. Moreover, the maxims that agents act on are not typically general; they contain the particulars of their circumstances of action thought to be relevant in the rational selection of means and ends. Since moral judgment should reflect relevant particulars, it would seem that restricting the CI procedure to general maxims is self-defeating. But if the adequacy of the CI procedure is measured by its ability to render clear judgment on particular, situation-specific maxims of agents, there is little hope of success. Any significant increase of detail in the maxim makes it less likely that universal action on the maxim would be impossible (or impossible to will).

This is the same fact that was exploited in the old criticism that "tailored" maxims could make it through the CI procedure. Although tailoring maxims is not legitimate, the criticism based on it did not misunderstand the CI procedure. Moreover, strategies to defeat tailoring cannot be employed when the situation-specific elements of a maxim *are* legitimate: I would not make a deceitful promise unless it was for the sake of a best friend. The very features that make it impossible to will universal deceitful promising do not arise in willing this more specific maxim to be a universal law. The moral results are unacceptable.

---

3. The remarks that follow summarize results I argue for in Chapter 7.

There is a different way of thinking about the CI procedure that takes advantage of its success with very general maxims. We might think of the formal CI procedure (the two tests) as designed to assess the most general form of a given kind of maxim ("generic maxims," if you will), *not* to show that there is a duty or prohibition with respect to some class of actions, but to introduce a *deliberative presumption* against certain kinds of action done for certain justifying reasons (certain maxim types). So, for example, when deceitful promises are rejected in the *Groundwork,* what the CI procedure shows is that reasons of self-interest cannot justify deceitful promises. Agents whose justifying reasons are different (they would make a deceitful promise in order to save a life), could be acting on maxims whose generic pattern is different and possibly permissible.[4]

Deliberation that takes account of the more specific action descriptions of the agent's actual maxim would work (very roughly) in this way. Suppose a generic maxim of killing is rejected. An agent proposes acting on a maxim of killing alpha persons (persons with a distinguishing set of characteristics). The agent then must show that alpha characteristics are such that a prohibition applying to persons per se does not apply to alpha persons. Something about the nature of an alpha person must rebut the deliberative presumption against killing persons. (Alpha persons might be candidates for compassionate euthanasia—the fact of terminal illness, extreme suffering, or a plea for death could be offered as reasons to rebut the presumption against killing persons per se.)

If we are to rebut a deliberative presumption, however, the CI procedure argument that establishes the presumption must have content. That is, we can only argue that alpha persons are exempt from a general prohibition on killing if we know what it is about killing persons that makes it impossible (if it is) to will a generic maxim of killing as a universal law. Thus the requirement that the CI procedure give results in a way that has moral content is not just some desire for a supplementary or psychologically useful extra feature. It is central, as I see it, to the form of moral deliberation the CI procedure seems best able to support.

Let us return to our case. We begin with the general maxim, "To kill whenever that is necessary to get what I want": a maxim of convenience killing. Universalizing the maxim we get, "Everyone kills when that is necessary for them to get what they want." The CI procedure directs us to consider a world with this universalized maxim as one of the laws of human action. We are to ask first whether such a world can be conceived without contradiction and, if it can, whether it can also be willed

---

4. A similar strategy may be at work in O'Neill's account of the CI procedure that has it assessing agents' "underlying intentions" rather than their maxims of action. See her "Consistency in Action."

(thought of as an effect of willing the original maxim) without that will contradicting itself.

But what of this imagined world? If everyone killed as they judged it useful, we would have an unpleasant state of affairs. Population numbers would be small and shrinking; everyone would live in fear. These are bad consequences all right. Still a world that looks like this is conceivable: Hobbes described it in some detail. And if there is nothing inconceivable or contradictory in thinking of a world that contains a Hobbesian law of killing, it looks as though we must conclude that the CC test does not reject the maxim of killing.[5]

If the CI procedure is to reject the maxim of killing, then, it will have to do so through the CW test. This result surprised me. I had always thought it obvious that the maxims that failed the CC test were somehow morally worse than those that "merely" failed the CW test (worse not in terms of consequences, but as forms of willing). A lying promise or deceit (as I understand Kant's hierarchy of value) is a graver offense than the refusal to provide aid or failure to develop one's talents, the *Groundwork*'s two examples for CW. (Saving a life, after all, does not justify lying.) Could killing not be among the graver offenses? Moreover, one would expect killing to be a violation of perfect duty (an injustice)—yet in the *Groundwork*, at least, Kant appears to identify the CC test and perfect duties. It would be very odd to think that the problem with a killing is in an agent's ends (or general policy maxims) and not in what she does.

As a possible explanation for the failure of the CC test to rule against killing, one might try to make something of the fact that the CC test works best with "conventional" actions—promises, theft—where one comes to the CI procedure with maxims that already include normative concepts. (Even its rejection of slaveholding depends on the assumed moral fact that slaves cannot hold property.[6]) The CC test shows that it is part of what a moral convention (institution) is that we must not have or use them in a way that cannot be willed a universal law (at least within the territory of

---

5. This is a strict, though I think correct, reading of the CC test. Some have thought that the CC test should be understood a bit differently—as requiring that it remain practically reasonable to will our original maxim in a world in which the universal form of our maxim was a law of nature. See Christine M. Korsgaard, "Kant's Formula of Universal Law," *Pacific Philosophical Quarterly* 66 (1985), 24–47. It works from a reading of the deceitful-promise example, which is said to show that in a world in which deceitful promising is law, I can no longer use deceitful promises as means. Thus the maxim of deceitful promising cannot be conceived as a universal law without practical contradiction. But in a world with a law of convenience killing, although I may not know whether I'll be around to do what I will, I ought nonetheless to be able to will in the face of uncertainty, and so be able to will to kill others. So, on this interpretation of the CC test as well, the maxim of convenience killing *can* be conceived of as a universal law without contradiction.

6. See O'Neill, "Consistency in Action," p. 96.

the institution or convention). Where there is a moral convention, we cannot both use it and legitimately exempt ourselves from its requirements. (The test is silent about what conventions we should have.)

If this were all there is to the CC test, we would have an adequate explanation of why it could not reject a "natural" action like killing. But it is not. There is, on the one hand, Kant's suicide example. Whatever one makes of his argument there, it is clearly intended to reject a natural action. Of greater interest is the fact that the CC test seems adequate for maxims of deception and coercion. Universal deception would be held by Kant to make speech and thus deception impossible. And there is something arguably impossible in the idea of universal coercion—where the will of each is to be under the control of the will of the other—though I do not want to develop such an argument here. If we think the CC test might work for coercion, then we need an explanation for its silence about killing.

Although many violent acts are coercive (and so pose no special problem for the CC test if coercion is rejected by it), it will not do to claim that killing is a limiting case of coercion. A coercive act aims at the control of a person's will; killing does not (at least not of the will of the person killed). In killing, someone is prevented from doing anything at all, but he is not made to do something against his will. There is a significant difference between threatening pain or twisting your arm (or even threatening to kill) to keep you from joining the opposition party and killing you to achieve the same result. The coercive act looks to alter what will happen by controlling what an agent wills. In killing, the victim is not prevented from *doing* something— the killing prevents something from happening. Killing (and noncoercive violence in general) poses a moral problem that needs to be kept separate from that of coercion.

So either the CC test works for no natural acts, and killing as well as deception and violence must be rejected by the CW test, or there is a moral distinction between acts of violence (simply) and coercive acts (including acts of coercive violence) that we should expect the CW test to make use of.

II

Let us turn now to the CW test. It requires a positive answer to the question: can I will the killing maxim a universal law of nature without my *will* contradicting itself? There are different ways of understanding this requirement. An obvious route is to follow out the observation that a world in which each kills as it is judged necessary or beneficial is a Hobbesian world. We then read the test as asking: could it be rational for me to will that a Hobbesian world come into existence? The answer seems to be no—given that I am a being with all kinds of purposes, the insecurity I introduce through my willing of a universal killing maxim would (as a psychological fact?) render all but the most minimal purposes futile. It would have to be all right with me that, in willing to kill, the Hobbesian world of all against all should come into being. And isn't it irrational to create a situation of risk to the possibility of (my) successful activity in general?

How does this amount to a contradiction in will? We want to say that willing a Hobbesian world conflicts with what we must will, if we will at all. To be an agent is to will that one's actions and projects succeed (insofar as this is in one's power). To will a Hobbesian world is to will the diminution of the likelihood of success of one's actions in general. And doesn't this contradict what one must, as an agent, will? But how is this different from ordinary risk taking, where you are willing to trade some hoped-for benefit against the possibility of loss? Well, the Hobbesian world promises the certain depression of one's capacity as an agent. Is this right? Would the argument work against one of Mrs. Foot's tough atheistic characters? Isn't this just an argument that would show that for those who are weak, and dependent on the rule of law for their effectiveness as agents, it would be irrational to will a Hobbesian world? But a strong man, confident of his agency or willing to take the consequences—how could the argument apply to him? It is not certain that his agency will be diminished. (This is of course the argument at issue in the first two books of Plato's *Republic,* and it was not answered there either through an appeal to risk.)

The interpretation of the CW test in Chapter 3 suggests another way of looking at this argument. To will a world where everyone acts against one's life when it is convenient to do so is not just to impose a likely increase in the failure rate of one's actions and projects. It is to will a world in which the fact that a life would be lost or taken provides *no reason* to refrain from acting. The life of a person is merely something that may be moved out of the way. The question I take the CW test to pose is whether it can be rational to will a world where one's life can have no value in this reason-giving sense. What we need to see is if this conflicts with something that we must will insofar as we are rational agents. If it does, there will be a contradiction in will.[7]

Among the things normally necessary for my successful willing is the noninterference with my agency by other agents. In the real world, this is something I need; it is not something I can will. (There is an important difference between what I can try to bring about—your noninterference with me through my noninterference with you, for example—and what I can will. I cannot will, have as an end of mine, that *you* will in a particular

---

7. Servility, as Tom Hill describes it, involves such a failure to will the means necessary to have oneself viewed as a source of reasons. See his "Servility and Self-Respect," *Monist* 57 (1973), 87–104.

way or take such and such a consideration as a reason.) But whether you do or do not take the fact of my life as a reason not to kill me is something I *do* will under the hypothetical conditions of the CW test.

As I understand it, the CW test asks this: can you *guarantee* that in all circumstances you can will that others not regard your life as a reason not to kill you, without your will contradicting itself? The argument of the test thus does not turn on the likelihood of others killing me because they all have maxims of killing (or trying to kill) when that is useful. This would be a frightening world, but one in which some "I" could stand fast, if the freedom to kill seemed valuable enough. Instead, the argument moves from the fact of our mutual vulnerability—the weakest in the Hobbesian world is able to kill the strongest—to a conclusion about what it would be rational to will *if* our willing altered the principles of other agents' actions.

In the fictional world of the CW test, I will that others not regard my life as a reason to refrain from taking it. Given the Hobbesian condition, I cannot guarantee that I will avoid a contradiction in willing. For if I will anything at all, I must will the necessary conditions of continued agency (or I must will, as I can, the omission of what would undermine the conditions of my continued existence).[8] And, given my inability to guarantee avoidance of the Hobbesian condition or its consequences, I cannot guarantee that I will not also have willed the cause of the loss of my life. A maxim of convenience killing would pass the CW test only if the agent could guarantee that the willed universal principle of indifference to life cannot conflict with what else he must will, if he wills at all. No human rational agent can guarantee this. Since I must will, as I can, that others take my existence as a limiting condition on their actions, the maxim of convenience killing is rejected. One cannot will the universalized killing maxim and acknowledge the conditions of human agency.

The CW test thus does not ask whether it would be rational to will the world of indifference to life in the sense of assessing the risk. The test should rather be seen as *defining* a conception of rational willing through its procedural requirement.

This interpretation of the CW test involves a departure from the accepted view of the rationality constraint used in the CI procedure. Clearly when I am asking what it can be rational to will, more is involved than is captured by the formal notions of consistency and noncontradiction. The concept of rationality in "rationally will" has content: not normative content, but

---

8. If the single thing I want will happen only if I die, I need not will the necessary conditions of my continued agency. There is no objection to the CW argument in this, for the procedure applies to generic maxims offered as candidate policies for agents' ongoing willings. The fact that my purposes would be better served if I were dead is not likely to provide grounds that can rebut the presumption against killing derived from the CW argument rejecting the generic killing maxim.

clearly content with normative import. There are certain things that a rational will cannot rationally will. Among them is the (systematic) undermining of its capacity to will effectively. There are thus certain things a *human* rational will cannot rationally will, given the conditions of human willing.

The fact that features of human agency show up in the argument is no cause for alarm. Consider the Kantian claim that "willing the means" is contained in the concept of "willing an end." Is this true for all rational beings? Imagine a rational creature (call it a god) whose every willing makes it so (it can even will ex nihilo). It is not true of its willing ends that it will then will the necessary and available means. Perhaps it would be better to say that such a god never wills ends, as such, because it need not will means. Maybe so. But this would be to admit that at the center of accepted Kantian argument there are constraints derived from the kinds of wills that nondivine rational beings have. So why not more specific constraints suited to the facts about the *human* will?

Although the Categorical Imperative applies to all rational beings, duties and prohibitions can be species-specific (species of rational beings, that is). Only rational beings who communicate can lie; only those who are mortal require prohibitions on killing; only those who interact with (or have use for) material things can need an institution of property.[9] It is certainly possible to imagine a world of invulnerable rational agents who could be indifferent to the homicidal intentions of others (of course they also would not find it rational to adopt maxims of killing). When duties and prohibitions are species-specific, we should expect that the arguments establishing them must include aspects of that specificity in their premises. The *kind* of rational being we are, and so the constraints on what *we* can rationally will, enters through what I call the "conditions" of our agency. The CW argument against the generic killing maxim appeals to a special condition of human agency—our vulnerability—in its conclusion that we cannot rationally will a universal law of killing.[10]

Let us for now agree that we have an argument from the CW test showing that the convenience-killing maxim must be rejected. While this is reassuring—the CI can deal with this kind of action—the *way* the CI procedure rejects the killing maxim does not so much resolve the situation as introduce

9. At the end of the *Anthropology* Kant describes mutually transparent beings for whom deception is not a possible project. It is a useful exercise to see just what about us calls for what sorts of moral concepts.

10. The CI procedure seems to work this way: the CC test eliminates maxims that cannot be rationally willed on grounds that are the same for all rational beings (the maxims it rejects are not possible universal laws), while the CW test works from the conditions of human rational willing.

a battery of new questions. First of all, there is the oddness of sorting killing with nonbeneficence. They now sort together for formal reasons (they occupy the same slot in the *Groundwork*'s fourfold classification of duties) and because of the similar way the CW argument shows their impermissibility. Of course killing might be seen to involve, in an essential way, not helping. But surely what is wrong with killing is not the same as what is wrong with not helping. Killing (typically) introduces harm; not helping does not correct a situation in which the harm is already present or threatening. One expects such differences to register in an instructive procedure demonstrating impermissibility. In addition, certain things we might think about the CW test may produce uneasiness here. The CW test is usually taken to reject impermissible policies (or maxims of ends), not specific actions. Further, the duties supported by the CW test are said to be of wide obligation, leaving *Spielraum*—some area of discretion for the agent to determine how she would fulfill the duty. This does not fit well with killing, where we expect a more stringent prohibition. The prohibition we would seem to get, following the beneficence example, is a duty not to have a general policy of killing for self-interest. But although we must not have a policy of never helping, we may sometimes not help. Does it follow that, though we must not have a policy of killing, we may sometimes kill? We need to see whether these questions and the assumptions behind them are well founded.

If the CW arguments show that maxims of killing and nonbeneficence *are* deeply similar, because they both involve failures to acknowledge inescapable conditions of human agency, they also show how they are different, in that the condition of human agency that each would discount is different. What is wrong in the maxim of killing is its denial of the claim of vulnerability. What goes wrong in a maxim of nonbeneficence is its denial of the claim of need. The full content of the claims of vulnerability and need are derived from elaboration of these conditions of human agency. Within the CW arguments, in willing that maxims of nonbeneficence or killing become universal laws, the agent wills to forgo something (the help of others, their restraint) that he must, as a rational agent, will that he have (or not will that he not have). It is because we as human rational agents cannot exempt ourselves from the condition of need (and so cannot withdraw from the possibility of making claims on the help of others) that we may not ignore their claims of need. And it is because we cannot escape the conditions of our mortality and vulnerability that we may not take the lives of others at will. Looked at this way, it seems appropriate that killing and nonbeneficence be sorted together.

But this response does not meet the objection that any such argument neglects the distinctive wrongness of killing. What makes killing wrong, we may think, is that the loss of life unjustly harms the person who loses it.

There is a natural inclination to connect the nature of a wrong to the complaint of the recipient of the action. So we expect the analysis of violent actions to be in terms of harm inflicted (gratuitous pain, frustration of interests, loss of some good). But the CW argument does not lead one to conclude that we may not act assaultively because that would harm others, or that we may not kill because in so acting we cause loss of life. The burden of the CW argument, as I interpret it, is that the agent who would kill in pursuit of his interests fails to acknowledge what follows from the fact that the life he would take is the life of a person. He fails to count the life of the other as in itself providing a reason not to kill—a reason that outweighs (independent of any calculation) the reasons for killing derived from the agent's pursuit of private ends. We might put it this way: the CW argument shows that it is impermissible to discount the value of human life to the currency of our purposes. In effect, then, what makes such killing wrong, when it is wrong, is some erroneous valuation, and not the causing of death or harm. The correct moral complaint from the victim does not speak of pain or loss, but of the lack of proper regard for him as a rational agent.

This result should not be surprising. In Kantian ethics it cannot be what happens to an agent as a result of what is done that makes an action morally wrong. That is, killing is not wrong because it brings about death, and mayhem is not wrong because it brings about pain or harm. Moral wrongness is not a function of consequences but of willings. And according to the argument of the CW test, what is wrong with the killing maxim is that the agent fails to accord proper weight to the value of life of rational agents (including his own) in what he wills.

This is the result that should surprise, because it looks as if the conclusion of our argument is that rightness and wrongness are a function of correctly or incorrectly *valuing* human agents. And if considerations of value play this role in determining permissibility, the analysis in Kantian theory of right and wrong would seem to depend on the theory's conception of the good. What has happened to deontology?

We must not be misled by modern views about deontology or become fixated by the prominence of rules, principles, and the idea of duty in Kantian theory. It has, as it must have, a conception of value to provide the foundation for moral assessment. In the terms of a more recent Kantian enterprise, we can say that what the CI procedure shows is that the value of rational agency is lexically superior to the value of desire per se. It is not that desire (the satisfaction of desire) has no value, but that there is a strict hierarchy such that the value of rational agency cannot be outweighed by that of (any) desire. Failure to assign correct value to rational agency—discounting the conditions of human willing—is the "content" of morally wrong action.[11]

---

11. The elaboration of a value-based interpretation of Kantian ethics is the subject of Chapter 10.

I think we must take seriously the passage in the *Groundwork* where Kant describes the value of a rational being. It is *autonomy,* he says, the capacity to will what is in itself good (and so unconditionally good), that gives humanity a value *(Wert)* called dignity *(Würde)*—a worth that puts it "infinitely beyond all price, with which it cannot in the least be brought into competition or comparison without, as it were, violating its sanctity" (G435).

The appearance of a conception of value at the heart of Kantian theory does not imply that we can drop the CI procedure and make moral judgments directly according to some scale of values. Knowing that the autonomous will has value beyond price does not tell us *when* our actions discount that value.[12] The procedures of judgment for the CI explicate the conception of value that is at the foundation of Kantian moral theory. The role of the CI procedure, through its two tests, is to tell us when our willing is good—when we succeed in acknowledging the true worth of rational agents (ourselves and others) in our maxims. The arguments of the CI procedure at once describe the form of good willing and bring it to bear on the conditions of human agency. Good willing is a matter of deliberative commitment, in which formal procedures of deliberation express the basic value conception. It is not the concept of duty but the ultimate reliance on the CI procedure for judgments of value that makes Kantian ethics "non-teleological."

III

The arguments of the CI procedure—under both tests—introduce constraints on what may be rationally willed that are ultimately based on those constitutive features of human agency that can be affected by the actions of ourselves and others. It may help to survey what these are. Kant views action as beginning in a conception of interest or desire that prompts an agent to adopt ends according to principle; we act in the way we believe is a means to realizing our end, which we take to be in some sense good. These general features of willing contain the points at which the will is subject to possible manipulation and interference, where agents' actions may be brought under the control of another. Beliefs can be manipulated, desires can be altered, induced, enhanced, and so on. This is the arena of the CC test. The conditions of agency that enter

12. This is why one cannot replace the Formula of Universal Law with the Formula of Humanity. Although the Formula of Humanity gives more direct expression to the idea that rational agency has value, and so must be accorded respect (treated as an end), the formula cannot be applied without use of the CI procedure. To treat someone as an end is to act in such ways that the person can "hold the very same action as an end" (G430). What sorts of actions can be "held as an end" is, I believe, best understood as those actions that can be rationally willed: a determination that needs to be made by the CI procedure.

CW arguments are not characteristics of willing as such. They are the features that characterize the limits of our *powers* as agents: we are both physically vulnerable and mortal; we are not always able to sustain ourselves without help; not all of our capacities develop with the mere passage of time.

Here is where one might draw the line between violence and coercion. Earlier I supposed that maxims of coercion would be rejected by the CC test. What remained to be explained was why coercion was rejected on other grounds than killing. Now one might say: coercion involves a more direct attack on agency than does any act of (mere) violence. Its intent is to subvert and control the will of another. What we find through the CI procedure is that, in willing maxims of deceit and coercion to be universal laws, one wills a world in which one's own desires and beliefs are to be available to all as means for their purposes. In willing that our desires or beliefs be so manipulated, we in effect give over our agency to the agency of others (we become but one of many who determine what we will). A universal law involving the dispersal of agency cannot be conceived as a law for rational agents.

Unlike coercion or deception, which involve assault on the integrity of willing itself, the object of violent action is not the will but a person's body. (Threats of violence and threats involving violence are other matters.) Coercion involves an attack on agency; violence, an attack on its conditions. Although violent actions usually prevent an agent from *doing* what he wills, they do not (they cannot) control willing. The agent in the hands of violence has his will obstructed, as he would if the general circumstances of his action turned recalcitrant. This is why a world of universal violence is conceivable.

It is appropriate to note here that the extension of the CW argument from maxims of killing to maxims of violence requires no new argument. However we regard the body—as universal means, as our embodiment as causally effective agents—it is the material condition of human agency. Having a body is not a necessary condition of agency per se. There might be beings characterized by "agency at a distance": able to effect what they will through no intermediary entity or through the body of other persons. We are not such agents. Since the CW argument requires that we take the conditions of *human* agency as the bases of reasons not to interfere with them, generic maxims of killing and noncoercive violence are rejected for the same reason.

The CI procedure would seem to sort morally wrong "natural" actions into two kinds: (1) impingements on the constitutive elements of willed action (threats and coercion manipulate desires; deceit manipulates the circumstances of deliberation), and (2) discounting the conditions of agency (violence, indifference to self-development or the true needs of others). Perhaps the reason that conventional or institution-based moral wrongs sort with coercion and deceit is because those institutions with moral foundation (promising, property) are constitutive of the possibility of coordinated free human activity (what coercion undermines).

IV

The CI procedure shows, in its rejection of generic maxims of killing or violence or deception, that reasons of self-interest cannot be offered as justification for actions (maxims) that assault the will or the conditions of human agency. But when agents act impermissibly, they do not normally intend to subvert rational activity or consciously refuse to acknowledge the conditions supporting rational agency. (Violent acts are vicious, not just impermissible, when their attraction is in part the fact that the victim is a person.) People are drawn to impermissible actions by a situation-specific error in relative valuation: in special circumstances, where the felt pressure of need is great, where it seems impossible not to act, actions that impinge on rational agency, even ones the agent recognizes are normally wrong, present themselves as suitable means to ends (G424). I may know that I intend to deceive, but justify my deceit by the extremity of my desire and the belief that it will do no real harm. Another may feel there is no choice but to act violently—sure that whatever harm she causes is justified by the harm she would otherwise suffer or the loss she thereby avoids. Agents look away from the moral fact that the claim of interest cannot justify discounting the claims of rational agency or its conditions.

The error of "devaluing" or "discounting" rational agency describes what is morally wrong in maxims judged impermissible by the CI procedure, showing what it is about our impermissible maxims that makes them fail.[13] This does not mean that we can instruct moral agents by directing them to avoid errors in the relative valuation of persons and interests. The identification of impermissible forms of willing is the task of the CI procedure's two tests. Likewise, when an agent acts morally well (when her will is good), it is not helpful to say (even though it is true) that she values rational agency and its conditions. Rather, as a moral agent, committed to the deliberative constraints of the CI procedure, she will refrain from treating others in certain ways (on *formal* grounds) that we may say amount

---

13. If I am right in holding that the CI procedure directly assesses only generic maxims, an agent's specific maxim is judged impermissible when its justificatory claim (to do *x* for reason *y*) is insufficient to rebut the presumption against an action or policy established by the CI procedure's arguments. A rejected particular maxim will be rejected because it exemplifies the form of "moral devaluation" of the relevant impermissible generic maxim.

to regarding them or valuing them as ends-in-themselves. Talk of respect for persons or the value of rational agency must always be understood as an intuitively appealing shorthand for the outcome of a deliberative commitment to the CI procedure. The idea of "devaluation" brings these results closer to intuition and guides further deliberation.

The CI procedure shows that certain patterns of reasoning—certain forms of willing—are not legitimate. This establishes directly some duties and prohibitions. In addition, the arguments of the procedure's two tests reveal categories or rules of moral salience that are to be used to sort the details of cases, carrying with them certain presumptions about forms of impermissible willing. In rejecting the general maxim of violence, the CW argument shows that acts that use or harm the human body may not be regarded simply as available means for our various purposes. This sets the relevant principle of casuistry. It establishes a moral presumption against violence (moral devaluation of the body), putting the burden of argument on the agent who would be violent to explain why what he would do is not governed by the terms of the presumption.

Although it is to be part of the defense of this interpretation of the CI procedure and the CW argument that it can guide moral judgment in hard cases, the detailed development of this defense is a project well beyond the scope of this chapter. Nonetheless, I think we can get a sense here of how the casuistry of acts of violence will work out. Let us take self-defense as the test case for using the principle of casuistry for violent actions.

Self-defense is particularly difficult in Kantian ethics, for it is not clear how one could ever be morally justified in taking someone's life. How could killing an aggressor be compatible with the regard we must have for him as a rational agent? The fact that an aggressor acts on impermissible maxims could not justify withdrawing from him the value or moral standing he has independent of what he does. Insofar as he is no less a rational agent for being an aggressor, his continued existence instead of mine seems, from the point of view of rational agency per se, equivalent. If we follow this line of thought, no act of violence could be morally justified. This seems to leave us, morally, at each other's mercy (or throats).

One might consider a counterappeal in the fact that what I lose if I do not act in self-defense is my life—a necessary condition of my agency. But if I am justified in doing whatever I must to preserve my life, then it looks as if I can take your food or your heart if I need it. And if we say to that, "It is not that you can do whatever you must to save your life, but you can do whatever you need to do if your life is the object of *aggression*," then it is not the fact that I will lose my life that explains the permissibility of self-defense. (This reasoning would also not protect innocent bystanders, but that is another problem.)

It is reasonable to require of any Kantian account of self-defense that it answer three questions. What is it that gives moral significance to loss of life through aggression when death itself is not morally bad (and in itself does not justify acts of violence)? What blocks reciprocity of complaint—why can't the original aggressor accuse the self-defender of aggression (and now renew his aggression with moral support)? If I can save my life without taking the life of the aggressor, must I? (That is, can we motivate proportionality of response?)

Interpreting the CW argument as establishing a principle of casuistry prohibiting the devaluation or discounting of the material condition of human life to a means takes us some of the way toward understanding self-defense. We should consider the possibility of a maxim of taking life (in self-defense) whose justification is not self-interested or based in any erroneous valuation of the aggressor. If we can base answers to the three questions on this, we will have as much case support for the interpretation as we could reasonably expect at this stage.

So, first, why may I kill to resist aggression? What reasons could I offer to rebut the presumption against violence? It is not that I may kill in order to keep myself from becoming dead—something I do not want to happen. Death is part of the fate of human agents. The kind of value or moral standing I have as an agent is not lost or compromised in dying. What a maxim of aggression or violence involves, morally speaking, is the discounting of my agency. The aggressor would use me (take my life) for his purposes. This is what I resist and claim moral title to refuse. Just as I cannot agree to become someone's slave, so I must not assent to be the victim of aggression.[14] This gives more than permission for an act of self-defense when that is necessary to resist the aggression; it imposes a requirement that aggression be resisted. Though I may not be able to prevent the aggressor's success, I may not be passive in the face of aggression. Passivity here is like complicity. It does not follow from a requirement of nonpassivity that I must act in self-defense. I might have a commitment to resist and have reason not to do any of the things available as acts of resistance (suppose they involved loss of innocent lives). What is clear is this: it is not the fact of death but the death as a means to the aggressor's purposes that gives moral title to resistance and self-defense. The circumstances of aggression rebut the presumption against violence.

This same fact blocks reciprocity of complaint. The aggressor acts on a maxim that involves the devaluation of my agency. I do not. I am not acting to save my life as such, but to resist the use of my agency (self) by another. Acting to save my life (as something valuable to me) would be to act for

14. That is, maxims that involve the abandonment of autonomous agency are impermissible—they cannot be willed a universal law.

just another purpose. The moral standing of my agency—what makes it the source of reasons for others to refrain from acting against me—is not the good (to me) of being alive. Acting to sustain the integrity of my agency is to act for a morally necessary end. Thus, since my maxim of resistance is not a maxim of aggression as a means, the original aggressor cannot renew his attack on morally superior grounds. I am not acting to preserve myself through violent means. In stopping aggression with force, I am asserting my status as a rational agent. It is an act of self-respect.

The justification of self-defense does not devalue the aggressor because he is guilty of aggression. He forfeits no moral title; I have no claim of moral superiority. If I may act with violence against aggression, I must do so without ignoring the fact that the object of my action is an aggressing *agent*. Moreover, the fact of his undiminished agency and value grounds a proportionality of response, not because it is better that there be more agents around but because, in limiting my action where possible, I demonstrate the moral regard he is still owed. It may be possible to defeat or defuse the threat, or even remove myself from the other's sphere of action. The justification of a *maxim* of resistance does not justify every action that would stop the aggressing agent. The action of resistance needs to be guided by what is necessary to defuse the actual or perceived threat, constrained by other regulative maxims and concerns. If violence in self-defense is justified as an act of resistance to aggression, it would seem to be justified as an act of last resort.

Having answered our three questions, we have casuistical material that takes us a bit further. For example, the argument that justifies violence in self-defense does not justify violence against innocent threats (persons whose actions, or the effects of their actions, threaten life but who do not intend any harm or violence). Self-defense is permitted as a way of resisting a willed attack on my agency. Since the innocent threat is identified as having no agency-discounting maxim—no maxim of aggression—I may not act against him in self-defense.[15] For the same reason, I may not take the life or the organs of another to stay alive. In neither case would I be acting to sustain the integrity of my agency—only its duration.[16]

---

15. A troubling consequence of this view is that the justification of self-defense requires knowledge of another's maxim. While there are circumstances in which we can infer an agent's intentions with great confidence, in all too many others we cannot. It is not clear how we are to deal with this kind of uncertainty. I am not troubled by it here since my much more limited goal is to see if actions of violence in response to acts of aggression are *ever* justified. One consequence of the fact of uncertainty would be to add weight to the idea of proportionality of response.

16. It does not follow that we cannot act against innocent threats. The deliberative question is whether the need to remove a threat to life is sufficient to rebut the presumption against violence.

If resisting or refusing the devaluation of agency in a maxim of aggression provides the principle of justification in self-defense, there is no special issue with third parties. Since the justification for resistance is *not* that I may act to save my life, but to resist the misuse of my life or body *as* the life or body of a rational agent, it is not clear what difference it makes if the self I protect is not mine. The requirements on victims and third parties might divide if there is an argument to show that victims must adopt maxims of resistance.

May I protect myself from aggression by letting it spend itself on someone else? Could I defend such an act as protecting the integrity of my agency? I do not myself assault the other, and if he is well positioned I need use no force—perhaps I just step behind him so that the aggressor shoots him instead of me. I think we will want to say that redirecting the threat is not an act of resistance but of defense in the literal sense.

While I think there is good support for the first set of results, these last remarks are clearly speculative. And the questions multiply. Suppose the aggressor protects himself from my response with an innocent person? May I still resist, viewing the loss of one of our innocent lives as inevitable and therefore acting to save my own as permissible? What may I do to resist aggression that does not threaten my life? May I kill to prevent the loss of an arm, take only an eye for an eye? What may I do in the face of threats? Given the condition of human agency, does a threat that puts me at risk already count as an act of violence? Quite obviously, the casuistical method we have begun here is still too crude to resolve these questions or the many others they spawn.

Where does this leave us? That we could proceed at all in the discussion of self-defense is ground for confidence that the principle of casuistry derived from the CW argument against killing can do the kind of job we hoped it could. Further results will require extensive work on the role of principles of casuistry in deliberation and, in particular, on developing a method for using the rejected generic maxims as deliberative presumptions in judgment directed at morally complex cases. Although this way of working with the CI procedure does not preserve the idea of a simple technique for maxim assessment, that loss (if it is a loss) will be more than made up if the CI procedure can actually be used.

7

Moral Deliberation and the Derivation of Duties

INTERPRETERS and critics of Kant's ethics are heavily invested in the Categorical Imperative as a principle of moral judgment. There is endless discussion about how or whether the CI works, about whether the results it would give if it did work are acceptable, and so on. A question that is much less frequently asked is: what role does the CI have in moral judgment? That is supposed to be obvious. I am increasingly sure it is not. What I want to do here is review some of the reasons for rejecting the received view (actually views) of the CI, and then sketch an alternative role for the CI within a more complex Kantian theory of moral judgment. If we have been wrong about the role for which the CI procedure was designed, the fact that no one has been able to make it work would be much less significant.

I

There are two roles that are commonly assigned to the CI procedure. It is thought either to support a derivation of duties or to provide an algorithm for moral deliberation. (I will refer to the two interpretations by these functional descriptions.) The derivation-of-duties model has been the most enduring in the history of interpreting the CI procedure, and it is probably the source of most of the stock criticisms of the substantive results of Kant's ethics. The idea is that with the CI procedure in hand, we will be able to produce an "N Commandments" of morality: Thou shalt not make deceitful promises, neglect the needs of others, and so on. The more recent view of the role of the CI procedure, and the one I have thought to be most interesting, takes it instead to provide a set of instructions for moral deliberation or judgment[1] whereby an individual, in specific circumstances

---

1. In the first half of this chapter I will follow common practice and speak of moral deliberation and moral judgment interchangeably. I will have reason in the second half to assign

with particular intentions, can determine the permissibility of a proposed action or end.

The chief objection to the derivation-of-duties model is that it generates a rigoristic ethics of duties and standing obligations. Relying somewhat on Kant's *Groundwork* examples but more on his various normative pronouncements, the CI procedure is taken to be the source of absolute, exceptionless prohibitions. Such a theory is rightly charged with insensitivity to moral complexity and righteous absurdity in requiring, as it is sometimes thought to, that we keep all promises, tell no lies, regardless of the consequences. It would seem to produce a moral life inevitably riddled with moral conflicts without providing any way of resolving them or determining the priority of moral claims.[2] There is little to recommend such an account of morality, and few endorse it. Those sympathetic to Kant's foundational claims or his analyses of moral worth or autonomy generally look for ways to get around the derivation-of-duties interpretation of the CI procedure.

What of textual evidence in support of the derivation-of-duties model? It is mixed. On the one hand, Kant says in the introduction to the four examples of the *Groundwork* that he will show that you can "derive imperatives of duty" from the one principle that is a CI. On the other hand, there is the surprising fact that the CI procedure is not used in either part of the *Metaphysics of Morals,* where Kant explicitly derives duties of virtue and justice. (He uses a new principle for the duties of justice and a version of the Formula of Humanity for the duties of virtue.) Of course Kant could have changed his mind in the later texts about the utility of the CI procedure for deriving duties, but it is more than a little odd that he never indicates that he has done so, especially since he makes such a point in the *Groundwork* that "one does better if in moral judgment he follows the rigorous method and takes as his basis the universal formula of the CI" (G437)—that is, the CI procedure. Surely a natural explanation of the absence of the CI procedure from Kant's more extended derivations of duties is that it was never intended for that role.

---

them separate roles.

2. In the introduction to the *Metaphysics of Morals* (223), Kant denies that "conflicts of duties" are possible. (Actually he says that such conflict is "inconceivable.") If we take him to hold that duties carry some kind of practical necessity, and he believes that there are in the usual way a number of duties, then indeed he must deny the possibility of conflicts of duties. It would be perverse if this meant he was denying that any conflict between moral requirements could occur. This is not the only interpretation of the denial, however. He could equally well be (and I think he is) denying that we have duties (plural) in the strict, necessitating sense. We have a duty, in cases of conflict, that is determined according to the stronger of what Kant calls two conflicting "grounds of obligation." We will return to this material later, when we are in a position to see what some of these distinctions might amount to.

Although the CI procedure is not used in the *Metaphysics of Morals*, Kant does offer a variant of it in the *Critique of Practical Reason* as the rule of judgment by which our maxims of action can be evaluated. He calls it the "Typic of pure practical judgment." The Typic account does not say whether we should use its method for deriving duties or for moral deliberation. It is, however, presented as the formal statement of the rule by which everyone does decide if actions are morally good or bad—a rule of deliberation.

Given the absence of decisive textual evidence for a derivation-of-duties model and the strength of the moral objections to its results, hope for the CI procedure has seemed to reside with the moral-deliberation model. There is no decisive textual evidence against the moral-deliberation interpretation of the CI procedure. Even Kant's remarks about "deriving imperatives of duty" as he introduces the CI procedure can be read to support it. His object at that moment in the *Groundwork* was to show that the formal principle derived from analysis of the unconditioned "ought" of morality (the CI) is a moral principle by showing that it can explain the judgments we take to be incontrovertibly moral. Then we can understand the four examples as demonstrating that a set of canonical pretheoretical moral prohibitions ("imperatives of duty") follow from the principle. What the examples show is that if an agent brought a maxim violating what we typically think of as a duty to the CI procedure, it would be rejected: a maxim of deceitful promising for gain is not a possible universal law. It does not follow from this rejection that the CI procedure has thereby derived (in the strong sense) a duty of honest promising.

There is support in other places for the idea that the role of the CI procedure is to regulate moral deliberation. Kant expresses a Rousseauian conviction that the Moral Law functions in the conscience of every normal person, leading us to assess actions by an intuitive appeal to a criterion of universalizability. If we think of the moral theory as the formal analysis and elaboration of our intuitive manner of moral thinking, the CI procedure provides the formal explication of the natural manner of moral deliberation familiarly expressed in the "What if everyone did that?" query.

The most persuasive evidence for the moral-deliberation interpretation comes from attention to the fact that the CI procedure is addressed to *maxims* of action—the subjective principles of agents' willing. To the extent that maxims are viewed as circumstance and interest-specific—doing x in circumstance c for the sake of an end e—applying the CI procedure to maxims could yield duties only if every maxim of a certain action (or end) kind was rejected. With maxims as the objects of assessment for the CI procedure, it seems more reasonable to view the role of the procedure as directing an agent's moral judgment or deliberation.

The great appeal of the moral deliberation plus maxims view is the degree to which it makes the CI procedure sensitive to the morally relevant particulars of agents' circumstances. Such a method of judgment would not be likely to introduce the rigid moral requirements that have been the complaint of recent critics of Kant's ethics. Indeed, not only is the theory unlikely to produce rigid requirements, but it could permit agents to act in quite different ways in similar moral circumstances *if* they were sincerely acting on different maxims. Permissibility—the outcome of the CI procedure— would to an extent be a function of each agent's perceptions.[3]

Although such a version of Kantian ethics would be radical—reflecting social, personal, and historical variation—it would still be a theory with objective results, issuing from an impartial procedure impartially applied. Any variation in moral requirements would be a function of real differences that, though introduced through agents' perceptions, knowledge, and such, would not signal any corrosive subjectivism. The same maxims would always be judged the same way. The moral-deliberation interpretation seems to liberate Kantian ethics, allowing it some of the creative sweep claimed by consequentialism, while remaining true to the strictures of rationalist theory.

Two sorts of problems might dampen enthusiasm. First is the reasonable concern that no such principle could support or generate public moral rules. Uniformity in upbringing, conformity from social sanctions, could produce people who would see things the same way and so act on the same maxims. But there might be no moral justification for producing the convergence, and no moral grounds to criticize sincere deviance. Perhaps there would be classes of maxims that we would agree no one could act on and ends that most of us would have sufficient reason not to adopt. But such clumping phenomena would not replace duties.

As a theoretical objection this has little weight, for its point is really to gainsay the force of the revision. If the role of the CI procedure is to assess maxims, and maxims are context-sensitive, then we will have a theory that has a formal and objective procedure for moral deliberation or judgment that does not generate duties.

There is more bite to a practical version of the criticism. The absence of duties or public moral rules may suit a society of moral saints whose known sincerity and wish to be moral would provide grounds for tolerating differences in moral behavior. Where such ideals were not realized, as among ordinary people, morality could not do its job (if it is its job) of producing a certain kind of order and confidence of expectation about the behavior of others. A crucial question for this project would be whether independently justified rules of public order (laws) could introduce socially necessary uniformity without undermining moral sensitivity and diversity.

3. Though only to an extent. Social uniformities and pressures of mutual intelligibility would produce convergence in content.

However attractive this direction of thought, there appears to be a decisive obstacle to the view that the CI procedure regulates moral deliberation: on either of the most plausible interpretations of the CI procedure's two tests, the introduction of circumstance-specific maxims of action causes the procedure to break down. Some of the questions that arise in showing this to be the case suggest a different way of thinking about the role of the CI procedure in moral deliberation and judgment.

II

Internal criticisms of the CI procedure have usually focused on two issues: the nature of the input to the procedure (the problem of maxim description) and the nature of the contradiction that the procedure is designed to detect. There is now a more or less standard set of views that explain how the contradiction is to be understood.[4] I do not want to add to them; they represent the interpretive options reasonably well. My questions concern their adequacy in accounts of the CI procedure's role in moral judgment. In particular, I want to look at the features of impermissible maxims that are said to produce contradictions under universalization. An interpretation of the CI procedure will be satisfactory only if it produces the right results *and* allows us to understand what makes wrong actions (maxims) wrong.

The opening moves of the CI procedure are the same for all interpretations. You start with an agent's maxim; the maxim is universalized; you ask whether the agent can will that such a universalized maxim become (through her will) a universal law of nature. A maxim fails if it cannot be willed a universal law without contradiction (in conception or will). It is at this point that the different interpretations diverge. I will consider two of them called, following Christine Korsgaard's useful typology, the practical and the logical interpretations.[5]

According to the practical interpretation, a maxim is rejected by the CI procedure if, when we imagine a world in which our universalized maxim is a law, it is no longer a world in which it is rational (in a practical sense)

4. See John Rawls, "Themes in Kant's Moral Philosophy," in *Kant's Transcendental Deductions,* ed. Eckart Förster (Stanford: Stanford University Press, 1989); Christine M. Korsgaard, "Kant's Formula of Universal Law," *Pacific Philosophical Quarterly* 66 (1985), 24–47; and Onora (Nell) O'Neill, *Acting on Principle* (New York: Columbia University Press, 1975), chaps. 4 and 5, and "Consistency in Action," in *Constructions of Reason* (Cambridge: Cambridge University Press, 1990).

5. Korsgaard, "Kant's Formula of Universal Law," p. 25. Korsgaard sorts the interpretations into three kinds: logical, practical, and teleological. I will not have anything to say about the teleological interpretation, in part because it does not introduce any special features into the problems I will be discussing, but mainly because the assumptions of natural and necessary purpose it uses are hard to defend.

for us to will according to our original maxim. There is a contradiction in our willing the original maxim *and* its universal form. The contradiction is practical because, in the imagined world, the universalized maxim subverts the original maxim's ability to serve our purpose. Because it is pointless or self-defeating to pursue purposes with a deceitful promise in a world of universal deceitful promising (the universal practice removes the conditions of trust that make deceitful promises a useful means in the first place), one cannot rationally will a deceitful promise (for a purpose) *and* a universal law of deceitful promising without practical contradiction.

This is the form of argument in the contradiction-in-conception test, associated with the first two examples in the *Groundwork*, interpreted as a practical contradiction. The contradiction-generating idea behind the second, or contradiction-in-will, test is that maxims will be impermissible if, when willed a universal law, they conflict with purposes that we must as rational beings also will. Although the two tests are of equal importance in understanding a Kantian account of moral judgment, the central argument of this chapter is keyed to the contradiction-in-conception test. This is so for two reasons. First of all, unease about talk of essential purposes makes it hard to see the moral point of requiring that maxims be universalizable (whereas, once we see the point, we can motivate the introduction of essential purposes). Second, the differences between the rival interpretations that are instructive for this project do not show in the contradiction-in-will test.

The logical interpretation works from the most literal rendering of the texts that describe the contradiction in conception. According to the logical interpretation, maxims that fail the test cannot be *conceived* or thought a universal law without contradiction. You cannot conceive a universal law of deceitful promising because nothing can be a universal *law* that cannot have an instance. The very possibility of a deceitful promise depends on it *not* being the case that there is a universal law of deceitful promising. (The idea of the argument is that the possibility of deceitful promising requires a viable institution of promising, which does not exist where deceitful promising is a universal law.[6])

The reasoning in the logical and practical interpretations in the canonical deceitful-promise case appears to make use of the same feature: the parasitic

---

6. The logical interpretation is clearest in Allen Wood, "Kant on False Promises," in *Proceedings of the Third International Kant Congress,* ed. L. W. Beck (Dordrecht: D. Reidel, 1972), pp. 614–619. Maxims that fail the contradiction-in-will test according to the logical interpretation do so because when willed a universal law they contradict something that one must will insofar as one wills at all. I am not concerned with working out the details of the supposed contradiction arguments at this stage. In a sense I want to work backward: first we need to see what kind of argument does the job (and what kind of job the job is); then we can worry about whether there is an argument that works.

dependence of the proposed maxim on the fact that others do not act in the same way. It is because, and only because, promises are not routinely deceptive that I can make a deceitful promise and pursue my purposes by its means.

I want now to look at a kind of case that reveals how, despite their apparent similarity, the logical and practical interpretations pick out different features of an agent's volition in the way they judge impermissibility. Consider two examples of "timing" or "coordination" maxims:

1. A acts on a maxim of saving money by shopping in this year's after-Christmas sales for next year's Christmas presents. If everyone acted as A does, the practice of Christmas sales would die out, and A would not be able to pursue his economies as he now does. What makes A's maxim rational is plainly his knowledge that others do not act as he does.

2. B knows that the best time to play tennis is Sunday morning when her neighbors are in church. At all other times the courts are crowded. B acts on a maxim of playing tennis Sundays at 10:00. If everyone acted as B does, the courts would be crowded Sunday mornings as well as all other times. What makes B's maxim rational is her knowledge that others can be counted on not to act on the same maxim.[7]

As one proponent of the practical interpretation explains: "the contradiction that is involved in the universalization of an immoral maxim is that the agent would be unable to act on the maxim in a world in which it were universalized so as to achieve his own purpose—that is, the purpose that is specified in the maxim." And again, "What the test shows to be forbidden are just those actions whose efficacy in achieving their purposes depends on their being exceptional."[8] If the practical interpretation of the contradiction-in-conception test rejects maxims whose rationality is based on others acting differently, the actions in these two cases are impermissible. We may not shop in after-Christmas sales; we may not organize our tennis playing to take advantage of our neighbors' religious commitments. This unfortunate result follows from the "success condition" used in the practical interpretation. A maxim is impermissible if its *success* would be undermined by universal action on that maxim.

No such result follows from the logical interpretation. That an action could not serve its intended instrumental purpose in circumstances in which others acted similarly does not show that action in those circumstances is

7. The example is borrowed from T. M. Scanlon, "Kant's *Groundwork:* From Freedom to Moral Community," manuscript, 1983, lecture 2.
8. Korsgaard, "Kant's Formula of Universal Law," p. 36.

in any sense *inconceivable*. "Foolish" or "pointless" would be the more likely terms of criticism. According to the logical interpretation, under universalization the deceitful promise is not intelligible as a deceitful promise, because promising (and so deceitful promising) is not possible in the world of universal deceitful promising. Given universalization, a "tennis at 10:00" maxim will not achieve its purpose (finding an empty court), but it is not for that reason inconceivable or impossible. The logical interpretation, therefore, does not reject coordination or timing maxims as impermissible.

This is an important result. We may expect that the fault a universalization procedure will show in such maxims as deceitful promising is "free riding." The problem with the practical interpretation, as I am reading it, is that it fails to distinguish free riding from coordination. Why should there be anything wrong with my using others' known patterns of behavior to my advantage? This is not a matter of abuse. We want to think here about the range of normal cases. I select my driving route to school by observing where others don't like to go. I go to the movies at 6:00 because there are crowds at 8:00. The intention is to do what others are not doing. The condition of success for such actions is that others not act the same way.

Following the practical interpretation it might even seem reasonable to conclude that these ordinary coordination actions were morally worse than deceitful promising. The deceitful promisor might be free riding without thinking of his action that way, whereas the coordinators choose their actions on the basis of their beliefs that because others do x doing not-x will be instrumentally successful.

The upshot of this is that, whatever is wrong with actions like the deceitful promise, it is not (or not just) that they are actions "whose efficacy in achieving their purposes depends on their being exceptional." There is nothing wrong with actions so described.

There are possible rejoinders to this line of argument. One might argue that there are better (or equally accurate) descriptions of the original cases which would not lead to the objectionable results under the practical interpretation. One might replace the after-Christmas sales maxim with a maxim of shopping whenever it is cheapest to shop (or whenever the balance of cheapness and convenience is right). Everyone could happily act on such a maxim (indeed "the market" assumes they do). In similar fashion, the "tennis at 10:00" maxim could be replaced by a maxim of playing tennis when the courts are least likely to be used. And so on.

It is possible that this could be done for all the difficult cases we could find. I am uneasy with this strategy. Were it successful, it would not be adequate to say that there are "equally accurate" noncoordination descriptions, since that would leave actions permissible under one but not another description. We would need to argue that the coordination description is erroneous. But since coordination actions are routine, and conceived as such by agents, there should be maxims where that feature of the action is a natural part of the description. Eliminating the countercases by claiming that they do not really occur is belied by the fact that the form of reasoning they represent is an ordinary and, one would think, permissible form of means-end reasoning.

Whether we come to regard the role of the CI procedure as the generative source of duties or as the procedure for moral deliberation about cases, when the CI procedure rejects a maxim it ought to do so for reasons that explain what is morally wrong with the maxim. On the practical interpretation, it fails to do this.

Moreover, even if the practical interpretation can be made to work (that is, not produce false negatives) by redescribing the troubling coordination maxims, this begs the question of demonstrating that a given maxim is or is not permissible. For whether or not the maxim is to be redescribed seems to depend on our understanding its moral status prior to assessment. We could redescribe the deceitful-promising maxim too: "to make use of others' expectations in order to secure advantages." What we of course want to respond is that such a redescription omits the morally salient feature of the maxim, the deceitful promise. But how do we tell that we have not similarly omitted the morally salient features of the shopping and tennis maxims when we redescribe them? Only by already knowing that deceitful promising is, and after-Christmas shopping is not, morally suspect.

If the logical interpretation has the advantage of sorting the coordination maxims correctly, it must also provide the right sort of account of the moral wrongness of the maxims it rejects. Under the logical interpretation of the contradiction-in-conception test, maxims are judged not to be possible universal laws when their own nonuniversality is a condition of their possibility as maxims. (The assumed nonuniversality in the background of the coordination maxims is not a condition of their possibility but of their *success*.) It is not immediately obvious what moral bearing this fact has. The practical interpretation draws strong intuitive support when it seems to pick out free riding on the activities of others as the morally salient failure of impermissible actions. We take such actions to be unfair. It would be helpful if we could give a comparable intuitive gloss for the logical interpretation.

What the logical interpretation captures and the practical interpretation misses in the comparison of the deceitful promise and the coordination cases is the *deception*. In the coordination case, the behavior of others is a public fact that I take into account in determining how to act in pursuit of my interests. It is like the weather: knowing that it will be sunny in July, I plan my vacation. Knowing that others will do *x*, I do *y*. In the deceitful-promise case, I use the fact that others participate in the institution of promising as a way of controlling or manipulating their behavior. The very possibility of my deception depends on the presence of the institution it deceptively mimes. That is why general knowledge of coordination maxims will not affect their efficacy. No one would be bothered by knowing how I shop or when I plan to play tennis. Others are acting as they wish and would continue to act as they do given the knowledge that their actions afford me opportunities. Deception is not possible when the intention to deceive is known. In its reliance on the success condition, the practical interpretation fails to elicit this feature.[9]

One could amend the success condition so that maxims whose efficacy depend on secrecy are judged impermissible. But this again begs a key question: why should possible publicity be the key to permissibility? It also fails to explain in any easy way why activities such as surprise parties are all right. No doubt further ad hoc amendments can take care of such cases, though at the cost, it seems to me, of weakening the intuitive explanatory power of the success condition.[10]

The success of the logical interpretation in rejecting the right maxims for plausible reasons does not mean that it has no difficulties. Chief among them is its inability to produce results for maxims that contain action descriptions that are not general. Imagine a paternalistic analogue to Kant's deceitful-promise case. Suppose I know that you will gamble away money saved for your child's education, a deed you will later regret. You will also loan the money to me, if I tell you I am in trouble and need it. So I decide to ask you for a loan, though I do not in fact need the money. I promise to repay the loan, but do not intend to. I will instead keep the money for your child. The possibility of such a maxim, its coherence, does not depend on others not acting similarly in similar situations. Although the nonuniversality of deceitful promising is assumed as a condition of the maxim, the nonuniversality of paternalistic deceitful promising is not.

If we are tempted to think that this result is acceptable because paternalistic deceitful promising may be permissible (or is not obviously impermissible), we should note that the formal feature that distinguishes paternalistic

9. We might put it this way: the difference between coordination and deceit that the practical interpretation misses and the logical interpretation captures is the difference between taking advantage of others' actions and taking *unfair* advantage of them (or taking advantage of others' *actions* and taking advantage of others).

10. In his unpublished lectures on the *Groundwork*, Scanlon suggests a different interpretation of the CI procedure that avoids this result. In his account the test asks whether one could reasonably permit all others to act on one's proposed maxim. Clearly this does the job with coordination and timing maxims as well as the surprise party. The considerable advantage is gained, however, at the cost of giving up the notion of a contradiction playing any central role in the CI procedure. See also Thomas W. Pogge, "The Categorical Imperative," in Otfried Höffe, ed., *Grundlegung zur Metaphysik der Sitten: Ein kooperativer Kommentar* (Frankfurt: Vittorio Klostermann, 1989), pp. 172–193.

deceitful promising from deceitful promising tout court is present in morally corrupt or trivial deceitful promises: a deceitful promise in support of racism; a deceitful promise in order to injure; even a deceitful promise in order to surprise you later. So although the logical interpretation distinguishes deceitful promising from timing or coordination cases, it is unable to distinguish among maxims of deceitful promising that are adopted on more restricted grounds. If the logical interpretation rejected all such maxims, it would at least be consistent with the more rigoristic moments of Kant. What makes this a serious interpretive problem is that the logical interpretation instead *passes* all restricted maxims when quite obviously they are not all permissible.[11]

The problem cannot be solved by restricting the CI procedure to maxims with general action descriptions. It is not just that the consequences of such a move are rigoristic moral requirements that vitiate any hope that the CI procedure can be morally supple. The deeper difficulty is in the arbitrariness of general descriptions. How would we determine the correct level of description except as the one that produces the desired moral result? As with the practical interpretation, any such solution to the problem of erroneous results undermines the independent authority of the CI procedure.

Another proposal involves testing the set of maxims based on all intentionally relevant act descriptions, at all levels of generality. An action would be judged impermissible if any of its intentionally relevant descriptive variants failed.[12] But even if the idea of "intentionally relevant levels of description" was clear, there is no reason to suppose here either that we will reach the "right" level of generality to get the logical interpretation to reject the maxims it ought to reject. If I have a restricted maxim of action ("deceitful promise for purpose x"), I will run afoul of the CI procedure if I am acting on that maxim as an instance of my general policy of deceitful promising, but not if I do not have such a general maxim. Further, if the intentional description on which the action fails happens not to mention deceitful promising, we would have a procedure of moral judgment unable

11. The problem of false positives affects the practical interpretation as well, although its use of a practical contradiction captures a somewhat greater range of maxims. I do not think the problem of false positives is the distinctive problem with the practical interpretation, but it is serious nonetheless.

12. This was O'Neill's strategy in *Acting on Principle.* In the more recent "Consistency in Action" she interprets the object of the CI procedure as identifying moral worthiness and unworthiness through assessment not of maxims of action but of maxims of agents' underlying intentions. Since I do not want to abandon the idea that CI procedure can be used in action assessment, I will not explore this revision. What O'Neill gets right is the power of the CI procedure when it is applied to certain sorts of maxims. My disagreement concerns the implications of the location of this success for understanding the ambitions of moral judgment in Kantian ethics.

to say that there was anything morally untoward about the deceitful promise as such.

There is much more tinkering we could do. But past experience suggests a permanent fix-it situation: the correction of one difficulty or apparent oversight creates space for new problems to emerge. At a certain point it becomes reasonable to consider the possibility that the source of the difficulties is systemic. I think we do best to stop with the practical interpretation generating false negatives and the logical interpretation generating false positives, with the practical interpretation more effective in dealing with maxims as they are willed, and the logical interpretation superior in the kind of account it gives of what is wrong with the maxims it directs the CI procedure to reject. These problems can be understood as setting reasonable goals for a successful interpretation of the CI procedure. With this in mind, I want to try another way of thinking about the CI procedure. This is a useful thing to do quite independent of the possibilities for further tinkering.

III

Both the practical and the logical interpretations accept the role of the CI procedure as providing a method for the moral assessment of maxims. It is a method of judgment to be used by agents in determining the permissibility of their own maxims. Difficulties with settling maxim content then undermine the adequacy of the method of judgment. I want to suggest instead that we approach the CI procedure *from* the side of maxims. Knowing more about what maxims are and why they are central to Kantian theory of action and judgment will suggest a different task for the CI procedure.

It has been argued that maxims are Kant's solution to what is called "the problem of action description."[13] This is not wrong, but it is misleading if it suggests that maxims solve "the" problem of action description. Kant introduces maxims in order to present actions in a form suitable for assessment by principles of practical rationality. For Kant, the question of rationality in action is a question about an agent's willing: her subjective principle of action. This principle is the agent's maxim. What belongs in a maxim—Kant's solution to *his* description problem—is then a function of the relevant terms of assessment.

In willing, a rational agent acts for what she takes to be sufficient and justifying reasons. The representation of an action-as-willed in a maxim should provide a description of an action (a proposed, intended action) *as* purposive voluntary activity initiated for the sake of an end that the agent judges herself to have sufficient reason to pursue. It is in this sense that a

13. O'Neill, *Acting on Principle*, chap. 2.

maxim is the agent's subjective principle in acting. Since rational agents take themselves to act for sufficient reasons—to satisfy the standards of practical rationality[14]—descriptions of an action for a maxim are incomplete if they do not include material sufficient to justify the action from an agent's point of view. Correlatively, no description may be included in a maxim unless it fits the agent's conception of her action as willed, even if the description that fits excludes morally significant information.[15]

Consider a simple example. Normally, when it is my turn to do the grocery shopping, I go to the supermarket. It is nearby, large, and its prices are reasonable. But today I decide to do my shopping in the Yuppie Farm Market Store across the street. Groceries will cost more; I will not have the same selection for some of the things I want to buy; but I am tired of mediocre fruits and vegetables and want, just today, the best. I will my action with and from a conception of its value to me. In these particular circumstances, what I value at the Farm Market Store provides sufficient reason to go there, when normally it does not. Without that information included, my maxim does not present the rationality of the action *as I will it.* My maxim when shopping at the Farm Market Store is in significant ways different from my maxim when shopping at the supermarket, though it is possible to describe both actions in the same terms (say, "shopping in the store that most suits my mood").

In the normal presentation of maxims, the justificatory elements may be submerged or omitted in descriptions of normal actions. "To go to the cafeteria after my noon class" is a well-formed maxim that does not need to mention its justificatory purpose (getting lunch to satisfy midday hunger). When the justificatory value of the action is transparent, bringing the justificatory material into the maxim will often make it seem artificial. Explicit inclusion of the justification of routine actions is always possible and will be called for when the circumstances of action suggest something unusual, as when an ordinary pattern of action is interrupted or called into question. I would do some action *x* for routine end *e,* but that will prevent my doing *y* for *f.* Then I must think about the relative priority of *e* and *f* or search for some other route to either one. Or suppose my proposed action will bring about what I want now, but what I want is not good for me later. I need to evaluate the relative weights of long- and short-term interests. Because the relative priority of two ends is a function of the interests they serve, the conflict between long- and short-term interests cannot be resolved

14. The principles for judging the sufficiency of reasons are the hypothetical, prudential, and categorical imperatives.

15. For more on maxims and their connection to subjective justification see Chapter 10, section III; Chapter 5 looks at the effects on moral assessment of the fact that maxims may not include all morally relevant data in agents' circumstances of action.

without examining the framework of actions—the life plan, if you will—that gives them sense. In order to deliberate in such cases, the justificatory content of the proposed maxim must be made explicit.

Establishing the content of a maxim can be a complex business: not only is much of the content assumed when maxims are offered, some elements of description will not be forthcoming without a degree of self-examination. This does not imply that maxims are unconscious or willings opaque. The kind of immediate unavailability at issue is like the background beliefs that support ordinary empirical judgment; we are not conscious of their role in routine judgment, but they are available and brought forward in anomalous circumstances.

There is more. Implicit in the willings of a normal moral agent is the commitment to a moral standard for her actions that is only rarely part of proffered action descriptions. That I believe my routine actions are morally permissible goes without saying, we say. This is the way the motive of duty works in what I have earlier called its limiting-condition role. As a normal moral agent, I am prepared from the outset to let moral considerations constrain what I can will in pursuit of my ends (and in the choice of my ends). This condition on what I will becomes explicit when there is reason to believe or suspect that a proposed action or maxim is not morally acceptable. One often responds to a moral challenge by insisting that one only acted in such and such a way because one believed it was right (or all right): the action may be deviant, but it is justified.

This fact about maxims, if we agree that it is a fact, bears directly on the question of the role of the CI procedure. For if the maxims of moral agents have implicit moral content, moral judgment does not function only *after* maxim formulation: it is not in that sense external to an agent's willing. And in circumstances where moral deliberation is appropriate, the deliberative conclusion is not arrived at as the product of the employment of the CI procedure on a maxim that itself has no moral content.

In order to understand the different sources of moral content and their connection to the CI procedure, it will be useful to distinguish moral deliberation from moral judgment. This is not a distinction Kant makes, nor one that ordinary language insists on. But there are two distinct activities that are often referred to as "moral judgment" and that are usefully kept separate in working out the role of the CI procedure. What I call moral deliberation is occasional, in the sense that something occasions it; moral judgment is routine. While all moral action requires moral judgment, we do not need to deliberate morally in order to act morally. We deliberate as a way of figuring something out.

Normally we act within a moral framework that is without further thought adequately action-guiding. I have made a promise to do whatever; the time to act has come and I set about doing what I promised. This is a matter of moral judgment: recognizing what ought to be done, and being aware that there are no competing claims, appropriate action follows. There is nothing to deliberate about when what one ought to do is plain. (Deliberation about means is not normally *moral* deliberation.) There is also nothing to deliberate about when one is simply uncertain that there is any moral matter in the air. If I know that a deceptive action is wrong, but I do not know whether an action is deceptive, this is a matter for inquiry or investigation, not deliberation.[16]

The characteristic moments of moral deliberation will occur when an agent perceives her circumstances as exceptional or as containing conflicting moral considerations or directives. There is need to deliberate when, for example, you would do something you know is usually wrong but you feel that the action is justified, or even required, in this case; or when considering the effects of a proposed action makes you aware of opposing moral claims. The perception of such conflict elicits the fuller justificatory structure of the willing, setting the terms for beginning moral deliberation.

We should resist the thought that deliberation is always in order or always possible. There are some reasons why one might think this, but I do not find them persuasive. We tend to assume an equivalence between procedures of deliberation and justification so that, if we take agents to act with the sense that what they do is justified, it must be possible to elicit at least latent deliberation (demonstrating justification). This will seem all the more natural if we take the CI as establishing a unique procedure that yields moral judgments of permissibility and impermissibility as deliberative outcomes. We already have good reason to doubt that the CI procedure is able to perform such a function.

Another reason why one might suppose deliberation is always in order is if one thinks that there is a standing moral injunction (as some think there is in strict utilitarianism) that puts the permissibility of every maxim in real doubt. There are some moral data here. In a certain mood, I can feel the inescapable and inexhaustible presence of moral claims. How can I sit here writing when . . . and then comes the list: El Salvador, rape, child abuse, world hunger. Justifying normal action can seem both necessary and impossible in the face of this. These moments suggest the omnipresence of the moral question and thus the presence of a standing issue for deliberation (may I continue my work, take a vacation, when . . . ?). But this is misleading. These moments may instead reflect moral uncertainty about the nature of our obligations and the kinds of circumstances that call for our response. It is not unusual to respond to overwhelming unmet need with the thought

---

16. I am not supposing that these brief remarks make the distinction between moral deliberation and moral judgment perfectly clear. The nature and point of the distinction will become sharper in the context of its use.

that one must do everything—or nothing. Both responses leave the kind of intractable guilt that undermines moral seriousness and commitment.

We should expect a moral theory to tell us when and how these facts make demands on our lives and resources, and to regard a theory as defective that leaves demands open-ended. Moral demand must find a place in a scheme of deliberation. I would say: an insatiable "do more" leaves little room in morality *for* moral deliberation. In any case, there is no evidence of such a demand in Kantian ethics.

IV

If moral deliberation is called for when there is perceived moral conflict in an agent's circumstances of action, the method of deliberation must itself rely on a set of moral results (judgments) derived in some predeliberative way. What I want to argue now is that this predeliberative moral knowledge—which both provides the content of moral judgment and sets the terms for moral deliberation—is to be had from the CI procedure. This is a task the CI procedure can perform and, I believe, the only one it can perform. This will take some explaining.

One of the lessons we can take from the earlier discussion of the logical interpretation is that the CI procedure *can* yield results (and in the right way) for general maxims of the form: to do *x* to promote my purposes. We could not use this fact to make the CI procedure work as a general method of moral deliberation or judgment because this is most often not the level of generality of description appropriate for particular actions as they are willed. But a result showing, for example, that "deceitful promising for my purposes" is not justified *is* at an appropriate level of generality for establishing a principle that contains the moral knowledge necessary for both routine moral judgment and moral deliberation.

The idea is that we are to think of the CI procedure as applying not to actual maxims of action but to a type of action-justification pair: to do *x*-type action for *y*-type reason. I call these pairs "generic maxims." Generic maxims are not maxims of any agent's willing, though it could happen that some general policy willings would be described by a generic maxim. The point of using a generic maxim is not to represent an agent's willing but rather to present a general pattern of justification to the CI procedure in the form of a possible principle of willing. The rejection of a generic maxim by the CI procedure shows that a certain kind of action may not be done for a certain kind of reason. This in effect establishes a principle of moral judgment that can set terms for moral deliberation. The power of this result will depend on the scope of the reasons that appear in the resulting principles. Since, as I shall argue, the standard form of a deliberative principle is derived from a generic maxim of self-interest, the results are very powerful.

If actual maxims are not the input of the CI procedure when viewed this way, neither are duties its output. We can think of what is rejected by the CI procedure—a kind of action for a kind of reason—as setting a deliberative principle in the form of a presumption. The deliberative presumption can be rebutted by reasons (justifications) of a different sort. (The fact that the result of deliberation is the rebuttal of a deliberative presumption and not the overriding of a duty will make the casuistry of this view distinctive.) This strategy takes advantage of the features of the CI procedure that have been taken to support a derivation-of-duties model of its use, but because the output is an element of a deliberative scheme and not a duty, we do not have the derivation-of-duties problem of rigorism.

The results of generic maxim assessment are themselves action-guiding. If there were a principle barring deceit for reasons of personal advantage, this does not introduce just *a* reason against, say, failing to tell you about a recent accident I had in order to keep you interested in buying my car. Given my reason for deception, the presumption against deceit is not rebutted, and so the action is directly *judged* impermissible. Normally such a situation will provide no occasion for deliberation. I will simply recognize that these are circumstances in which deceit is presumptively impermissible.

Actions whose maxims raise a moral question (provide the occasion for moral deliberation) are flagged by deliberative principles derived from the CI procedure. The presumption that the principles carry is open to rebuttal in a given case by the agent's actual justificatory reason. The burden of proof is on the agent to show that her circumstances deviate in a morally significant way from those specified by the principle. (This assumes normal moral agents with knowledge of deliberative principles.)

A few things need clarification. I have suggested that generic maxims will have the form of maxims of self-interest. This is not because there is some inevitable conflict between morality and self-interest, or because the interests that are self-interests are either selfish or concerns for oneself. The designation "self-interest" signals the moral or justificatory status of the reason in question. The agent has a reason for acting solely because the action or what it will produce is something she wants.[17] So understood, morality is simply the regulative norm for our interests. And if the object of morality is to introduce norms (and so limits) for agents' willings, what an agent may do in the rational pursuit of her interests is the natural object of moral judgment.

---

17. Rawls has suggested that reasons so characterized be called "own-interests" to make it clear that one was talking about grounds of interests and not the object of interest.

The first moral question, then, for any type of action (kind of willing) is whether it is a morally possible (permissible) means to ends that have no moral standing apart from the fact that they are ends we are interested in. This is why the rejection of a generic "maxim of self-interest" by the CI procedure establishes a moral presumption against a certain type of action. For if a certain kind of action may not be taken as a means to ends in general—ends we act for simply because we care about them—this shifts the burden of proof to showing that a particular end, for whose sake we wish to take the action in question, has moral standing for us beyond its being an end in which we have an interest.[18] What the CI procedure shows is that actions of a certain kind are not to be counted as "routine means."

Differences among the various sorts of things that are reasons of self-interest do not have different justificatory weight. It does not matter whether I make a deceitful promise because I need money for the movies, for my career, or to please my child. Each of these is a reason because it is something I care about or want. Although they are not equal reasons to me—I do not care about them equally or in the same way—these differences do not make a difference in the standing of the reasons in moral deliberation. Even an agent who acts morally because being moral seems appealing can be thought of as acting morally for reasons of self-interest.

Moral reasons, on the other hand, are of interest to a moral agent, but unlike reasons of self-interest the condition of their being reasons is not the agent's subjective, contingent, interest in them. Insofar as one accepts a moral reason *as* a moral reason, one acknowledges a kind of interest that is not dependent on what one subjectively wants.

An actual maxim of action can rebut a deliberative presumption only if its justificatory basis is something other than self-interest. Let me give an example. In order to help A, who is my friend, I must make a deceitful promise to B. Suppose there is a deliberative presumption against deceitful promising in pursuit of one's interests per se. Insofar as my concern for A is a concern of self-interest—I do not want someone I like to suffer—there is not even occasion for moral deliberation. (Given the deliberative presumption, I already know that deceitful promising is not a routine means.) But if the deception of B were for the purpose of saving A's life, something of value independent of its value to me (say because saving A's life is called for by the duty of mutual aid), then there is a legitimate deliberative question (only) of whether in this case the deception is justified. The deliberative outcome in such a case need not be affected by the additional fact of my

---

18. Of course ends are not the only considerations that enter deliberation. The point here is merely that for an end to rebut a deliberative presumption it must be willed for some reason other than mere interest.

self-interested concern for A's welfare. Overdetermination does not pose the same problem for deliberation that it does for moral worth.

The occasion of moral deliberation is some question of the type, "Is *this* (some justificatory feature) sufficient reason to act contrary to such and such a moral presumption?" So the maxim relevant to deliberation must include the special justificatory features of the end or circumstances (special needs, other moral values) that the agent takes to warrant acting against the presumption. Inclusion of detail in the maxim description is controlled by the structure of deliberation. If I believe that what justifies my doing *x* (a presumptively wrong action) is that in so acting I am helping a friend, *that* qualification of my end may not be introduced for purposes of deliberation unless it is supported by reasons not already excluded by the deliberative presumption.[19] So if I would help because I take that to be part of the obligations between friends, inclusion of the detailed description is appropriate. But if I want to help because a friend's unmet need causes me distress, it is not. As a justificatory reason, it is a reason of self-interest. (Accordingly, one maxim is a maxim of self-interest, the other a maxim of fulfilling obligations of friendship.)

The requirement that descriptive detail may be included in maxims only as it plays a justificatory role in willing provides a way of dealing with what might be called the "scope" problem in maxim assessment. Suppose I sincerely act on a maxim of deceiving or refusing to aid only people of a certain kind (call them alpha people). If maxims were judged directly by the CI procedure, and if maxims express what we sincerely intend to do, many such scope-restricted maxims would pass. This is the sort of difficulty that has led John Rawls to introduce the veil of ignorance into the CI procedure.[20] When one must judge, aware of the possibility that one is oneself an alpha person, what can be rationally willed is properly constrained. The pattern of deliberation I am sketching does similar work, but it accommodates the agent's conviction that who she and others are matters in a more direct way.

The veil-of-ignorance strategy prohibits the use of special information in the deliberative premises. The deliberative strategy (as I might call it) permits the use of any information the agent can argue distinguishes her case from the conditions of the relevant deliberative presumption. So, if we knew that one may not fail to aid others regarded simply as persons, one might claim a maxim of not aiding alpha persons *only if* one could show that alpha persons are unlike persons per se in ways that show that the

19. Recall that different questions elicit different elements of description; we rarely have reason to construct a complete maxim.

20. John Rawls, "Kant Lectures," manuscript (1987), lecture 2, and his "Themes in Kant's Moral Philosophy," p. 86.

reasons for helping persons do not apply to alpha persons. It is thus not only interest types that can be brought forward to rebut a deliberative presumption; equally relevant are features of one's circumstances of action that one judges to be morally significant.

In Chapter 4 I argued that the activity of moral judgment depends on agents being able to recognize that their circumstances or their proposed actions are in some way morally significant. Morality (a moral culture) educates agents in a moral language, using rules of moral salience. These rules instruct about the sorts of actions that need moral justification and the sorts of circumstances to which morality requires a response.[21] What I am arguing here goes further. For the purposes of moral *deliberation,* these rules need to establish not just salience but also a deliberative presumption for justifying reasons. Prior to deliberation the agent must *both* identify her proposed action as of a particular moral kind (this sets the deliberative presumption) *and* determine the nature of her interest in the action (or its end) that is to ground a possible rebuttal of the presumption.

It may be difficult to identify the nature of one's interest in an action— there are all of the usual problems about motivational opacity and overde- termination. Nor are we all equally sensitive to such matters. We are not evenly sensitive across our own various interests. This is not, however, a problem peculiar to moral deliberation. The task of identifying interests is of general practical import: how well and in what terms I understand my interests in my activities centrally affects any deliberation about what to do. Epistemic difficulties in identifying interests are not responsible for our failure to understand the complexities of Kantian moral deliberation. That responsibility lies in our not recognizing how the evaluation of subjective concerns sets the framework for deliberation.

V

From this point on, let us accept the distinction between deliberation and judgment and the restriction of the CI procedure to the derivation of principles of deliberative presumption. We need next to see what form deliberation has when judgment about moral facts suggests that a recog- nized presumption should not be decisive.

The test case will be the classic conflict between the requirement of mutual aid and the prohibition on deceit (a variant of the problem posed in Kant's "On a Supposed Right to Lie"[22]). The agent in the story has a

---

21. Here see a brief but very good discussion in O'Neill, "The Power of Example," in *Constructions of Reason.*

22. It is only a variant because it is not clear that Kant saw the conflict in Malebranche's

maxim that carries a pair of conflicting moral considerations: to lie or deceive to save a life. In a case of simple deceit for self-interest, no deliberation is necessary because self-interest per se does not rebut the deliberative presumption against deceit.[23] We assume that our agent knows this. Deliberation is called for because the agent thinks her maxim of deceit does not fall within the scope of the presumptive judgment. She must determine whether "saving a life" rebuts the presumption against deceit.

In traditional Kant interpretation the next step—the step of moral deliberation—would be to run the restricted maxim, "To deceive to save a life," through the CI procedure to determine which of the moral considerations at issue will hold the field. One is to ask whether a universal law of deceiving to save lives is a possible universal law. It seems clear that it is.[24] Then, contrary to Kant's infamous treatment of this case, deceit in these circumstances is permissible.

But recall that almost *any* maxim that is more specific in its end than the generic maxim of deceit will survive the CI procedure (the problem of false positives).[25] This gives reason for concern that the features of the restricted maxim that make it pass are not the moral features of the case. While it may be all right to deceive to save lives, the CI procedure will show that it is also all right to deceive to save slugs. Would it then turn out that, for purposes of moral deliberation, slug lives and human lives have the same moral standing? (There is some sort of radical anti-speciesism that might welcome this, but it is surely not a view that Kant could endorse.) More seriously, because it might be the mere fact of its specificity that moves the maxim through the CI procedure, we do not get an answer to the question whether there was something about the particular reason for action (saving a life) that justifies an action that is normally prohibited.

The revised account of the role of the CI procedure is formally responsive to just such questions. We have a moral agent recognizing a need to deliberate when the action or policy she would pursue is flagged by deliberative principles *and* she believes her reasons for action are such as to rebut the presumptions against the kind of action she intends. Surely the

---

example to be between two grounds of moral requirement. I believe Kant's objection was directed quite precisely at the claim that one had a *right* to lie based on altruistic feelings.

23. I am assuming for simplicity that generic maxims of deceit will fail if the maxim of deceitful promising fails. Nothing in what follows depends on this.

24. See Christine M. Korsgaard, "The Right to Lie: Kant on Dealing with Evil," *Philosophy and Public Affairs* 15 (1986), 325–349, where she interprets the result of applying the Formula of Universal Law to the "lying to save" maxim this way.

25. Assuming the logical interpretation. The problem of false positives also surfaces in the practical interpretation's treatment of restricted maxims of deceit. Deceit, unlike a lie, allows flexibility. Because you act on a maxim of saying whatever is necessary to conceal the truth, your maxim is not defeated under universalization. See Korsgaard, "The Right to Lie," p. 330n.

deliberative question ought to be whether her reasons are of a kind or of sufficient weight or gravity to justify her intended action.

Ignoring the strictures of traditional Kant interpretation, we might try to imagine what would allow her to proceed. A natural solution would be an account of the deliberative presumptions set by the CI procedure in terms that support some kind of comparative judgment. Simply knowing of a generic maxim that it cannot be willed a universal law does not give deliberative guidance. One wants a way to rank or compare or weigh different moral considerations. The difficulty is that any talk of weighing and comparing is supposed to be out of court in Kantian ethics. While it is true that Kantian ethics cannot accommodate value comparisons of states of affairs or weigh the good of one person against another, these options do not exhaust possible value resources. Kant's ethics is, after all, an ethics of good willing. Although later, in Chapter 10, I will present arguments to show that Kant's ethics is best understood as an ethics of value, here I will try to show how considerations of value might be connected with the CI procedure and where they might enter in deliberation.

The place to look for the bases of comparative judgments is in the arguments through which the CI procedure rejects generic maxims. Every universalization test has to set a condition that an action must meet or else be judged impermissible. Consider two familiar non-Kantian universalization tests. According to one, an action is permissible only if its universal performance is *acceptable* (or not rationally rejectable) from all points of view (or from the point of view of some privileged superagent); according to the other, an action is permissible if universal performance would *promote utility* at least as much as the universal performance of other available actions. The notions of acceptability and utility are necessary if universalization is to show anything. In this sense we can think of the CI procedure's "possible law" requirement as the argument that gives Kantian universalization determinate content.

The relevance of this claim about universalization tests to comparative deliberative judgment is the fact that the argument of a universalization test directly or indirectly introduces a theory's conception of value into its procedures of judgment. For the argument of a universalization test to produce determinate moral results, it must reveal something that matters.[26] Even a minimal requirement of coherence (that x universalized be logically possible) has bite only as coherence under universalization is (in some sense) of value. Consider the standard query, "What if everyone did that?" There is supposed to be something wrong with an action that, if performed by all, would have negative consequences. Without a value interpretation—say, it

26. This is not incompatible with the claim that universalizability is part of the meaning of moral terms.

is wrong because it would be unfair—the merely possible negative consequences of everyone doing x are surely irrelevant when not everyone is.

Kant makes use of a universalization procedure because good willing—
the condition of all justified action and choice—is found only in maxims
that have the form of universal lawgiving. A maxim is not a possible maxim
of a good will, and is therefore impermissible, if its goodness (the condition
of its subjective choice-worthiness) depends on its nonuniversality. This is
a requirement of practical rationality, and it sets the argument of the CI
procedure. (A procedure is necessary because whether a maxim has the form
of universal lawgiving is not routinely perspicuous to self-reflection.) That
we may not act on a maxim that cannot be or be willed a universal law for
all rational beings—or human beings insofar as they are rational—locates
the wrongness of impermissible maxims in a failure to include the conditions of rational agency as a constraint on willing. In this sense the argument
of the CI procedure invokes rational agency as a value constraint: the value
of rational agency is to be expressed in the commitment to refrain from
adopting principles that are not possible for all others of one's (rational)
kind. Positively, each must view her maxims as candidates for principles
that could constitute a community of free and equal persons.[27] That is why
universalization matters.

Those features of a maxim that depend on the maxim's not having the
form of universal lawgiving explain its impermissibility; they also point to
the aspect of rational agency that the resulting deliberative presumption
requires us to respect. To see this, consider again the argument rejecting the
generic maxim of deceitful promising.

The maxim of deceitful promising cannot be willed a universal law
because the deception requires the background institution (or set of conventions) of nondeceitful promising if it is to succeed in producing belief.
Universal deceitful promising annuls the institution and, in making deceitful
promising impossible, reveals nonuniversal deceitful promising as a condition of the deceitful-promising maxim. This is the formal wrong-making
characteristic of the maxim.

The basis of this formal result is a fact about human rational agency: we
depend on convention-controlled communication for information essential
to normal action and choice. What the rejection of the maxim of deceit
signifies is the inappropriateness of principles that exploit the vulnerability
of human agents to manipulative control.[28] Such principles fail to respect

27. This interpretation of Kantian requirements is eloquently developed in O'Neill, "Reason
and Politics in the Kantian Enterprise," in *Constructions of Reason,* and in T. M. Scanlon,
"Contractualism and Utilitarianism," in Amartya Sen and Bernard Williams, eds., *Utilitarianism and Beyond* (Cambridge: Cambridge University Press, 1982).

28. It is neither the falseness of the beliefs nor the intention that you will as I want that is
the problem. The first can be accidental; the second is equally the case if I tell you some truth

the integrity and separateness of will that is constitutive of rational agency. The CI procedure has then shown that the pursuit of our interests does not justify interfering with the integrity of another's will. This is a conclusion drawn in terms of *relative* value.[29]

Now if the deliberative question is, "May I deceive (or make a deceitful promise) to save a life?" we need comparable knowledge concerning the relative value of the claim to aid. We should then look to the CI procedure's rejection of a generic maxim of neglect (nonbeneficence) to see how it argues against justifying a refusal to help by reasons of self-interest.[30] The argument identifies the material conditions of rational agency (Kant calls them "true needs" [DV392]) as what we may not neglect for reasons of self-interest. That is, when someone has a life- or rationality-threatening need that we are in a position to meet, reasons of self-interest are not sufficient to rebut the claim of need.

The deliberative question can now be asked in value-based terms: may I manipulate a rational agent's will (violate its integrity) for the purpose of supporting the conditions of life of a rational agent? If the value translation puts the moral question in a more theoretically tractable form, it does not make the answer obvious. This is so because the value commitments that emerge in the CI procedure's arguments are not "scalar": failing to save the life of a rational agent is not half or twice as bad as deception. Deliberation is therefore not a weighing of amounts of value.

Let me briefly try to explain. In Kantian theory of value, the autonomous will ("humanity, insofar as it is capable of morality") has dignity, a kind of nonrelative value (G435). What I have called the "integrity of the will" represents the fact that the wills of human beings are separate, individuated as persons are individuated. A will's integrity is the empirical form of its autonomy (rational agency). If we view the will not as a special entity or faculty, but as a certain way of bringing about effects unique to rational beings (G412), respecting the integrity of the will is to regard that way of bringing about effects as having nonrelative value. Manipulative interventions in the process of willing (deception, coercion) that regard the will as

---

intending thereby that you will act as I want you to act. The moral question turns on whether I tell you what I believe to be true *as* information of use to you as well as me (and so contribute to the process of deliberation), or whether what I tell you is controlled by a commitment to regulate the flow of information in such a way that you can deliberate only as I will. Because our deliberative capacity is vulnerable to manipulation in this way, respect for rational agency requires a commitment to avoid intentional falsehoods *and* misleading truths.

29. I have intentionally blurred the distinction between deceit and deceitful promising. I believe that it is more accurate to view the deceitful promise as a kind of deceit instead of as a defective kind of promise. Because it conveys sincerity of intention, promising provides an avenue for the deceitful manipulation of agency.

30. The argument for this is in Chapter 3.

just another route toward ends are therefore impermissible. Such actions do not respect the integrity of the will (the maxims of such manipulative interventions cannot have the form of universal lawgiving): they accord the will only relative value. The mistake is not in the fact that the manipulator accords the integrity of the will *lower* value than her ends, but in the fact that the integrity of the will is on the scale at all. Since we come to the idea of the integrity of the rational will as an interpretation of the CI procedure's argument, it has the standing of a moral constraint—a limiting condition on what we may take to be justifying reasons.

Deceiving to save a life involves an assault on the integrity of a rational will. This fact is deliberatively determinative unless failing to give aid is also incompatible with respect for rational agency. And it is not: we may fail to aid. What one may not do is fail to give aid when true needs are threatened *for* reasons of mere self-interest. In so acting one mistakenly discounts the claim of need to one of mere interest. Still one may fully acknowledge the claim of need but be in no position to help because one does not possess what is needed, or the action necessary to provide help is impermissible, and so on. To the bare question, "May I deceive to save a life?" the answer seems to be that one may not.

It is not clear that there is good reason to find this conclusion objectionable. "But," someone will ask, "suppose what was necessary was only a small deception?" I'm not sure there is such a thing. There are of course deceptions that have benign or tiny consequences. This misses the moral objection to deception in Kantian ethics. Deception is not wrong because of the harm it does. That is why beneficent or paternalistic deception is not justified by its good effects. Formally, the fact that loss of life does not by itself justify deception should be no more uncomfortable than any other nonconsequentialist constraint on anything short of life-for-life. We are used to thinking that we cannot take someone's house to save a life or her arm—even if we plan to give it back. Now we have an argument that we may not "take" someone's will.

Even if, as I think is the case, the value of agential integrity never permits exceptions (violation) for the sustenance of life or the provision of true needs, it will not follow that we may never deceive when life is at risk. There is no a priori reason to suppose that no act of deception can accord with necessary respect for rational agency. It depends on the nature of the justifying reasons.

Consider some further detail of cases where one might think it justified to deceive A in order to save B's life. (These are presumably all cases where I cannot save B on my own. I recognize B's need, but the only resource I have available is deceit.) A might have some resource that B needs in order to live that he will not give freely. Suppose A ought to help B: B's claim is valid, and A can help but refuses to for no good reason. I could get A to help by deceiving him (say, about the importance of B to some cause A supports). We might be tempted to argue that deceit is justified here because it simply gets A to do what he in any case ought to do. But what A ought to do is acknowledge B's need and help, if he can, for that reason. My deceit cannot get A to do that. Absent good-samaritan laws, I have no grounds for compelling A's external action.

In the famous case A does not merely withhold something B needs to live, but A threatens B's life. It is not clear that the only or best way of justifying deceit here is as a means to save a life. That leaves out the aggression. One might then offer a different ground of justification, arguing that a maxim of deception to repel or prevent aggression has as its object A's abandonment of his impermissible maxim. The deception would then be in the service of a morally necessary purpose: a manipulation of a will to bring it into conformity with its own defining principles.

It is not relevant to this discussion to determine whether or why bringing someone to abandon an impermissible end rebuts the presumption against deceit—why it is not an assault on the integrity of a will. The point of the argument sketch is rather to illustrate that there are ways of thinking about some deceptive (or coercive) actions that work from significantly different deliberative principles from those used in the standard treatments of difficult cases.

As a methodological matter, it is an open question as to what sorts of reasons will rebut a deliberative presumption. It is a substantive claim of Kant's ethics that only a competing deliberative presumption can. The role of these presumptions (Kant calls them "grounds of obligation") in averting the conflicts-of-duty problem in Kant's ethics is the subject of the next chapter.

To summarize: my objective has been to indicate the structure of the occasion for moral deliberation and to provide some idea of the background conditions of moral judgment that must be present for deliberation to be possible. The discussion of the test case has shown that there is really no new procedure for moral deliberation. Moral deliberation is called for by circumstances of moral conflict (or uncertainty) that are flagged by the deliberative principles (presumptions) derived from the CI procedure. If they are to be able to resolve complex and unfamiliar cases, agents must not only recognize the morally significant features of their circumstances and of their proposed action, but they must also be able to make the necessary value translation of the flagged features of action and circumstance into the terms of rational agency.

The point of the value translation is to permit deliberation to take place in its terms. What a moral agent should do is to "respect rational agency" (the value translation of good willing). An agent respects rational agency by accepting the deliberative presumptions against certain kinds of action (and so excluding certain useful sorts of action from the lexicon of "routine means"). Deliberation in cases of conflict seeks a practical conclusion by examining the values present in the competing options. Because there need not be one answer for all circumstances where deliberative principles appear to conflict, a great deal of the work in moral deliberation will be to get the deliberative question right. Hasty presentation of the conflict may obscure deeper issues of value, as will employment of terms of conflict description that do not permit value translation (terms that are not derived from the arguments of the CI procedure).

It is not to be supposed that moral deliberation is simple or that it is (in most lives) engaged in frequently. Clearly it presupposes a manner of thinking that is difficult and ill suited to the haste of practical life. Mostly we are to imagine moral judgment being guided by deliberative presumptions, and circumstances of conflict to come in familiar forms. Moral knowledge accumulates. It is neither reasonable nor necessary to expect a moral theory to do better than this.

8

Obligation and Performance

CONFLICTS of duty pose practical problems for agents and theoretical problems for philosophers. The theoretical problems track the practical less than one might hope: the extensive discussion of such moral dilemmas in the literature is not about the dilemmas—about their resolution, occasion, or cause.[1] What are of concern to philosophers are the theoretical difficulties that the mere possibility of practical dilemmas introduce.

This chapter is also not really about conflicts of duty. Its subject is the philosophical discussions of conflicts of duty insofar as they present one of those nodal points at which seemingly benign shared assumptions reveal the strains they impose on theory. In explications of occasions when we are said to have more than one obligation or duty without being able to act to satisfy each of their conflicting claims, routine assumptions about the application of theory to its domain (here, practice) make this conflict a sign of theoretical inconsistency.[2] One then has a dilemma *between* theory and practice. If one accepts that there are conflicts of duty, then moral theory lacks consistency insofar as it allows them. If, giving priority to consistency, one denies the possibility of conflicts of duty, then one must explain away the phenomena of conflict in moral experience. Either choice imposes fairly large costs as it has been worked out—one to morality (to its ambitions of deliberative authority), the other to the integrity of moral experience. The

1. For the purposes of this chapter, there is no need to distinguish conflicts of duty and moral dilemmas. In the literature with which I am concerned, the latter is of interest only as it appears to be an instance of the former.

2. Whatever important differences there may be between "duty" and "obligation" in some moral theories, in discussions of moral dilemmas they do not function differently: each carries a moral requirement, an ought, that is not canceled by the fact of conflict and cannot be set aside at the discretion of the agent. Because I am most concerned with this fact of our being obligated, with the "practical necessity" of morality, I will sometimes talk about conflicts of duty as involving competing obligations.

question is whether we must accept that these are the alternatives. I think we do not.

Of first importance is the fact that conflict of duty is not a theory-neutral phenomenon. To produce conflicts, morality must contain (or set) independent moral requirements that can apply simultaneously in circumstances of action. But it is not a necessary feature of morality that it generate duties or obligations (plural), even when the account of morality is deontological. Indeed, morality as I believe Kant understands it does not impose duties or obligations (plural) and therefore, as he claims, *cannot* generate conflicts of duties. The frequent accusations to the contrary mistake the nature of Kantian moral requirement.

What the Kantian requirement of obligation is and how it supports Kant's claim that "conflict of duties and obligations is inconceivable" are the central concerns of this chapter. But they are not the only ones. There are reasons to welcome the Kantian concept of obligation that go beyond its resolution of difficulties associated with conflicts of duty. Chief among them is its effect on the structure of moral experience. I want to argue that it introduces greater narrative coherence into the life of a moral agent than does either the view of obligation usually imputed to Kantian morality or the view that is taken for granted in most conflict-of-duty discussions. The idea of narrative coherence is in turn a vehicle for an interpretation of autonomy and self-legislation that can counter criticism of Kantian ethics as incompatible with values of agential integrity (having a life that is one's own, that one can care about in a human way). Because such criticism relies on a conception of obligation foreign to Kantian ethics, it has the effect of an alien species brought into a friendly environment, driving out the native inhabitants. This chapter is to be seen, then, as part of a project of rehabilitation.

I

If you survey the literature on conflicts of duty, it is clear that these conflicts disturb moral theory insofar as they cannot coexist with two basic moral postulates. Generically, a conflict of duty involves two moral requirements applying to an agent in circumstances that do not permit the satisfaction of both. If failure to satisfy a valid moral requirement implies wrongdoing, then agents can be in circumstances in which wrongdoing is unavoidable. But "unavoidable wrongdoing" does not sit well with the "Ought implies can" postulate. Normally we say that if you cannot do x, then it is not the case that you ought to do x. But if we appeal to this postulate, it is hard to say what remains of the phenomenon of conflict of duty. For if it must be possible for an agent to negotiate the moral terrain without fault (because agents must be able to do what they are morally required to do), then either there are no conflicts of duty or, in violation of the second postulate, moral requirements do not obligate (where being obligated to do x implies that one may not omit doing x). Yet if moral requirements do not obligate, "conflict of duty" would seem to signal no more than the presence of a hard moral question. The tension is thus between the claim for the phenomena and the moral postulates. Something needs to be abandoned or modified.[3]

There are some who would deny the phenomena. They do not dispute that we experience conflicts of duty, nor that we have feelings of guilt and remorse that we believe appropriate to having failed to meet a moral requirement. What they deny is that the experience of conflict implies any actual conflict of duties.[4] Concerned to defend the consistency of morality or the possibility of determinate moral reasoning, they explain the experience by appeal to agents' lack of full moral awareness or their lack of knowledge (moral and empirical). Guilt and remorse are justified because they support useful character traits, even though, or even because, they reinforce the false belief that there are conflicts of duty. Indeed, the experience of moral conflict *as* conflict of duty and the attendant feelings are sometimes thought to be necessary to secure reliable performances in difficult circumstances.

These are recommendations for "indirection" in morality. One says that if we must permit agents to do things that are generally wrong (and possibly very wrong), we risk making them able to do what is truly wrong too easily unless they suffer guilt based on their belief that they have done something wrong (even if unavoidable). The moral character of ordinary agents cannot withstand knowledge that such actions are even moral possibilities (for them or for others); moral psychology requires the conventional distinctions and prohibitions. Guilt and the belief in wrongdoing keep them sensitive to the awfulness of what they might do. But since it does not follow from these beliefs and feelings that an agent acting for one of the requirements in a conflict-of-duty situation does anything wrong (or does any wrong thing) in failing to act for the other, we do not, in our theory, admit the reality of moral conflict.

3. There are some who do not think morality contains, even in theory, a consistent set of requirements. If the requirements are not internally ordered, and there is no set of principles that can sort them, then moral agents are left with the practical task of developing a kind of character that can withstand the effects of moral indeterminacy without collapse into cynicism. For examples of this view, see F. H. Bradley, *Ethical Studies* (Oxford: Oxford University Press, 1927), and Thomas Nagel, "The Fragmentation of Value," in *Mortal Questions* (Cambridge: Cambridge University Press, 1979).

4. See, for examples, T. C. McConnell, "Moral Dilemmas and Consistency in Ethics," *Canadian Journal of Philosophy* 8 (1978), 269–287, and Earl Conee, "Against Moral Dilemmas," *Philosophical Review* 91 (1982), 87–97.

The cost of saving the consistency of morality in this way is the competence and integrity of character of the moral agent. This joins a recurrent tendency in moral theory to divide theory and practice in a manner that demeans most moral agents (particularly those ordinary moral agents who are not privy to the indirectness arguments). Though we are not now tempted to see morality as Plato saw justice, or Aristotle virtue—as a way of life suited to the few—we often share with them the belief that although moral behavior is socially necessary (and thus legitimate to impose on people through law or socialization), people (people in general, that is) cannot be expected to (really) understand morality or to be motivated by such understanding. Indeed, it is often argued that for many people understanding morality would defeat its authority for them. Because people cannot internalize or work with "true morality," they must be given a different version of morality that will cause them to act approximately as they would act if they could act in accordance with an understanding of the dictates of true morality.

I do not dispute the claims about our character and situation on which the indirectness theses rest. What I object to is the program of holding morality apart from the very features of human character that make morality necessary. The danger sign in indirectness arguments is that the morality they most often recommend for "us" is "commonsense" morality. (If agents cannot act as "direct" moral theory would dictate, it is hard to know what could command assent in practice other than commonsense morality. Any other practice would require indirect (false) justification and false content.) If one is at all worried about what may be enshrined in commonsense morality, one should be all the more sensitive to arguments that depend on the supposed incapacity of people, especially ordinary people, to act according to "true moral principles." It is anything but obvious that the content of commonsense morality is neutral to the interests of those whose lives it regulates. The very thing that gives commonsense morality its authority—the accumulated wisdom of the ages—should ground skepticism and suspicion.

There are good grounds to accept a presumption against a moral theory if it requires indirectness to work. And if one is friendly to morality, there are especially good grounds to reject any theoretical account that imposes indirectness *without regard to the content of moral requirements.*

Independent of theory, we would say that the phenomenon of moral conflict is an ordinary part of moral experience. You don't need Agamemnon or stories of Third World bandits to establish that agents may be faced with situations (brought on by themselves or by the actions of others) that leave them with no choice that does not also involve apparent wrongdoing. To the contrary, one might hold that moral conflict is the stuff, the data, that moral theory ought to be about. If we started from experience, instead of supposing that we have in place moral theory whose principles ought to yield consistent results (if they are any good) but do not (and so fail), we might take it that the determining data for theory are the experience of conflict and the need for its resolution. Our understanding of what moral principles are (or do) ought to accommodate that.

If we are hesitant to accept the phenomenon of moral conflict because it sets off theoretical disorder, we should look again at the two postulates that set the engine of disorder running. We need not accept without question that they are the fixed points around which everything else in moral theory must circulate.

Rejection of the idea that obligations necessitate may seem the most appealing strategic move, especially since it is less than clear what kind of necessitation could be involved. If, as one might first suppose, it were the practical necessitation of "best reasons," we would have reason to reject the idea that obligations necessitate if only to accommodate the unexceptionable fact that there are cases of moral conflict where one has better reasons to act for one duty rather than the other. On the other hand, if obligations do not necessitate, we do not generate the phenomenon of conflict of duty. Without a better account of the necessity that obligation introduces, we cannot make this move. There is greater opportunity with the usually sacrosanct "Ought implies can" postulate.

In the sense that enters the conflict-of-duties discussions, the "Ought implies can" postulate is implausible. Consider a simple case. If I am obligated to repay a debt on Wednesday but I squander the money on Tuesday, it seems reasonable to say that my inability to repay my debt does not remove my obligation. Surely it is not the case on Wednesday that I have no obligation to repay my debt. So we need to see what it is about the way we are reading the postulate that has to be wrong.[5]

The intuition that supports the "Ought implies can" postulate is that morality, or the possibility of the moral ought, requires that we must be able to do what we are obliged to do. The intuition is sound enough. But there are narrow and wide interpretations of what the intuition represents. The narrow reading requires an ability to perform whatever is in the scope of the ought (or obligation).[6] The wide view holds that we can be obliged to do actions only of a *kind* that it is possible for us to do. So we cannot be obliged

5. This problem could be elicited directly from cases where it may seem that one ceases to have an obligation to do x once one chooses to do y, even if one chooses to do y in order to avoid doing x. There are of course solutions to such cases, but they too undermine any simple inference that inability shows absence of obligation.

6. If the narrow reading is defensible, it is hardly self-evidently so. Perhaps I have no obligation to pay my debt on Wednesday when I cannot; a theory that accepted this could plausibly do so only if it had other resources to account for the obligations I do have in virtue of the reasons why I no longer have the obligations I did have.

to know what someone else is thinking or to alter a past event. Rather than determining the conditions of moral responsibility (what an agent can legitimately be obliged to do), one might say that "Ought implies can" in the wide sense establishes the necessary condition for the *possibility* of responsibility. Knowing what *kinds* of things morality can require, we are then able to consider in a given case whether it is reasonable to hold someone responsible for an action he could not, at the time of the action, avoid.[7]

This is Kant's point in the *Critique of Pure Reason*. He argues that obligation (the possibility of a moral ought) would be unintelligible if we (as moral persons) were fully determined—if we did not have in any sense a free will. Free will is the condition of our ability to act on moral principle. It does not follow from *this* "Ought implies can" that there will be no limitations to our ability to act to satisfy moral requirements, though it does follow, Kant thinks, that we cannot be unable to *will* as we ought.

If we accept the wide interpretation of "Ought implies can," there is no particular tension generated by moral conflict. Each of the moral requirements is, if valid, a kind of thing the agent is able to do. If the circumstances are such that the agent is unable to satisfy both requirements, this sets a practical problem that a good theory will have a way to resolve. There is no theoretical problem since it does not follow from "Ought implies can" that a given agent in particular circumstances must be able to satisfy all moral requirements that apply.

II

At this point one might object that it has become hard to see what is involved in the very idea of moral requirement or obligation. On the one hand, I want to insist that obligation necessitates, and on the other I speak of the possibility of moral requirements obtaining even when agents are unable to act as they direct. Surely, to say that obligation necessitates is to say that if one has an obligation (or duty) to *x*, nothing could be a reason justifying not *x*-ing. (The sense of "necessity" here is not logical or physical but *practical*.) But if it is possible that one may (even faultlessly) be unable to satisfy moral requirements, then it would seem that, at the least, one is "not unjustified" in not *x*-ing. To explain why there is no inconsistency here, I want to reset the problem of the conflict of duties through close attention to the one passage in which Kant discusses it and declares its impossibility. We can find there the lineaments of an account of obligation and moral requirement that saves both phenomenon and theory.

7. Perhaps confusion about the wide and narrow readings of "Ought implies can" explains our puzzlement over Aristotle's insistence on responsibility for parts of our character we cannot now change.

The text is the famous passage in the *Doctrine of Virtue* in which Kant argues that conflict of duties is impossible:

> A conflict of duties would be a relation of duties in which one of them would annul the other (wholly or in part). —But a conflict of duties and obligations is inconceivable. For the concepts of duty and obligation as such express the objective practical *necessity* of certain actions, and two conflicting rules cannot both be necessary at the same time: if it is our duty to act according to one of these rules, then to act according to the opposite one is not our duty and is even contrary to duty. But there can be, it is true, two *grounds* of obligation *(rationes obligandi)* both present in one agent and in the rule he lays down for himself. In this case one or the other of these grounds is not sufficient to oblige him *(rationes obligandi non obligantes)* and is therefore not a duty. —When two such grounds conflict with each other, practical philosophy says, not that the stronger obligation takes precedence *(fortior obligatio vincit),* but that the stronger *ground of obligation* prevails *(fortior obligandi ratio vincit).* (223)

Alan Donagan provides a more literal translation of the key sentence: "When two such grounds of obligation are in conflict, practical philosophy does not say that the stronger obligation holds the upper hand . . . but that the stronger ground of obligation holds the field."[8]

The crucial claim is this: if there were conflicts of duty, one duty would "annul" the other (wholly or in part). But since the concept of duty expresses practical necessity, there can be no annulling. The necessity that comes from the concept of duty makes it the case that failure to act for either duty is "contrary to duty." An un-acted-upon duty does not lose its necessity; it is not annulled.

We can see why Kant talks about annulling a duty if we look at how one resolves conflict between Kantian pragmatic oughts. When, because of two ends I pursue, I find that I am in circumstances in which what I must do for one end conflicts with what I must do for the other, I resolve the conflict by backing off from at least one of the ends. The object of some want or desire can, at that time, no longer be an end of action. One could say that my choice to act for one end annuls the ought set by the other (wholly or in part, as circumstances permit). It is part of the concept of the moral ought that I cannot annul its requirement by choice or by abandoning an end. From this it would seem to follow that a system of pragmatic oughts that allows conflict is possible, but a system of moral oughts that allows conflict is not.

---

8. "Consistency in Rationalist Moral Systems," *Journal of Philosophy* 81 (1984), 294. The German is: "Wenn zwei solcher Grunde einander widerstreiten, so sagt di praktische Philosophie nicht: dass die starkere Verbindlichkeit die Oberhand behalte . . . sondern der starkere Verpflichtungsgrund behalt den Platz."

Although Kant appears to agree with those who deny the possibility of conflict in order to save the consistency of morality, he does not adopt their secondary "indirectness" arguments to explain the experience of moral conflict. The shift from conflict of obligations (or duties) to conflicting *grounds* of obligation "saves the phenomena" directly.

The easiest reading of "grounds of obligation" is by analogy to W. D. Ross's prima facie obligations.[9] Grounds of obligation would provide reasons for action but no necessity. Conflict between grounds of obligation would be possible and resolved by having the stronger ground (reason) obligate. This strategy preserves the experience of conflict without producing a conflict *of duties*. (One could only have duties when the grounds did not conflict.) The necessity of the resulting obligation would be the necessity of best reasons.[10]

Kant's metaphors suggest that something else is going on. He says that if conflicts of duty *were* possible, the stronger duty would "hold the upper hand." That is, it would have compelling power, defeating or controlling the conflicting duty. This fits with a "balance of reasons" story. Conflict resolution through a balance of reasons is possible if the reasons (duties) present have different weights. One goes with the best or strongest reason, the duty that holds the upper hand. But the metaphor governing conflicting grounds of obligation is different: the stronger ground "holds the field." The metaphor is exclusionary and suggests that the weaker ground of obligation cannot gain the field at all—it has no effective weight in these circumstances.[11] There is no balance of reasons in the resolution of conflicting grounds of obligation. So we need to think again about what a ground of obligation could be.

If obligation marks moral requirement (practical necessity), then a ground of obligation ought to be that in virtue of which one is obliged. In Kantian ethics, the ground of obligation would be that which constrains what can be willed a universal law (under the rules of the two tests of the Categorical Imperative procedure). Consider the duty (or obligation) of mutual aid. Because we cannot will a maxim of nonbeneficence a universal

---

9. *The Right and the Good* (Oxford: Oxford University Press, 1930).

10. Ross is not always consistent in what he understands a prima facie obligation to be. At times he presents prima facie obligations as reason-giving, and conflict is resolved through the balance of reasons (what one is obliged to do emerges only after the balancing of reasons). At other times what it means is that a prima facie obligation is one we would have had except for the presence of another, weightier, obligation. Then conflict is not between two duties or obligations or between two prima facie obligations. There are two instances of duty kinds, one of which is prima facie my duty, the other is my duty. I think this second picture of conflict is much closer to Kant, though Ross's view of obligation is hardly the same as Kant's.

11. Of course, what is kept off a field may exact some toll in its exclusion. It does not follow, however, that it therefore has weight in the "balance of reasons" sense.

law—we are dependent rational beings for whom a law of mutual neglect cannot be rationally willed—we are directed by the CI procedure to acknowledge the needs of others as a possible moral reason for action. The ground of the obligation is the fact that we are dependent beings, a fact that is salient in an agent's circumstances of action through the claim of need.

The ground of the Kantian prohibition on deceit is the integrity of the rational will itself. Deceit is a means of controlling the will of another. A universal law of deceit is not possible, because it is not consistent with the integrity or separateness of agents. There is thus a prohibition on deceit (strictly, on maxims of deceit as a routine means). The ground of obligation in the circumstances of action is the conditions of the integrity of the will.

What these argument sketches are meant to suggest is that grounds of obligation are *facts* of a certain sort. They have moral significance because they are defining features of our (human) rational natures that limit what we can rationally will (as defined by the CI procedure). Following the model introduced in Chapter 7, we should say that these facts enter moral deliberation carrying the deliberative presumption that they will generate decisive reason for action (obligation) unless other "moral facts" in the circumstances of action rebut the presumption. For example, if I am faced with someone who has a valid claim of need, I cannot appeal to facts of self-interest in deliberating whether I should offer help, because self-interest per se cannot rebut a moral presumption. I may consider (include in deliberation) any danger or risk to my life that may be involved in helping; these are morally salient facts. If there is no danger, and I have the resources to meet the need, I must help.

Because grounds are facts, they cannot conflict. Facts may occasion conflict, given certain theoretical or practical constructions. The potential for moral conflict occurs when an agent must take account of more than one ground of obligation, and she cannot directly take care of (act for) both. Moral conflict occurs when there are "two *grounds* of obligation *(rationes obligandi)* both present in one agent and in the rule he lays down for himself." Moral conflict, then, is *in the agent,* in her maxim of action. In other words, if an agent recognizes more than one moral fact (ground of obligation) in her circumstances of action, she *may* adopt a maxim of action that brings them into conflict. Recognizing both that her friend needs help and that she has a promise to keep, an agent may set herself to act on both grounds of obligation only to discover that acting on one will make acting on the other impossible. "In this case one or the other of these grounds is not sufficient to oblige." Conflicting grounds of obligation so understood are not the mark of inadequate deliberative procedures but indicate an occasion in which deliberation is necessary.

There are two things to note here. (1) The location of the conflict in the agent's rule or maxim provides the strongest sort of evidence that Kant does not restrict the idea of autonomy to the metaphysics of morals. This treatment of moral conflict suggests a quite literal understanding of autonomy as self-legislation. There is conflict because of the rule an agent *lays down for herself.* (2) Resolution of conflict in an agent's maxim requires a principle of deliberation. It is not a matter of weighing independent reasons. The question is whether the claim of need (of friends) rebuts the presumption (whatever it is) against promise breaking. If it does, then she ought to aid her friend and break her promise. If not, then she may not help her friend in these circumstances. (I am assuming here and in what follows that the CI procedure supports principles of deliberation able to deliver results. It is not to the point of this discussion to argue this. The task here is the more limited one of describing the kind of moral results that the Kantian deliberative principles were intended to produce.)

The *result* of deliberation is obligation. The practical necessity that is the core of Kant's view of morality arrives as the agent determines which of the grounds of obligation present "binds to duty." Guided by the CI procedure, deliberation takes up grounds (plural) of obligation and determines obligation (singular). So we can say that a ground of obligation "holds the [deliberative] field" when it is not rebutted by the other relevant moral facts in the agent's circumstances of action *as* determined by deliberation. Grounds of obligation by themselves do not give reasons for action at all. They are presumptive: reason-giving only in the sense that they set terms of moral deliberation. The ought that Kantian deliberation yields is a moral ought, the ought of obligation and practical necessity.[12] In holding that moral deliberation issues in a requirement of practical necessity, one might say we have offered Kant's interpretation of the idea that the conclusion of the practical syllogism is action.

Whatever merits this kind of account may have in negotiating conflicts of duty, as an interpretation of Kant it seems incompatible with his commitment to juridical duties and duties of virtue (both plural). If there are such duties, they would surely seem to undermine the account of obligation I have just described as Kant's and make conflicts of duty, in the traditional sense, unavoidable.

Conflicts of duty are unavoidable when duties (or obligations) are conceived of as *performance* requirements, that is, as obligations to *do* certain actions (or kinds of action). What we must show then is that, understood as *moral* duties, the Kantian duties of virtue and justice are not "performance obligations."[13]

---

12. It does not follow from the claim that deliberation resolves conflict that the ground of obligation that does not "bind to duty" is to be ignored. It can occasion *further* deliberation. This and related issues are taken up in section III.

13. Moral duties are here contrasted with juridical duties in a public order. Such duties are

This is easiest to see with the duties of virtue. They do not constrain the agent to specific actions or courses of action, but require the agent to take certain ends as her own (as "obligatory ends"). Actions that will promote one obligatory end can conflict with actions that support another. But since one has no obligation (or duty) to any particular action in support of an obligatory end, the incompatibility of actions promoting obligatory ends does not constitute moral conflict. This is not to say that these duties are "imperfect" in the sense that one is in any way free to determine when the duty applies. (The *Spielraum* of obligatory ends leaves one to determine how, not whether, one will act.)

The necessity that comes with an obligatory end constrains not action but the will. The obligatory end of mutual aid requires that I attend to need. I am to acknowledge its claim on my actions and resources and accept a deliberative constraint or presumption on my maxims where there is a valid claim of need. Other duties of virtue require sensitivity to different facts and impose different deliberative constraints. One can think of the duties of virtue as elaborating the parameters of a single deliberative obligation: we must attend to a set of moral facts and give them deliberative standing in practical judgment. While it may be impossible to pay attention to some different sets of things at once, this possibility does not generate dilemmas: attention always has circumstantial limits. What is required is that we *not ignore* what is there.

Let us compare this account with a traditional conflict-generating one. Suppose that the lives of identical twins are in jeopardy and that through force of circumstance I am in a position to save only one. (The example is from Ruth Marcus; following her, I think of this and similar examples as "Buridan cases."[14]) Conflict of duty can seem unavoidable if we assume that there is an obligation to save each and that there are no moral grounds for choosing to save one twin over the other. No matter which twin I save, I had an obligation to the other that I did not meet.

Something blocks the natural thought that in such a case where the claims of the twins are of equal weight, where it makes no moral differ-ence which of the twins I save, morality can underdetermine outcomes. I believe this option is rejected because the traditional account is commit-ted to something like the following. If I have an obligation to help A,

---

identified as actions that can be legitimately coerced by public authority. Treating promising as a duty that also belongs to ethical theory, in the sense of having a derivation independent of law, may not be something Kant would have accepted. However, given the recent habit of regarding promises as canonical examples of ethical duties, and given that nothing in this discussion depends on promising being an ethical duty, I will proceed as if it were.

14. Ruth Barcan Marcus, "Moral Dilemmas and Consistency," *Journal of Philosophy* 77 (1980), 125. Marcus uses this example to show that no single-principled theory can avoid conflict. It is therefore quite suitable to my purpose here of explaining how Kantian theory is both single-principled *and* conflict-avoiding.

then there is no reason that could justify not helping A (if I can and the means are not impermissible). But if I also have an obligation to help B, and I can only help A or B, then I will necessarily act in a way that cannot be justified. In such circumstances, the underdetermination of outcomes is unacceptable. One cannot honor both obligations, and morality gives no grounds for choice.

These difficulties do not arise for the Kantian obligation to aid in the Buridan saving case. One is obliged to acknowledge claims of need and to be prepared to help as and if one can. This obligation can be met for *both* twins. It remains true that if one acts to save A one cannot act to save B (and vice versa). But in not saving B, one has *not* left one's obligation to B unfulfilled. One had no obligation to save B (or A). Having acknowledged the claim of both twins' needs and with no moral reason to prefer saving one twin over the other, everything that ought to be done is done in saving either one. (Acknowledgment plus preparation is not just idle talk; if one is ready to help both and circumstances change—the current suddenly sweeps the twins together—one is *already* committed to saving both.)

The Kantian account of the Buridan twins directs us through a set of problem cases. If someone's life is in jeopardy but we are separated by a deep river gorge, I can do nothing beyond acknowledging need and being prepared to act. I must act if I can; if I cannot, that is (morally speaking) the end of it. This is also the case when we judge that I do not fail to act as I must if, having acknowledged a claim of need, I defer to someone better situated to save (another's help is preferable or more safely given). No obligation is left unfulfilled in these cases, though there is no action taken.

Performance obligations cannot manage these cases without strain. If I have no obligation where I cannot act to save, shifting circumstances may make my obligations come and go. In the river gorge, when I discover a bridge around the bend I then, for the *first time,* can have an obligation to save. (This makes it hard to explain any obligation to seek means that are not at hand.) In the "defer to the better saver" case, if we think I have no obligation when my help is not necessary (or preferred), then an obligation will once again pop up if it turns out that the better saver falters. (If we think I do have an obligation, then since only one of us can help, there will be an unmet obligation. Would this give us reason to compete to avoid this demerit?)

The Kantian model has no suddenly appearing or disappearing obligations. The cases are situational variants of the same obligation to aid. In each case I am obligated throughout: I acknowledge need and am prepared to act. I do not become obligated only as there is opportunity to act. In each case, whether I act or not, I can have fulfilled my obligation. This is equally so when I am unable to act (the gorge and Buridan twins) and when I have good reason to refrain from acting (the better saver). As circumstances change (action becomes possible), the obligation that I *already* have is sufficient for action.

Since it may seem that the Kantian account depends on features special to the duty to aid, let us also look at the obligations associated with promises. They certainly seem to involve performance requirements and so to be occasions for conflicts of duty.

Take a second Buridan case, again from Marcus. "Under the single principle of promise-keeping, I might make two promises in all good faith and reason that they will not conflict, but then they do, as a result of circumstances that were unpredictable and beyond my control. All other considerations may balance out."[15] The conclusion is that conflict is both possible and unresolvable. As before, the assumption behind this conclusion has to be that if I have an obligation to do x (here, keep a promise) and I am able to do x, I am not justified in not doing x.

Let us look at the obligation-generating "single principle of promise keeping." To support the conclusion, it must give an agent an obligation to do what she has promised to do. This is a performance obligation: in promising to do x, I incur an obligation to do that thing. But if obligation carries practical necessity, this is at odds with the fact that we frequently think we have good reason not to do what we have promised to do.

There is no evidence that Kant believes we have a perfect duty of promise *keeping*. There are three grounds of obligation relating to promises. They concern making, keeping, and breaking promises. (One breaks a promise when one believes one has sufficient reason not to do the promised thing; failure to keep a promise does not involve belief that one's action is justified, as when one has forgotten.) It is implausible to think we are obliged never to break a promise or never to fail to keep a promise. Insofar as we have a perfect duty to do anything, it is *not to make* a deceitful promise.[16]

Having made a promise, I have constrained my future deliberations in certain ways. This constraint on deliberation is in fact the content of the promising obligation. (I take this to be part of the elaboration of the claim that what is constrained in Kantian ethics is not deeds but willings, where will is the active face of practical reason.) I know that not wanting to keep the promise (or wishing I had not made it) is not a deliberative ground that rebuts the presumption that I am to act as I promised. On the other hand, if at the time when the promise is to be kept I have good (moral) reason to

---

15. Marcus, "Moral Dilemmas and Consistency," p. 125.

16. This is not quite right, for it suggests that we may never make a deceitful promise. I think the perfect duty that Kant has in mind is more restricted: one may not make a deceitful promise for reasons of self-interest. Some reasons for thinking this are suggested in Chapter 7, section V.

do something else, then the deliberative presumption can be rebutted, and I am not required to do what I promised. Since the obligation in promising is a deliberative constraint, it is possible to be unable to do what one promised without failing one's obligation.[17]

In the Buridan promising case, whichever promise I keep (and it makes no moral difference which of the two it is), it follows that I will not be able to keep the other promise, but it does *not* follow that I have not done what I ought to have done *with regard to the promise I have not kept*. I can have satisfied the obligation (in the sense of deliberative constraint) imposed by both promises.

Furthermore, since among the deliberative constraints that reasonably come with making a promise is that we not knowingly do what will make keeping the promise impossible, we can explain why, if I have promised to repay a loan on Wednesday but squander the money on Tuesday, I have violated the obligation incurred by promising. Indeed, even if the cause of my not having the money on Wednesday is not my own doing (bank failure, theft), I do not cease to have the obligation. What will change is what I am to do given these new circumstances. It also does not follow that the promisee who failed to get what she was promised has no claim. That is a question for the casuistry of promising: the moral fact of an unkept promise may require some further action.[18]

For Kant, all obligation set by the duties of virtue and of justice issues from moral judgment or deliberation. When grounds of obligation conflict (they cannot both be taken up into an agent's maxim of action), one's obligation follows one's deliberative determination of the ground that "holds the field" or, as when the grounds are the same, one's choice of action. There remain, of course, many differences between duties of virtue and duties of justice in the particulars of their deliberative requirements. What I have argued is that, insofar as Kantian duties necessitate, they do not do so directly. Necessitation (obligation) is always the outcome of deliberation.

The Kantian concept of obligation protects the idea of practical necessity without generating dilemmas by not placing us under multiple standing or voluntary performance obligations. Moral conflict is experienced by an agent in circumstances where she is responsive to more than one ground of obligation and at least one of them cannot bind to obligation if the others do. There is no moral dilemma because the grounds of obligation do not each obligate. The experience of conflict, of there being a moral problem,

---

17. Even Nietzsche does not think that it is our ability to perform the action we promised that makes promising defining of moral nature—we have no such ability. What promising signifies is our ability to stand guarantor for ourselves for what we will.

18. There is further discussion of this in Chapter 5.

sets the agent a deliberative task, the resolution of which reveals her obligation. Although procedures of deliberation do not always dictate what to do, they (in principle, at least) resolve the status of competing moral claims. If the agent still needs to choose, even if the choice is hard, it will not be one horn of a moral dilemma.[19]

III

Although this way of understanding obligation saves the experience of conflict without introducing moral dilemmas, it does not resolve the issue entirely. There are those who argue that there are certain basic facts of morality that we must preserve even if they force acceptance of moral dilemmas. I think of this as the problem of the three *R*'s: remorse, restitution, and remainders. Each of the three *R*'s includes something that an adequate moral theory must address, but each also carries dilemma-generating assumptions about conflict and obligation. The question is whether we can preserve the basic facts they contain within the Kantian account of obligation. First let us see why the three *R*'s in their customary presentation do not fit in the Kantian account.

Remorse. When an agent is unable to meet a moral demand or requirement present in her circumstances of action, we take it to be a good thing that the agent does not act without compunction (a feeling of moral concern and caution, an awareness of moral danger). But some hold that she ought to feel remorse (not just regret) for the action not done, especially when the consequences of not acting are grave. (It would be odd to think that one should feel remorse for breaking a promise that puts the promisee in the way of some great good fortune.) Eschewal of indirection arguments leaves the conclusion that if it is morally good for the agent to feel remorse, she has done something wrong.[20] If remorse is the correct or good response to situations of conflict, we cannot accept the Kantian account. The Kantian agent does nothing wrong in acting as deliberation directs.

Restitution. It is often held to be the case that the agent owes something in virtue of the un-acted-upon obligation, from as little as an apology to as much as damages for harm incurred. We would not owe unless we had done wrong: the very idea of restitution implies repair of wrongful damages. An

19. Faced with the prospect of having to let one twin drown, we would feel a deep sense of conflict at the prospect of having to choose where no reasoned choice is possible and where the costs are so large. This is wholly compatible with the absence of moral dilemma.

20. If we *excuse* the untaken action because of the circumstances of conflict (as with the Buridan cases), we are thereby committed to the thought that the agent did something wrong. In such cases some are tempted to say that the agent did not "act wrongfully" in "doing something wrong." Embedding the excuse in this way does not clarify the question of whether remorse is an appropriate response.

apology does moral repair work too. It averts the damage to moral stature that would be incurred if one's valid moral claims were left unacknowledged. (Some repairs are necessary for maintenance: their omission lets a damaging condition progress.) It is hard to see how the Kantian account could accept the appropriateness of restitution if it denies that the agent has done any kind of wrong in resolving a dilemma situation.

Remainders. Remainders support the claims of restitution. It can seem that if there were no moral remainders there would be no grounds to claim that something more needed to be done after the "right" choice was made in a dilemma. Then, one will conclude, if there is to be restitution, something of the unfulfilled obligation must remain. But the Kantian resolution of the situation of moral conflict leaves no unfulfilled or un-acted-upon obligations.

There is no good argument that justifies remorse or guilt in the absence of wrongdoing. If I am unable to do what I think I ought to have done, I often do feel guilty, even when I know my action is justified. But I also often feel guilty when I am unable to bring something about (say, a good thing for my child) that is neither mine to bring about nor something that is a matter of obligation or wrongdoing. I do not think we are clear enough about guilt—about its role, place, cognitive and affective content—to have much confidence in our guilt responses as foundations for theoretical claims. And surely the myriad psychological accounts of the etiology of guilt should make us hesitant to read guilt feelings literally.

Perhaps confidence in the suitability of guilt to circumstances of conflict comes from hard cases. We are unable to imagine a moral agent who would not feel guilt at leaving one of the twins to drown. And we do take the inability to feel guilt about certain kinds of action as a sign of moral pathology, if not insanity. But this does not show much. The power of guilt to move and define us is so strong as to make it unlikely that these feelings are not coopted by all sorts of private purposes and cultural projects (if it is not morality itself that has done the coopting). There are many reasons that it should be hard to do certain kinds of action. Some actions should be impeded by inertial forces; others need to stay behind the barrier of a taboo. These limits, held in place by negative moral feelings, are appropriate constraints for imperfectly rational beings, for rational agents who have a character.

Even so, I think that we unnecessarily spread the occasions of guilt beyond wrongdoing. There are other morally more precise feelings to do the required instrumental work (compunction, repugnance, regret) that can, in addition, withstand "the dissolving force of analysis." So if we do not need guilt to secure a strong negative reaction in the face of the normally forbidden, it is hard to see how it could be morally good for an agent to feel guilt when she has done nothing wrong. *If* Agamemnon acted as he ought, whatever the feelings he should have had (horror, a sense of pollution), guilt would not be called for.[21]

Some seem to think that guilt is simply a mark of good character in the face of those actions normally forbidden. No further purpose would need to be served by guilt any more than there is purpose served by the joy we feel at something gloriously beautiful. We might think that guilt, like joy, is constitutive of a certain sort of experience, the appropriate occurrence of which is the mark of a certain kind of character. Guilt is a retrospective feeling; prospectively it works as a form of fear. To encourage a guilt response independent of wrongdoing would create a certain sort of moral character, to be sure. But it seems a dubious thing to encourage dissociation of a moral feeling held to be constitutive of good character from correct moral belief.

There is a better case for the other two *R*'s. We want the agent to do *something* in the face of unmet obligation. And if restitution brings things morally back to a former condition, it is appropriate only if there is something for which we need to make amends. While remainders per se do not imply wrongdoing (actions leave all kinds of things behind), if the thought is that there is remaining unmet obligation, something that ought to have been done but was not, then of course remainders do imply wrongdoing (even if excused or justified wrongdoing). The claim of restitution is easiest to make if there are such remainders.

The problem is that the three *R*'s, as customarily presented, are basic terms in a particular theory of moral failures. If they seem natural to us, it is because we accept the performance theory of obligation that makes them necessary. When one holds that obligations require performances, the unmet obligation in a conflict situation is a justified nonperformance, an omission. It could not be the ground of any (further) moral requirement unless the unmet performance obligation leaves a remainder (the limiting case being the wrong done by leaving the obligation unmet). Only then is there something substantial to proceed from (and something to feel guilt about when restitution is not possible).

Accepting an account that depends on performance obligations brings costs beyond the theoretical difficulties that attend conflicts of duty. There are also serious practical consequences in the way performance obligations construct a certain kind of moral life. This is most easily seen by following

---

21. I find it hard to believe that our sense that he ought to have felt guilt is not rather a sign that we find his sacrifice of Iphigenia horribly wrong. We would do better, I think, to avoid Agamemnon (and like examples) in seeking either illustrations or evocations of our moral intuitions. The power of these stories is in their complexity and ambiguity, which are all the more exaggerated by their role in the purposes of the classical dramatists.

the economic metaphors that are often used in accounts of these obligations. Take the Buridan promises again. If we hold that an agent acting to meet the obligations of the first promise fails to meet the other obligation, we find it natural to say that because of the unmet obligation, there is a balance due, a debt that is owed. It is incumbent upon a responsible agent to discharge the remaining obligation, to clear the balance. Because it is inefficient not to have clarity and finality about the balance due, a likely demand on the casuistry of promising will be for clear determinations of the appropriate response to various kinds of broken promise. To have made a promise is to have set oneself to a certain performance. If justified promise breaking leaves remainders, then one is in the wrong unless one clears this up. The second performance wipes the slate clean. (This sort of thinking can lead to the view that promise keeping and promise breaking plus restitution are morally equivalent.[22] Making a promise opens an account that either action can close.)

These metaphors extend beyond promises to other forms of obligation: to our families, to the state, even to friends. Obligations are burdens to be discharged, interfering with the real business of our lives. If we are good, or better than good, we discharge our obligations cheerfully. If we are not so good (and far from bad), we just do what we have to do. Whichever we are, with this understanding of what it is to have an obligation, it is irrational not to want them to be over and done with.

I suspect that this view of obligation is one of the reasons that a recent strand of moral theorizing has been so opposed to accepting obligation as the basic category of morality.[23] It is argued that thinking of the moral relations between persons in terms of obligations produces estrangement from one's actions and from others. So an obligation to help others leads us to view their needs as demands on our resources, and the morality of obligation requires only that the need be met, not that one care. Of particular concern are special relationships such as friendship. If one wants to regard friendship as a moral relationship (or a relationship having moral components), then it is ill described in the language of obligations. It is because we view friendship as an ongoing affective relationship that the metaphors of "discharge of what is owed" and "clearing the balance" are not only inappropriate but destructive. The needs of friends are not to be thought of as burdens (though they may come to be burdensome), and acts

---

22. There is a view of contracts where what one has agreed to is *either* the performance of the terms of the contract *or* nonperformance and a payment that meets the original value of the agreed to performance. This is justified as giving protection to the parties when changing costs make staying with the terms of the contract unfairly burdensome.

23. See Lawrence Blum, *Friendship, Altruism and Morality* (London: Routledge and Kegan Paul, 1980), and Bernard Williams, "Persons, Character and Morality," in *Moral Luck* (Cambridge: Cambridge University Press, 1981).

of friendship are not discrete required performances but expressions of a continuing friendship.

The mistake in this critique is not in the view of the morality of aid or friendship, but in the uncritical acceptance of the performance conception of obligation. One of the reasons we hang on to this conception, I believe, is the need to support the three R's, especially remainders. Without remainders it is not clear how an agent could be further obligated (to apologize, make restitution, and so on) in cases of moral conflict, especially when her nonperformance is justified. But with remainders, we have to accept the theoretical consequences of unavoidable wrongdoing.

The deep attractiveness of the Kantian conception of obligation is that it can both do the work assigned to remainders and be free of the real defects of the performance conception.

The Kantian conception of obligation does not need to leave remainders to provide a basis for ongoing moral requirement. In circumstances of moral conflict, the agent is presented with a deliberative problem whose resolution leaves her obliged to act as deliberation directs. With Buridan promises, having done one of the things promised, the agent's circumstances change; they now contain the fact of the unkept (or broken) promise. This is a new situation, setting a new deliberative problem. If restitution is in order, it will be because of the circumstances the agent comes to be in having acted as she ought. Restitution does not require remainders. Because the unkept promise in the Buridan case does not mark an unmet obligation, there is no wrong done. And if there is no sense in which the agent has left anything morally required undone, there are no remainders. There is nothing to feel remorse or guilt about.

The language and metaphors of obligation are different as well. If what it is to be obliged is to be under the practical necessity of acting as moral deliberation directs, obligation is not a matter of required performances but of commitment to a way of determining how one is to act. The Kantian agent lives in a very different kind of moral space from that created by performance obligations. It is direct (as opposed to "indirect") in its requirements, morally transparent in a sense, and, as I will argue, able to integrate morality more intimately into an agent's life. When an agent acts as Kantian deliberation directs in conflict situations, it is not the case that she is meeting one obligation while failing to meet another (that is, she does not do two things—one good, the other requiring justification and leaving remainders, wrongs done, and such). She acts as she ought on the ground of obligation that is sufficient in these circumstances to oblige her. She does one thing. Because of what she does, it may turn out that she must later do something else, since in acting she moves from a situation in which she faces two grounds of obligation to one in which she faces a new one, or more than one, according to what is morally present in her new situation.

In changing the understanding of obligation, one also changes what particular duties are about. On the performance model of obligation, making a promise committed one to a performance or, upon failure, remainder management. Continuity of obligation across nonperformance was secured by remainders. On the Kantian model, the commitment is to a procedure of deliberation that not only includes concern with performance but is equally and from the outset responsive to the full moral features of the agent's changing circumstances of action.

Having made a promise, the agent has initiated an ongoing deliberative commitment to take into account the particulars of the promise, the conditions and opportunities of successful performance, as well as the deliberative significance of an unkept promise, justified or unjustified. (These need not be the only things she has committed herself to.) There is no guarantee that her obligation will have prompt closure. While it does not follow from the fact that not keeping a promise causes some harm that the agent who causes it thereby has responsibility for relieving that harm, responsibility is possible—even when not keeping the promise is justified—since neither fault nor remainders are required to sustain continuing obligation. The point of a casuistry for promises is not to produce an account of what one owes (the "alternatives" to keeping one's promise), but to provide a method of determining what is morally salient in the making, keeping, and breaking of promises. Casuistry does not settle the issues in advance; it gives deliberative guidance.

One might say that regarding promises as deliberative commitments does not so much give you a future task that you must perform (or else) as it alters to a greater or lesser degree the way your life will go on. As rational agents with autonomy, we make plans and prepare to create a future. Of course, our creative powers are limited and affected by the activities of others (thus the insistence in the *Rechtslehre* on enlarging external freedom compatible with like freedom for others).[24] But to acknowledge our autonomy is to refuse passivity (the practical denial of determinism); we view ourselves as making our lives. To make a promise is to introduce new deliberative considerations that carry weight against our other projects. We may need to alter present activities to prepare for doing what we promised; we know that we cannot guarantee performance and so may be responsible

---

24. One does not want to exaggerate the claims for autonomy. Although as a rational agent with autonomy I view my life as a kind of creative activity—the expression of my causality and plans in the world—it may be that my actual circumstances of living do not permit effective activity and may even undermine my capacity for conceiving of a life. Such facts can be grounds for the moral criticism of oppressive social institutions.

for events beyond the scope of the actual promise. And so on. The casuistry of promising describes the deliberative constraints that an autonomous agent accepts in making a promise. Analogous deliberative constraints constitute our other moral requirements (the "duties" of justice and virtue).

Morality shapes, perhaps codefines, what our lives will look like. If morality were about obligations—performance obligations—it would be reasonable to regard it as external to us, introducing limits and constraints from outside the course of our activity. It would then be natural to think of morality as something imposed, something we wish to be free of. Such a picture of morality makes it hard to explain attachment to morality; it is not obvious why one should want to increase one's burdens.

It might look this way: since we already have a variety of things limiting our activity—natural forces, physical limitations, the activity of others— why should we volunteer to decrease further our effective freedom? It will then seem that the only possible answer is that the very limits morality imposes actually increase our freedom—*if* enough others also accept them. This introduces indirectness and ambivalence at the outset. The burdens imposed by the obligations do not correlate with the conditional good produced. Even the agent who accepts this morality will, insofar as she is rational, experience it as external and estranging, as something she would elude if she could.

One cannot care for something when what you primarily want to do is discharge it at reasonable cost. A normal moral agent will feel morality separate from her life. She will accrue a goodness score and perhaps value herself on its scale of performance success. But her moral obligations take her away from her life, and she pursues them with a different structure of concern and care than the projects she takes to make her life worth living.

By contrast, the Kantian account of morality does not work from a set of constraining obligations. Its central notion is the agent as rational deliberator. Accepting morality involves deliberative commitment both to a way of thinking about one's life and choices and to acting as deliberation directs. One's deliberative frame no longer locates one's life at the center or places morality along with other constraints at the boundaries as external, confining, limiting one's possibilities. The basic field of deliberation contains not only my interests and private projects but also the interests of others as possible sources of claims on my actions and resources. The grounds of obligation partially create the practical world I live in.[25] Moral requirements are part of the fabric of the practical world that requires attention independently of my wishes.

---

25. The claim that moral facts alter the world is a claim within the domain of the practical, not a gambit in the metaphysics of moral realism. The world a rational agent lives in contains moral facts, features that demand attention and that carry deliberative significance.

This is why I believe the Kantian model of obligation is not destructive of friendship or of other care-based moral relations. If friendship is a moral relationship or has a moral dimension, then there will be alterations in one's deliberative field as one has friends (and different elements introduced as one has different kinds of friends). Morality does not cause the needs of friends to be regarded as burdens or in competition with the needs of strangers. If among the moral features of friendship is a more stringent duty of mutual aid, then the needs of one's friends will occupy higher ground in the deliberative field. One will be open to the needs of friends in a way that one is not to the needs of strangers. There is not only commitment to giving friends' needs some kind of deliberative priority, one is committed to being more attentive to the possibility and occasions of their need. There need be no separation between morality and caring.

The charge that Kantian impartiality requires that one give no precedence to friends' needs, that it requires rigid even-handedness, assumes that there is no distinctive moral dimension to friendship. It may well be that Kantian ethics challenges some assumptions about the content of obligations of friendship, but that would be as deliberation directed and not because the very idea of obligation excludes the value of special commitments. "That she is my friend" may be a very good moral reason to provide help. This does not preclude some circumstances in which attention to the complete deliberative field shows that giving preference to friends is not justified.

Many of the examples in the philosophical literature tell a story of moral requirement as an intrusion or interrupting errand. I am on my way to meet a friend, as promised, when I see an accident occur. I deliberate: may I (or must I) break my promise in order to rescue the accident victims? Walking across a bridge I see a child struggling in the water. Must I go out of my way, risk my health, be late to a very important meeting, to try to save her?

These moral tales have me on my way in morally neutral territory when something "outside" my narrative happens. Morality intrudes. Moral inquiry determines the nature and degree of this interference with my story (my "business"). The metaphor embedded in this narrative structure practically makes it the case that I must most want to be on my way, to get on with what I was doing. Interruption is bad enough; absence of closure is intolerable. So, concluding that I must stop to save the child, we do not even ask, in the philosophical story, "What must I do next?"

It is understandable that we should want what morality requires of us to be finite. We have our lives to live. And even when we are prepared to live our lives within the confines of morality, we expect our engagement with morality's positive requirements to be something we can negotiate and go on from, like a necessary errand in the middle of the day. We are thus somewhat more comfortable with the omnipresence of negative moral requirements, for they introduce limits on means rather than detours away from our ends.

Different moral conceptions carry different narrative models. How we think about the fit of morality with our lives affects what the narrative of a life looks like. Performance obligations yield narrative interruptions. Kantian obligation yields ongoing, narratively central, deliberative commitment. And, not surprisingly, each narrative structure offers different possibilities of integration into a self-conception or conception of oneself as particular kind of moral agent. The hero of Kantian narrative has a conception of herself as an autonomous agent among others. The hero of the conventional morality of performance obligations is well described by liberal theory's successful individual: triumphant in the face of obstacles (including morality) in the pursuit of private goals.

The different narrative models bring with them different views about closure. The agent who views herself as attentive to the moral features of the deliberative field has no special reason to wish for closure. As need is a sign of distress, she must wish for the end of need; as an unkept promise may cause hurt or loss, she has reason to respond. In neither case is her interest in closure per se. That moral requirement may be open-ended is the nature of moral requirement. Sometimes circumstances may be such that moral demands exhaust the deliberative field; at other times it may be easy to attend to what morality presents but exhausting to care for oneself. In living a moral life the agent knows there is uncertainty about the different demands that will be made on her resources. Some of these demands will be out of her control. (In this regard morality is not badly modeled by our view of the good parent: one simply cannot know in advance what having a child will do to one's life. It may be that life goes on much as before, amplified in some areas, restricted in others. But it may equally be that one's life is utterly altered in ways that have nothing to do with choice because of the actual needs of one's children. One then lives a different life.)

By contrast, the agent whose life narrative is constrained and interrupted by morality cannot be sanguine about open-ended requirements. One may accept that one's life has to be within the moral frame, but, as with most practical matters, excessive interruption undermines the possibility of successful activity. Some individuals may be able to accept high levels of moral demand under perceived conditions of emergency. But we talk then of "putting one's life on hold" to deal with the tasks at hand.

We are not free to think about the place of morality in our lives in any way we want to. The narrative fit of morality depends on the kind of moral requirement that is central to the moral conception we accept. This is not a matter of theory—something we can ignore "for practical purposes." Our self-understanding, our appreciation of our lives (what we do, what we have accomplished), is very much a function of how we understand our connection to morality.

It may seem that, in my account of the different ways one might look at obligation, I have located deliberation in only one kind of moral theory. That is not the case. Every moral conception requires that agents deliberate about what to do. What distinguishes the Kantian conception is the idea of a unified deliberative field.[26] What matters, what is of value, including both the agent's preferences (her interests, in the traditional sense) and the moral features of her circumstances, is presented in the field. (Attention to all of the elements of the field is not automatic and may not even be possible. But this is not a special problem for the moral elements of the field. We are equally familiar with difficulties in attending to some kinds of needs and deeper interests.) Because the field is unified, the agent does not engage in multiple courses of deliberation: what I want to do, what would be good for me, what morality requires. We do not determine what, on the one hand, morality requires and what, on the other, one ought to do "all things considered." It is incumbent on the agent to perceive the grounds of obligation and the grounds of other concerns that are present. The presence of the former may determine the deliberative status of the latter. One might say that there are differences in value *in* the deliberative field. Making a promise, for example, introduces a deliberative presumption against reasons of mere self-interest. An interest that gave sufficient reason to act before the promise was made may no longer do so. The mere fact of interest may not now be reason enough to occasion deliberation. The promise alters the terrain of the deliberative field.

A deliberative presumption introduces value considerations whose effects are not correctly described in terms of greater weight. Their presence may exclude some sorts of considerations altogether and give others authority in the deliberative field. This contrasts with the usual view of reasons and deliberation. When "x is a reason" (or "x is of value") implies that x has a certain practical weight (either in itself or relative to other sorts of reasons), then x must be counted in deliberation. For most x, some sum of other reasons (values) will be equivalent in weight. This kind of arithmetic is not implied by the concept of value itself; it is a particular conception of value with strong normative consequences. It not only makes us think of deliberation as a kind of summing; it suggests that there must be some kind of currency of value in which value weight can be expressed. Indeed, it can

26. John Rawls develops a similar interpretation of Kant in the idea of a moral framework through which the autonomous agent constructs a complete conception of the good. See his "Themes in Kant's Moral Philosophy," in *Kant's Transcendental Deductions,* ed. E. Förster (Stanford: Stanford University Press, 1989), pp. 90–95.

seem that unless this is so the heterogeneity of value would make deliberation impossible.

Kantian deliberation protects the heterogeneity of value by excluding nothing from the deliberative field. The principles of obligation regulate what will be salient in deliberation in view of the facts of the agent's actual circumstances of action. An autonomous moral agent sees a complex world containing physical, social, and moral limits *and* possibilities. Some of what the agent finds is unalterable. Other features are reflections of contingent circumstances and structures. The principles of deliberative morality introduce practical order, making the world a human one.

9

Agency, Attachment, and Difference

IT IS for no trivial reason that Kant's ethics is the standard model of an impartial ethical system. Persons have moral standing in virtue of their rationality, and the morally dictated regard we are to have for one another reflects this deep sameness: we are never to fail to treat one another as agents with autonomous rational wills. This yields impartial treatment of persons and impartial judgment across cases. Although these features of Kant's ethics have traditionally been a source of its appeal, in many recent discussions just this sort of impartiality has come to stand for a kind of vice—mostly a vice of theory.[1] To the extent, however, that persons embody the values of impartiality, it is sometimes thought to be in them, if not quite a vice, then a lack or limit or defect of moral sensibility.[2]

In this chapter I want to examine a cluster of criticisms of Kantian ethics associated with its impartiality. They arise from concern for the moral standing of relationships of attachment between persons and extend to claims for the nonrational nature of the moral agent and the moral relevance of difference. Each strand of criticism has this form: because of its commitment to impartiality (or one of the grounds of impartiality, such as rationality), Kantian ethics fails to make room for x, where x is something no acceptable moral theory can ignore. Without making a general argument in praise of impartiality, I want to see whether its Kantian instantiation really fails to accommodate things no moral theory can afford to omit.

Relationships of attachment pose a serious problem for Kantian ethics, if attachment is a source of distinctive moral claims that impartiality

1. The vanguard of this complaint is to be found in the work of Bernard Williams, Michael Stocker, and Lawrence Blum.
2. Criticisms of the so-called justice perspective find fault this way. See Carol Gilligan, *In a Different Voice* (Cambridge: Harvard University Press, 1982), and her later introductory essay to *Women and Moral Theory*, ed. E. Kittay and D. Myers (Totowa: Rowman and Littlefield, 1987).

disallows or if the features of persons that support and express attachment are devalued by its conception of moral agency. While friends of Kantian ethics have described ways to accommodate the concerns that motivate the criticism, *what* has to be accommodated has to a large extent been accepted in the critics' terms. It is among my purposes here to initiate a more independent examination of the value of partiality.

It is important to say at the outset that I do not intend this chapter in the spirit of endless defense of a favorite system. The cluster of criticisms are worth attention because they do point to important matters that have been omitted or ignored by Kantian theorists, though whether by Kant himself is another matter. Moral theories should not be static. As we discover (or uncover) things a theory as formulated did not know about or attend to, we have occasion to further elaborate or develop the theory in the light of what we now know. Sometimes a theory can absorb new things; sometimes not. Whichever, we do best if we make the effort and see what happens to the theory under strain. Its success may suggest we have misunderstood the theory all along. Its failure can only instruct if we are scrupulous in finding the source of the fault. The fact that a theory as traditionally understood omits something should be the beginning, not the end, of inquiry.

I

Impartiality per se is the requirement that like cases be treated alike. As a requirement on justification, it is not trivial. Differential treatment or judgment requires the demonstration of relevant difference. But as a substantive moral requirement, impartiality by itself demands little. Do we violate impartiality when we favor friends over strangers in the distribution of some good? Does impartiality show that if pregnancy is accorded the status of a disability, employment law will not be impartial between men and women? Because there is nothing in the idea of impartiality to indicate when or in what terms cases are alike, it can seem that impartiality is an empty (or uninstructive) moral value. It is then hard to see what all the fuss could be about.

There is an interesting asymmetry here. For if impartiality is empty, partiality (in its different manifestations) is the stuff our lives are said to be about: *my* life, *my* loves, *my* ideals. Then to the extent that impartiality defines the moral perspective, partiality creates tension with and within morality. When I attend specially to the needs of my children and friends because I am partial to them, either I have acted as I ought not (morality requires that I count their needs no more than others'), or I have done what I ought to do, because there are obligations to one's children and friends, but I have done it the wrong way: my actions were expressions of my partiality, not of my moral understanding and commitment. Partiality is then either a sign or an occasion of moral failure, or a value that morality cannot acknowledge in a direct way. Those unhappy with this will say: impartial ethics does not allow room (or the right sort of room) for the relationships and structures of attachment that constitute good or normal human lives. It devalues the affective life—the life constituted by feeling, intimacy, connection. And if affect-grounded connection creates partiality of attachment, then impartial ethics pushes us away from such attachments.

I want to think more about this claim and about the nature of what makes it disturbing. Of special interest is the argument that takes a positive moral attitude toward feelings to be the basis for asserting the disvalue of impartiality as a moral norm for relationships. What I want to show is that much of the conflict between concerns of partiality and impartial ethics is caused by a misunderstanding of the requirements of both.

Let us first survey the kind of room that Kantian ethics provides for actions motivated by care and concern for the other—what I will call "motives of connection." As we see where reasonable grounds for complaint remain, we will have the issues that need attention. In Chapter 2 I argued that Kantian ethics does not block the satisfaction of certain obligations from motives of connection as they are available or appropriate, so long as the agent's volition (her maxim) is regulated by the motive of duty functioning as a secondary motive or limiting condition. That is to say: in acting from a motive of connection I must also recognize that I am in circumstances in which action is morally required, be willing and able to act even if connection wavers, and act only on the condition that the particular action I am moved to take is permissible. But permitting action from motives of connection does not fully resolve the problem. Even though there is nothing wrong with acting from a motive of connection in circumstances of obligation, the Kantian is likely to insist that action so motivated has no moral worth. The Kantian position is that the value signaled by moral worth is action done from a motive that tracks morality (the motive of duty): only then is there a maxim of action with moral content. A dutiful action done from a motive of connection has a maxim with a different content. The critic of Kantian ethics objects to the fact that no moral value is assigned to maxims or motives of connection. Toleration is not enough.

There are countermoves the Kantian may make at this point. One may note that in most cases the actions at issue are ones required by "imperfect duties." What one is required to do is adopt morally required ends *from* the motive of duty. That leaves open how (from what motive) one acts for that end. An agent may act for a morally required end from motives of connection. Indeed, a helping action guided by connection may be more successful than one done from the moral motive working alone. The agent's complete maxim then includes not only the motive of connection but also the underlying moral commitment to the required end (from the motive of duty).[3] The complete maxim has moral content. If this treatment secures moral worth to the agent acting from motives of connection, it still fails to accord moral value to these motives, except indirectly. The motives of connection are placed among those that can lend support to a morally required end, but the moral value of connection remains in question.

One might try to argue that since there is an indirect duty to maintain one's happiness (to secure stability for moral character), and since attachments are necessary to human happiness, then the motives of connection have moral value as they are means to happiness.[4] But this will not really satisfy those who find the issue in the need to justify the motives of connection in the first place. Nor should it. This way of arguing the value of connection or attachment depends on its role in supporting the "mental health" of the moral agent.[5]

Perhaps we should have asked first: why should it matter that maxims of connection do not have *moral* value? Why can't we say: morality is one kind of value, connection another? Not everything that matters to us must have moral value. A reason for caring about this might turn on the relative value weight of connection, especially if one thought that regulative priority implied value priority. That is, if morality (impartial morality) trumps connection, the value of connection is diminished. But, of course, even assigning moral value to motives of connection would not resolve the priority issue unless we thought that the moral value of connection was at least sometimes greater than the value associated with the motive of duty. And this the Kantian cannot accept.

There is an additional worry. Given the association in Kantian ethics between morality and rationality, on the one hand, and connection with affect and feeling on the other, the assignment of (at best) subordinate value to the motives of connection supports the idea that our affective nature is not essential to our moral agency, or at least the idea that our moral agency would remain intact in the absence of the grounds of connection. We will return to this concern later.

---

3. An agent's "complete" maxim is the fully elaborated subjective principle of volition, including not only the motive and end of the action to be taken but also the regulative conditions the agent accepts in acting. In the case imagined, the complete maxim reflects the agent's commitment to the morally required end of helping and her belief that the best means of acting in the circumstances is in a way that is expressive of connection.

4. See G399. Henning Jensen offers an interesting variant of this, arguing that a perfect duty to maintain the rights of humanity in ourselves entitles us to act from motives of connection *from* the motive of duty. See his "Kant and Moral Integrity," *Philosophical Studies* 57 (1989), 193–205.

5. We should at least mark that there is a question about why something that is slotted as of instrumental value does not bear the value of its end. This may have to do with a tendency to believe that instruments are fungible. It does not seem to be a necessary truth about value.

Does regulative priority translate into value priority? I think not. When we require that belief and argument meet standards of theoretical rationality, we are hardly committed to the thought that we thereby care more about rationality than we care about the substance of our inquiry. Regulative rules may serve what we value. We think that caring about theoretical rationality is part of caring about our other projects because rationality has instrumental value.[6] But of course sometimes it does not—as when we may recognize that false belief will facilitate some important activity. However we diagnose the tension in such cases, the very fact that there is tension would seem to undermine any automatic translation from regulative to value priority.

If theoretical rationality draws authority from its relation to conditions of success in action and belief, perhaps the problem with impartial morality is that it does not serve our purposes. So it cannot just be part of caring about what we care about. An instrumental claim is made on behalf of morality by some contract theorists.[7] But it is hard to see how such a claim could be supported in Kantian ethics, given its rejection of heteronomous (subjective, interest-based) foundations and its commitment to there being substantive moral questions about ends. Morality can be seen as the expression of a highest-order rational interest (as it is in Rawls), but that does not join the question of the relations between morality and interests per se, and motives of connection in particular.

One might argue that, just as theoretical rationality and prudential practical rationality have their authority based in the fact that we are interest and truth pursuers, so morality has its authority based in some equi-primordial fact—say, of our sociality. We need not take the Humean circumstances of justice to be the full terms that define the moral agenda for success as a human being among others (of our kind, language, culture).[8] Along these lines, morality would be necessary (and in that sense instrumental) given the complex of requirements needed to support acceptable or suitable conditions of sociality. There is much to find attractive in this way of proceeding. And if sociality involved connection (as partiality) in an essential way, it would certainly ease the tension between morality and connection. But it is not clear what sociality in this role involves. And it is not in any case a form of argument that is readily available to the Kantian.

Where does this leave us? I want to accept that it is reasonable to expect a moral theory to give noninstrumental expression to the role that sociality and the partiality of connection play in a human life. To show that and how

6. In a Humean mood, one might conjecture that what we take theoretical rationality to be is the manner of thinking that promotes our ends: the method of thinking that works.

7. David Gauthier, in *Morals by Agreement* (Oxford: Oxford University Press, 1986), offers an extremely sophisticated version of such an argument.

8. An example of such an account can be found in Stuart Hampshire, *Innocence and Experience* (Cambridge: Harvard University Press, 1989).

Kantian ethics does this, we must restart the discussion taking instruction from the fact that the affective life is not in general independent of various norms of rationality. This creates space for the claim that connection itself could be partially dependent on or a function of moral value.

II

We begin then with acknowledgment that intimacy and connection are necessary not just to a happy human life but to the form of life we call human. (This is to be understood in the sense that deprivation of the possibility of intimacy and connection threatens a person's humanity—thus the peculiar violence of solitary confinement.[9]) And the relationships between parents and children, between friends, lovers, neighbors, are essentially partial. It is because someone is *my* neighbor, lover, or child that I have reasons for action of a certain sort. Having these relationships is to have these reasons. They are reasons of considerable strength and priority, and they are reasons such that acting on them (and not on other reasons that can produce the same outcomes) is important to maintaining the relationships that generate them. The importance of these reasons derives from connections of feeling, familiarity, love.

If my child is among those who are at risk, I do not act for my child as a moral agent but as a mother. That is to say, even when morality permits mothers to act for their children first among others (and it will not always do this), I do not act for my child because morality permits it, but because I am his mother. To be a parent is to be a person constituted by a set of motives and reasons for action. This is a matter of personal identity. The strength of these reasons, their priority and the fact that acting on them gives expression to constitutive commitments, all add to the sense that moral reasons—reasons that do not arise directly from the natural affective connection between parent and child—are out of place here.[10]

There have been different philosophical responses to these facts.[11] Some suppose they show the limits of morality as regulative of our concerns.[12]

---

9. That someone might choose a solitary life or live well without intimate connection to others no more undermines this fact about human beings than extreme physical stoicism or a high pain threshold undermines the fact that physical assault interferes with successful human activity.

10. Thus Freud identifies an antisocial rather than a presocial role for the family in the "origins of society." But then, as he sees it, there is a primal antagonism between the partiality of family and the sociality of "fraternal" bonds. See his *Civilization and Its Discontents* (New York: Norton, 1962), chap. 3.

11. I view them as facts about feelings we take to be reasons.

12. Williams' influential notion of constitutive "ground projects" provides the most direct version of this view (see his "Persons, Character and Morality," in *Moral Luck*).

Not only are moral reasons not ubiquitous, but they must stand aside when they conflict with personal commitments that are constitutive of selves. Others do not find in the facts reason to question the authority of morality but rather the claim of impartial morality to be the paradigm of moral concern. So, it may be claimed, just these sorts of reasons, with their grounding in feeling and connection, provide the model for a "morality of care" or, as some have argued, for the distinctive moral perspective of women.[13] With either response, any claim for the priority of impartial morality is rejected as a devaluing of constitutive human concerns.

Such arguments against impartial morality are based on the feeling that our commitments and relationships of connection are sometimes of greater or deeper importance than those of impartial morality. But because it feels this way is a reason to take such feelings seriously, not a reason to give their claims automatic authority. For example, part of what growing up as a parent involves is the recognition of the place and point of such feelings. I think it is generally true that you feel like hurting anyone who causes your child undeserved pain, but that is not sufficient reason to do it. That someone close to you may suffer terribly in failing to get what he wants is not reason to make it happen when that is inappropriate. Sometimes it is the welfare of the loved one that is jeopardized by what one would do out of feeling. So the feeling needs to mature (or we who have the feeling need to mature); we need to be able to ask whether a particular expression of love is good for the one loved. And we sometimes need to let changes in those we love change our feelings (or what will count as expression of those feelings).

Since accepting limits set by autonomy, maturation, and change do not necessarily interfere with the way our supporting actions give expression to our connection with others, why should we be so easily disposed to accept that morality will interfere? We mistake the nature of feelings and their role in constituting our character to think that they are "original existences" whose modification cannot or should not be tolerated.

Let us look a little closer at the moral dimension of a relationship of connection. In addition to involving a deep bond of connection, parent-to-child is a relationship of *trust* between unequals: an essential kind of moral relationship that Annette Baier has argued cannot be expressed in impartial morality. Trust, as Baier describes it, is a noncontractual moral relationship between persons where there is vulnerability on the one hand and an implied reliance on good will and caring on the other (explicit or not, conscious or not). Because they are centered on cool, voluntary relationships between

13. In addition to Gilligan and some of the essays in the Kittay and Myers volume, see also Nel Noddings, *Caring: A Feminine Approach to Ethics and Moral Education* (Berkeley: University of California Press, 1984).

equals, Baier contends that moral theories such as Kant's cannot provide guidance in these regions. Yet, as we must agree, "a complete moral philosophy would tell us how and why we should act and feel toward others in relationships of shifting and varying power asymmetry and shifting and varying intimacy."[14]

If there is tension between trust and the morality of impartiality, there is no secure alliance between trust and partiality.[15] From the fact that my child trusts that my concern for him will lead me to guard and preserve his well-being as I can, it does not follow that I violate his trust if I refrain from doing some things that will benefit him (because they are wrong or unfair) or if I act for someone else first, as when I tend to the younger child hurt in the playground or expend finite resources on a needier sibling. What my son has reason to trust is that I am committed to his well-being: among the things that matter to me most and that will determine how I act is that he do well and flourish. But, as I must often remind him (and myself), his interests are not the only ones I care about (there are not only my friends, my spouse, my students, and myself, but sometimes complete strangers or causes that claim my attention and resources), and further he will do fine, indeed he will often do better, if he relies on me less and if my life is increasingly separate from his.[16] Because I care about him, he can trust that I will count his well-being as among the basic facts that determine what I do, not as special reasons at work when I have to choose between his and someone's equal or greater claim, but as a set of changing needs that will partially determine the shape of my life.

How we understand the role of impartial morality here depends on how we represent its place in deliberation. I want to suggest that failure to recognize two quite different models of practical concern and deliberation leads to serious distortion of the problem thought to be posed by impartial morality to concerns of trust and connection. I will call them, for reasons that should become clear, the "plural interest" and the "deliberative field" models.

According to the plural-interest model, where there is connection, there are those I care about, and the effect of my caring is to give their interests greater deliberative weight: for me. They matter more. And they matter more to me because I care about them. When I need to balance or weigh interests—should I do some good for my son or his friend—my son counts more. Of course I have a variety of interests and concerns, and they have

14. Annette Baier, "Trust and Anti-Trust," *Ethics* 96 (1986), 252.

15. This is just an extension of Baier's point, reinforcing the claim that a moral theory must have the means to talk about connection, inequality, power, and such. A moral theory that cannot get it right about these relationships cannot generate the appropriate regulative norms.

16. Of course I would not have said this when he was six months old. But that is just the point.

different weights (as I care about them and as they matter directly or instrumentally). The interests of my child weigh more than the next career step, which weighs more than my enjoyment of movies, and morality (if it has regulative priority) weighs more than all of the above. Deliberation involves further weighing and balancing. Interinterest comparisons of various sorts will be necessary. The descriptions of interests will often need to be more qualified and situationally explicit: a minor desire of my child won't count against going to a film I've waited years to see. There will be tension between looking to get the most interests satisfied and getting the most important interests satisfied. Over all these differently weighted interests loom the requirements of impartial morality in which I am not only supposed to have an interest, but an interest sufficient to support its supremely regulative role.[17]

On the plural-interest model, when morality contends with attachments it forces one against the grain, attacking the immediacy of connection. It would be natural to feel hostile to or alienated from the requirements of morality if they in this way denied a deeply felt claim of partiality. I do not mean to suggest that one would necessarily feel alienated whenever one acts for morality in a context in which connection draws you in a different direction. There are many times, especially with children, when the fact that a choice must be made impartially provides the occasion for useful moral lessons. In such circumstances, acting impartially expresses trustworthiness. The problem arises when it looks like "over here" is what I most care about, what I want to happen (and cannot not want to happen), but "over there" is what impartial morality demands. There is then deep conflict and tension. And when impartial morality wins, it is not only at the expense of what I most care about, but it provides no deliberative space even to acknowledge my concerns. The fact that I care about my son in no way affects the deliberative outcome.

If this is the way I see it, I can learn to take these losses, even to believe they are necessary. They are the price you pay for . . . and then some account of the role of morality that presumably justifies such losses by pointing to greater gains elsewhere. What other kind of justification of morality could work, given the imposition of losses? And if I am unmoved by the greater gains to be had elsewhere, often gains to be had by those other than myself or those I care about—not because I am selfish, but because of who I am (a person who cares about such and such)—then my

---

17. It is not a necessary feature of the model that impartial morality have this role. I present it in this form because some such version of the plural-interest model is commonly introduced in preparation for criticism of the implausibility of the demands of impartial morality. Although I am primarily concerned with the limits of this model to represent that claim of morality, the causes of its failure in this area suggest more general inadequacies.

life will not seem to be valued from the moral point of view. I will act either morally badly or against myself. Clearly, so long as we stick with the plural-interest model, we will have difficulty negotiating the terrain between impartial morality and attachment.

Among the elements of a full moral theory, we should find an account of how one is to integrate the requirements of morality into one's life. One could be someone whose interest in morality was an interest (if a very strong or strongest interest) among others. But such a connection to morality is not in itself morally neutral; it will follow from the substantive nature of moral requirements. There is no unique atheoretic model of a morally serious or committed moral agent. Depending on how this feature of a moral theory is elaborated, there will be more than one answer to the question of the effects of moral requirements on the motives of connection. Since on the plural-interest model, commitment to morality is at the expense of other commitments, especially attachments, there will be reason to favor a different model if it is better able to integrate these elements in a morally good life.

On the second model, deliberation addresses a field only partially shaped by those commitments, concerns, and relationships that determine my conception of the good. They stand there as myself—as interests that I need no further or instrumental reason to care about. It is not that I care about my son and therefore, when interests are to be weighed, his weigh more. Rather, because I care about my son—because of the way I care about my son—his interests (his good) are part of my good: *the* good as I see it. But just as I know in advance that I cannot do whatever will promote my own well-being, so I know in advance and as part of my caring that I may not be able to promote his good in circumstances where it is inappropriate to determine the effective practical weight of interests by how much I care about them.

According to this deliberative-field model, the practical self does not have as its major task negotiating a settlement among independent competing claims. Insofar as one has interests and commitments, one is a human self. But a human life is not the result of a "bundle" of competing interests (among which is an interest in morality). One's interests are present on a deliberative field that contains everything that gives one reasons. Thus, in addition to interests and attachments, there are also grounds of obligation, principles of prudential rationality, and, depending on the individual, a more or less complex conception of the Good. Not everything that may seek a place on my deliberative field is good for me to have there: bad habits, destructive relationships, incompatible goals and projects. And if there is a real question about what enters (or remains on) the deliberative field—this is often a question about ends—the conditions for accepting desires or interests as ends may (and often will) shape the result.

An agent with a deliberative field partly constructed by moral principles recognizes from the outset, in the adoption of ends, that pursuit of important goals may unforeseeably lead one to means that are morally inappropriate (not permissible). The commitment to pursue an end is always conditional; this is so whether the ends are ends of interest or necessary ends. In this way ends are absorbed into a moral structure as they enter the deliberative field.

This resetting of ends in the deliberative field is not unique to moral requirements. Something analogous occurs because of potential practical conflict between different nonmoral goals. Wanting both to have a career and a family, I can pursue both and hope for the best, or I can give one end priority (absolute or weighted) over the other, or I can make action on one conditional on noninterference with the other. With other ends— say, teaching and writing—I have additional possibilities, including the revision of each of these ends to include aspects of the other (I value my teaching as an integral part of the process that leads me to successful writing, or vice versa). These need not be once and for all decisions: my sense of the relative importance of ends may change, the likelihood of conflict may diminish, still other relevant interests may come on the scene. But having set ends in a complex deliberative framework, my sense of loss on abandoning one is different than it would be if I thought of myself simply as acting for diverse and separate goals, having to give up or limit or frustrate one for the sake of another. Acting from a deliberative framework, I am in a better position to accept the outcome. This is not a matter of resignation so much as acknowledgment. Without such a framework, the decision will seem more contingent—more a matter of bad luck—and the outcome arbitrary.[18]

To make sense of the deliberative-field model (and so, I believe, of Kantian ethics[19]), we must resist the tendency to think of the Good—an agent's conception of what is good—as a composite cluster of objects of desire, perhaps structured by priority principles and other success-oriented practical devices external to the ends we have because of the desires we have. This leaves the desire-object relation too much intact, with the agent passive with respect to her bundle of desires. Desires do not give reasons for action: they may explain why such and such is a reason for action, or

18. I do not mean to imply that desire must be understood to have its practical effect only in one of these two ways—in the deliberative field or as an intensity-weighted reason. There are accounts of desire that build reasons into them. In the tradition of Kant criticism, however, the simpler Humean model of desire has been thought to suffice in showing the weaknesses of the Kantian account of practical activity. The deliberative-field model is intended both to describe more accurately Kantian practical deliberation and activity and to show certain limits of the Humean model.

19. Textual and other support for this claim can be found in Chapter 8.

even why something can be an effective reason for action, but the desire itself is not a reason. One can take the fact of a desire to be a reason, but that just is to hold that desire, or this desire, is good.[20] Nor is it enough to replace desire with "end that it is rational or good to have." That still suggests discrete sets of interests and ends. What is missing—what you are supposed to learn as a maturing agent—is the integration and transformation of the ends in light of one another, of one's practical situation, and of one's conception of place and importance understood through the regulative principles—aesthetic, moral, prudential—one accepts. One has, or tries to have, a good life.

We will be inclined to view deliberation differently as we take ourselves to be either active or passive with respect to our desires. If we take the paradigmatic deliberative situation to be either means-end calculation or the resolution of conflict between ends, it will look as if our starting point is the pursuit of discrete goods (the objects of desires or interests) whose compatibility is a matter of luck. Now sometimes this is just the way things are. Circumstances can sharpen conflict, as they can make deliberation look like a search for the least costly compromise. But focusing on these cases reinforces a sense of our passivity as agents: what Kant meant, I believe, by a heteronomy of the will.

Our sense of things is different if we look instead at the ways we are or can be active with respect to our desires. We have desires we do not want to act on; we have desires we act on but do not value; we come to discover that some of what we want is caused by needs that would be better met some other way (as when an underlying insecurity leads to placing excessive demands on others). Refusing desires of the last two types is importantly not like restraining one's desire for sweets: a kind of desire we like to think we can turn our back on at will (or fail at controlling because of "weakness of will," a kind of muscular insufficiency). Activity involves more than effective second-order wants.

When, for example, I hear my mother's parental anxieties in my own voice as I criticize my son, I cannot resolve the problem I discover just by abandoning some end or disowning some desire, however much distress I feel about what I am doing. Part of what I discover in these moments is who I am—or who I am as a parent. I listen and find out what I desire. But then it is not enough to say that I do not want to act on these desires, and also not enough to say that I do not want to have them. I want them not to have a place in the complex of desires and thoughts that constitute myself

---

20. I have borrowed this way of putting things from Philippa Foot (unpublished manuscript, 1988), who sees confusion about this occurring because often it is reasonable to satisfy desires. If we imagine a very different sort of creature who had desires that were not in general good (for it) to satisfy, it is not clear how we would then regard desires.

as a parent. This may be no easy thing, for the very desires I would disavow may hold together things I like about myself as a parent.

Someone who is otherwise a good friend cannot come through when there is illness involved; he simply cannot see what there is to do. Suppose he comes to believe that he acts inadequately in these circumstances. What can he do? He wants to act as a good friend. He has the relevant ends. The problem is that illness makes him panic. Perhaps as a child he was made to feel responsible for a sick parent. Now, confronted with illness in others, he feels inadequate; he withdraws in the face of what he feels will be certain failure.

When we discover that with our children or our friends we are acting in ways that do not match our values or ideals, the practical task involves special difficulties, in the sense that we must come to see why we would do what we do not seem to want to do (this is *not* weakness of will). Success at this task may still leave us trying to figure out what to do with, or what we are able to do with, what we find. This is a function of what we might think of as the enmeshedness or even geology of desire.

Encountering (or more often stumbling against) such a complex, we may be enlightened or transformed, or moved to therapy, or despair. Affective disorders alert us to inertial features of character. We cannot just choose to care (about some things), and we cannot just prize out an unwanted desire by identifying and rejecting its object. So also we come to see that you cannot just add ends: not only because there may be conflict in realizing ends but also because the adoption of some ends resonates in the deliberative field. For the good friend to lose his panic in the face of illness, he may have to revise his relations with his mother (now and in the past).

The point here is not to argue for therapy or discuss the relative merits of deep versus shallow psychological change, but to let the difficulty of these matters direct us to a different picture (or set of pictures) about the Good as the complex object not of desire, but of practical agency.

If the attempt to abandon ends may draw us into more complexity than expected, we should not suppose that adopting an end is any simple matter. Ends are not adopted in isolation from one another. It is not only that their joint pursuit may not be possible. Adopting an end is (or can be) wanting some interest to be effective in my life. This may alter other ends I already have and affect what ends I may come to have. Wanting friendship to play a greater role in my life does not just mean creating more time for friends (and so less for the pursuit of other ends). It may make me see in my present attachment to other ends a lack of concern for others. Or vice versa: coming to take my work more seriously may reveal a will to distraction in my absorption with others. (When everything works for the best, this kind of insight need not lead to a conflict with friendship: it can make me a better friend.)

Because of the complexity of relations among ends, it can be difficult to predict the outcome of deliberation—for another agent, but equally sometimes for ourselves. We may not know in advance what impact circumstances will have on ends. When situations are new or complex, what an agent wants can depend on her response to the situations she finds herself in and on the way she makes use of whatever knowledge and sensitivity she can bring to bear. Some deliberative outcomes will reshape ends; others can lead her to see the world in a different way. Deliberation itself will then reshape or reconfigure the deliberative field.

Deliberation structured by *substantive* regulative principles involves still more. If in all of my relationships I am to treat people as ends, then as this conception has deliberative priority, what is possible for me in relationships will be different. My ends of friendship and intimacy will not be what they would have been otherwise. It is not that I must replace motives of connection with moral motives; I will have *different* motives of connection. Perhaps I will be more sensitive to problems of exclusion or of fairness. Perhaps I will be less tempted to interfere "for the best." It does not follow from the interpenetration of motives of connection with moral concerns that these will be the changes: what the changes are will depend on what I discover about the structure and tendencies of my relationships.

This transformational process does not go only one way. Commitment to treat others as ends (or in accordance with the dictates of some moral conception or ideal) does not by itself guide deliberation. As I come to understand more of what is involved in friendship and intimacy, so I also come to see more of what the moral requirement amounts to. Without knowledge of how intimacy engages vulnerabilities, I cannot see that or how certain behaviors which could be acceptable among strangers are impermissibly manipulative among intimates, and vice versa. Where power and inequality mix with intimacy, questions of exploitation and abuse are raised. Such questions are not part of the concept of treating persons as ends. They are what we discover treating persons as ends amounts to, given what human relationships tend to be like, or what particular relationships involve. Without such knowledge, moral judgment is not possible.[21]

Let us briefly retrace our steps. The sense of conflict and loss that we think follows from the regulation of relationships and attachments by impartial moral principles might instead be a function of the way we understand the connection between ends and deliberative principles. My discussion of the difference between activity and passivity with respect to our desires and ends was aimed, on the one hand, to defeat a picture of an autarchy of ends slotted into a legalistic or merely formal deliberative framework and, on

---

21. A more general conclusion of this sort is argued for in Chapter 4, section III.

the other hand, to replace that picture with the idea of the Good as a constructed object of practical agency.[22] Locating attachments in a deliberative field, we uncover a mutual practical dependence between formal moral principle (as it applies to us) and the structure of attachment.

Some resistance to this move may come from a presumed tension between moral and personal reasons that follows from a split in the practical between the moral and the natural. There is the thought that personal attachments—and especially what is good in them—are in some special way natural or spontaneous or pure. So one might worry that moral transformation might involve loss of this natural good. This concern is to be met with the reminder that "natural" relationships are, among other things, the locales of abuse, infantilization, exploitation, and other sins of intimacy. Intimacy may be a natural need, or arise from natural motives, but the relationships among adults usually are, when healthy, complex and mediated descendants of spontaneous or natural attachments.

When there is moral criticism of a relationship, we should not think that morality aims to replace the structure of attachment. Love for another may be necessary to change a relationship whose premises or practices are morally faulty. Morality alone can do no more than indicate the fault and give reason not to accept terms of relationship in which the fault is embodied; it cannot by itself direct the parties to a satisfactory resolution *within* the framework of intimacy.

As our conception of the Good becomes increasingly complex (involving morality but also work and children and the various kinds of intimacy), our understanding of our activities and attachments should reflect that complexity. This is not a loss of innocence that we have reason to reject (or rationally regret).

If the deliberative field were empty[23] until the agent brought to it—from outside, as it were—her interests, projects, and commitments, looking to use its principles to maximize satisfaction while attending to the demands of morality, one could safely predict the frustration of one for the satisfaction of the other. If the deliberative field is not empty at the outset, things look different. The alternative, or Kantian, model suggests that we think of an agent's deliberative field as containing representations of her interests, projects, and commitments that have been "normalized" to varying degrees to the principles of practical agency, both moral and nonmoral. Kantian

22. See John Rawls, "Themes in Kant's Moral Philosophy," in *Kant's Transcendental Deductions*, ed. E. Forster (Stanford: Stanford University Press, 1989), pp. 90–95.

23. Using metaphors this way will eventually—if not immediately—be misleading. But since all talk about deliberation is metaphoric (formalized versions no less so), the limits and presuppositions of the different pictures are worth exploration.

deliberation requires the prior processing of the material it takes up. Maxims and ends we know to be impermissible, if attractive, are represented as such; tasks we would take up as means toward desired goals are not represented as independently valuable (unless they also are); and so on. The normalization of the material of interest and desire to the principles of practical agency minimizes the degree to which deliberation and choice must involve sorting and weighing things of incommensurable or conflicting value.

Desires and interests are normalized to beliefs and values as well. Take a nonmoral example. Suppose it is normal (given certain patterns of upbringing, socialization, and such) that, faced with certain kinds of situations, people have sharply competitive reactions. For one sort of person, these reactions may be taken as the direct and natural response to a challenge, and so give reason to act competitively. Someone else may have a view about the etiology of such reactions in herself (anxiety, status hunger, aggression) that leads her to conclude that they should not be taken at face value: in and of themselves they are not reason-giving. If one describes the effects of such psychological facts as introducing a deliberative problem when circumstances provoke the reaction in question, the second person is misdescribed in an important way. Suppose, in addition to recognizing the origins of the competitive impulse in herself, the second person believes that the kinds of action it generates are by and large counterproductive (or just contrary to what she holds is good). She need not be faced with a choice each time the reaction occurs, for she does not regard the reaction as making a claim or having automatic reason-giving status. One might say that the impulse to competition enters her deliberative field already discounted, if it enters at all.

Discounted impulses need not be entirely counted out. The agent in the second case may believe that letting a competitive response regulate action can sometimes be useful. But even when it is, the impulse to competition is normalized in the agent's deliberative field to the discounted value. (That is, it is indulged for a special purpose; acting on it is not, in the usual way, an expression of competitiveness.) One could, I suppose, think that such impulses are held in check and then in special circumstances set free. But it seems truer to the pattern of increased and practically effective self-knowledge that the desires themselves be modified, or at least be under principled constraint in the way they are given access to the deliberative field. It is not just the pressure they exert that gains them entry.[24]

---

24. The psychological models that moral theorists use in these contexts are frequently unwarrantedly simple. We might want to think about sublimation or other strategies of object shifting (the mechanism of delayed gratification involves not just a willingness to wait for some often indefinite good, but also a release of focused task-oriented energy).

The advantage gained from taking natural motives to be normalized to the principles of practical agency is that it eliminates the deliberative quandary of having always to choose between natural motives and moral motives (or even motives of prudence). Without this, the tension between natural and moral concerns seems unavoidable: the tension will recur within the domain of the moral between virtues and moral requirements insofar as the virtues rely on natural motives (like compassion). If the natural motive of compassion has as its object the well-being of another, normalized compassion—concern for another framed by a practical awareness of the place of compassion in the moral life (suppose this is right)—would not shift the object of compassionate concern. It is still the welfare of the other that is sought in acting. What would change is the impact of the motive in the deliberative field. A natural motive is as effective as it is strong. A normalized motive is effective as a function of its place in the deliberative field: expressing more than the natural impulse at its origin, standing aside (not pressing its claim) as there are more important concerns present, but also drawing strength from its place in an overall practical conception.[25]

There is great complexity here. Motives can be embedded in or connected to other motives. Some concerns can absorb deep constraints without damage, others are fragile. Requiring civility while doing the grocery shopping introduces no grave distortions in the activity. A demand that one justify all nonnecessary expenses from the point of view of world hunger might well interfere with reasonable enjoyments. But this is a problem, if it is, of a substantive moral requirement. It does not follow from the formal fact that motives (or interests or concerns) are normalized to impartial moral principles.

Let me be clear about what I am *not* trying to say. The normalization of a natural motive does not eliminate the possibility of conflict with other moral considerations and claims. This discussion has been about the *structure* of deliberative commitments. The likelihood that the world will throw up difficulties is not diminished, though perhaps one will be, in a manner of speaking, better prepared when they occur.

Still one might worry that too little is left for deliberation to do because the process of "normalizing" has covertly usurped its work. If one thinks that deliberation brings its principles to bear on raw data, this would be so. Part of what I have wanted to present here are reasons for thinking this not true to experience. Two larger theoretical concerns give me confidence that this way of treating deliberation is appropriate. First is the fact that Kantian deliberation, if it in any way engages with the CI procedure, applies to maxims, and maxims require exactly the normalized input I have de-

25. Bishop Butler's distinction between the strength and the authority of a motive might help here. See *Five Sermons* (Indianapolis: Hackett, 1983), p. 39.

scribed.[26] Second is a view about what a practical commitment to morality amounts to. The moral agent (certainly the Kantian moral agent) is not one who has some set of desires and interests and then introduces an onlay of controlling principles and rules (with a new motive to get the regulative authority right). She is rather someone who takes the fact of morality to be constitutive of herself (or her identity as a moral person) and for whom the normalization of desires and interests is a way of making them her own.

Deliberation is not called for unless the agent finds reasons in her circumstances of action or choice to believe that normal moral constraints should not apply. So, for example, in cases of threat or danger or pressing need, one may need to deliberate to determine whether such facts ground a rebuttal of the moral prohibition on, say, deceit. But such facts ground a rebuttal, if they do, not because of the degree of one's concern but because they mark the presence of additional moral facts in an agent's deliberative field.

The upshot of this discussion for the questions with which we started can be put somewhat simply. When understood within the deliberative-field model, the regulative or transformative priority of impartial morality does not cause the loss or corruption of motives of connection. We can resist the idea that any constraint of a natural motive, any move to relocate it in a structure of justification, gives it a new object. Once attachment is moved into the deliberative field, however, we must acknowledge that strength or intimacy of attachment alone does not provide grounds to rebut the demands of moral requirement.

If in deliberation moral requirement is not external to other motives, and if our understanding of morality and attachment are mutually transformative, then the motives of connection themselves can come to express the fact that attachment takes place in a world that attachment alone does not create.

III

Having argued that there is no obvious or necessary incompatibility between impartial ethics and the value of attachment, we still need to consider arguments that Kantian ethics is inimical to a sound notion of the person as moral subject.

A typical argument goes this way. In Kantian ethics, we are moral agents insofar as we have practical reason (an autonomous will). Other facts about us—what we feel, how we are connected to others, that we are empirically, socially, and historically situated—are not what make us moral agents. Since "Kantian" persons have moral value insofar as they are

26. This is argued in Chapter 4, section I.

moral agents, the moral value of persons does not reflect their situation or attachments (neither that we in general have them nor how, in particular, having them makes a difference). If these omitted features are central to our ideas of what a person is (and of the good for persons), then the substantive normative claims of Kantian ethics are derived from an inadequate and impoverished concept of the person as moral agent.[27] If this is true, it is a serious problem. For even if, as argued in section II, moral deliberation is informed by the facts of our attachments, interests, and specific needs, the moral principles that construct the deliberative field have their source in the "pure" autonomous self.

Kantian autonomy is the property that the rational will has of being self-legislating. This is a metaphysical claim about the nature of rational agency. Its role is to explain both the possibility and the authority of morality. Nothing follows from it to the effect that persons are radically separate, nor that insofar as we take the moral point of view we are not to pay attention to the distinctive features of other persons. As I need not, because I am an agent with interests, look out at the world and others from a fortress of own-interests and desires, so equally, as a moral agent, I do not look out on a world of featureless moral agents because I have an autonomous will. Whether I am preoccupied with myself or engaged with others and sensitive to differences depends on my circumstances and my conception of the Good. Perhaps it is this last bit that is the source of the problem.

Kantian ethics constrains a conception of the Good by requiring that one's deliberative field be given a certain structure (a structure implied by the nature of rational agency itself). In particular, we are never to act on a maxim that we cannot will all rational beings to act on. But, it is argued, this cannot be the right way to derive moral principles for persons, since filtering for what is possible for all rational beings (or even all human beings) cannot tell the full moral story about fully embodied and socially connected persons in specific historical settings.

We can see some of the force of this concern by looking at a second kind of criticism of Kantian autonomy. The identification of Kantian autonomy as the property of a rational will seems to ignore morally important ways in which we judge that human beings are or can fail to be autonomous. If one has Kantian autonomy as a rational being (able to act on self-given principles), Kantian autonomy may be a necessary but not a sufficient condition for "real" moral autonomy. Ordinarily, we have reason to think that the autonomous person is not merely one who can act on principles

---

27. As one critic writes, "Why assume that the sole form of human autonomy adequate to support our moral theory is one that an agent [has] in isolation from her contingent ends, her culture, history, and relations to others?" Sally Sedgwick, "Can Kant's Ethics Survive the Feminist Critique?" *Pacific Philosophical Quarterly* 71 (1990), 22.

but is, rather, the person whose situation or upbringing yields not only a character capable of practically effective critical reflection but also a character moved by desires and interests that are in some important sense her own: desires and interests that are neither the result of coercion nor the products of institutionalized oppression.[28] Lack of autonomy in this sense is compatible with Kantian autonomy. The question then is whether the Kantian conception of autonomy obscures a real issue of human autonomy, and, if it does, whether it implies that oppression cannot interfere with the most important kind of human freedom.

I want to argue that the Kantian conception of the autonomous agent neither elevates rationality to the only thing that really counts about persons nor forces us to deny that agency is compromised by the circumstances of oppression. It is true that the "worth beyond price" of the Kantian agent is in her autonomous will. This is the ground of the claim that persons are not to be valued only for use. The contested question is whether the constraints on action that follow from this ignore the real circumstances and full nature of persons.

The best way to answer the question is to look carefully at the way specific constraints work. What I will offer here is a summary examination of the restrictions on deceit and coercion: actions that are the archetypes of impermissible use of another. What the restrictions show is that the subject of moral protection is the fully situated human agent.

Deceit is an attempt to control how another will choose to act through the introduction of relevant false beliefs into her deliberative circumstances. In coercion, threats or force alter deliberative circumstances by evoking or strengthening desires that will bring the victim to act as the coercer wills. In both cases, the impermissible actions constitute an assault on the situated integrity of the victim's agency. You would not, for what deceit or coercion do to you, cease being an autonomous agent. Deceit and coercion invade the morally supported boundaries between autonomous agents in that the aggressor regards the *situated* will—the will as it draws reasons from beliefs and desires—as a possible means to her ends.

This story does not quite describe the moral wrong involved in deceit, for I look to control the will of another when I introduce true beliefs to get someone to act as I will. The problem clearly is not control of the will in the sense of contributory cause to a deliberative outcome, since that is the case whether what I tell you is true or (known by me to be) false.

What others tell us is one of the normal ways we have access to the facts in our circumstances of action (and belief). This is an inescapable fact about

---

28. I do not mean to suggest that such desires are easy to identify, though at critical times they may come to the surface not only as plainly alien—not mine—but as identifiably other (certain desires for approval, dispositions to defer, and so on).

human agency. Our reliance on what others say creates an area of vulner-ability—a point of access to the will. Although what I want in telling you the truth can be the same as when what I say is false—that you do what I will—the full story about how I am acting can be, in morally important ways, different. In some cases when I say what is true, I tell the truth only as what I need to say in order to get you to do what I will. I have no commitment to telling you the truth in telling you the truth. If the truth will not bring you to do what I will, I am ready to tell you something else.[29] When, by contrast, I tell you the truth as truth, though I believe that if you know this truth you will do what I will (and I even tell it to you wanting you to act as I will), I tell you the truth as information of use to you as well as me. Insofar as I conceive of what I give you as information, the intent is not to control your will, though it is to contribute to the causal (here, deliberative) conditions of your action. On this principle of action, I would not tell you something if I believed it was not the case.

Of course things are not so simple. If I tell misleading partial truths, I am equally taking advantage of our situation in order to create a view of the circumstances of action which will lead you to act as I want. This kind of truthtelling is a kind of deceit. You take me to be giving relevant informa-tion, in part because I lead you to believe that is what I am doing, but also in part because it is a normal expectation that I know of and rely on. This expectation is for you a condition of belief formation. That is why you must not catch on that I am controlling the flow of information if I am to get you to act as I will. You are deceived in that you are brought (encouraged) to believe falsely that I have told you whatever I know that is relevant to your deliberation, choice, and action. And this is why when I tell you a partial truth I am manipulating your will.

The importance of this for our question about Kantian agency lies in the fact that what counts as deceit varies with the persons involved, the social conditions of expectations, particular practices, and so on. If impermissible actions are those that fail in respect for the value of the autonomous agent, respect for the autonomy of another person in cases where we wish to influence deliberation requires detailed attention to specific facts about them. This will include facts about relationships (where one person has authority over another, or responsibility for another, expectations are affected), as well as facts about the social world that bear on their circum-stances of action.

The point of morality, one might say, is to regulate what can go on given the vulnerabilities of persons as agents—vulnerabilities we all share as human rational beings *and* vulnerabilities that are specific to our situations and relationships. Thus the constraints that morality imposes reflect the

29. There are problems involving counterfactuals that we can ignore here.

real conditions of effective human rational agency: the aspects of a person's circumstances of action (or deliberation) that are situated, historical, empirical. As I read it, Kantian morality not only does not ignore these features, but it makes them central to its "derivation of duties."

In effect, much of the critique of the Kantian conception of autonomy confuses autonomy and agency. Autonomy is the condition of the will that makes agency possible. If we were not rational beings, we would not have wills that could be interfered with. But *agency* is not completely described by identifying a will as rational. As human agents we are not distinct from our contingent ends, our culture, our history, or our actual and possible relations to others. Agency is situated. The empirical and contingent conditions of effective agency set the terms of permissibility because it is through effective agency that autonomy is expressed (made real). Here is a place where consequences matter.

The implications of the idea of deriving Kantian duties from the situation of real agents are far-reaching. If agency is situated, the conditions of agency will not be uniform. Certain features will remain constant: that we have vulnerable bodies, are mortal, are capable of acquiring new skills, that we are deceivable and vulnerable to duress. Other features will be a function of the social world in which a person acts. Matters of institutionalized subordination, dependency, questions of gender, class, and race, will need to be taken into account. This encourages us to move beyond the "agent-to-agent" limitations of traditional interpretations of Kantian ethics, where everything that is morally relevant is found in the actions and intentions of single, separate persons.[30]

Suppose, for example, social circumstances are such that the range of successful activities is dramatically limited by inability to read and write (both in terms of opportunities to act but also for gaining skills and developing talents). Illiteracy prevents the acquisition of information necessary to effective action. In such circumstances, denial of opportunity to become literate could be judged an impermissible refusal (under mutual aid) to provide for agency-necessary needs. Since literacy is not normally a good that functions outside an institutional context—schools, publishers—the moral failure in providing real access to literacy skills will not be one that is best or completely described as occurring between individuals. (I think a similar argument can be made for provision of a minimal standard of health

---

30. Textual support for such a move is not wanting. In elaborating the duties of beneficence, Kant attends to the special moral situation of the recipient of charity: a person receiving charity is in a position in which his dignity and sense of self-worth is fragile. Kant recommends that charity be given in such a way that the giver "make it felt that he is himself obliged by the other's acceptance or honored by it, hence that the duty is merely something that he owes" (DV453). And see Victor J. Seidler, *Kant, Respect, and Injustice* (London: Routledge and Kegan Paul, 1986), for a sensitive if highly critical treatment of Kant's views on these issues.

care.) It does not follow that one is committed to viewing literacy as necessarily making people better off regardless of their cultural circumstances. The point is to explain the circumstances in which literacy could become a moral requirement, the ground of a moral claim.[31]

In analogous fashion, there is room to talk about institutional or cultural assaults on the conditions of agency. If agent-to-agent coercion controls choice by manipulating desires (introducing penalties in order to block permissible choices), then when institutions penalize permissible choices, they act no less coercively. The chief difference in the moral analysis is, I think, that in the institutional case there can be coercion without specific intent. Quite apart from issues of dependency and lack of alternatives, it can be hard to understand the battered wife's refusal to leave her home, with its violence, without factoring in the effect of social pressures that measure adult success in terms of a woman's ability to maintain a marriage.[32]

On similar grounds I regard a recent controversy over the introduction of new brands of cigarettes targeted at particular, vulnerable groups as capturing the institutional variant of the wrong involved in agent-to-agent deceptive manipulation. Uptown and Dakota cigarettes were to be marketed to inner-city blacks and "virile females," respectively. Now the fact that advertising works by playing on beliefs and desires is not news. But since the conditions that make deceit possible vary from person to person and group to group, it is precisely the fine tuning of the ad campaign to trade on marks of social prestige among those both young and doubly disadvantaged that makes the moral case. (It is hard here not to see intent; but there will be other cases where the belief in the information conveyed is more credible. Certainly it was a stunning moment in the Uptown episode when a Philip Morris executive labeled as racist those who argued against the Uptown campaign on the grounds that it would exploit the special vulnerabilities of young blacks.)

On the basis of these brief remarks I want to offer two provisional conclusions. First, if agency is situated, then the fundamental moral equality of agents requires that we attend to difference when it affects the capacity for effective agency. Second, if agency is situated, and groups of people share vulnerabilities and needs that arise from institutional or nonuniversal cultural causes, then there are grounds for moral criticism of those causes that appeal to the same root values as ground agent-to-agent requirements.

---

31. Kant, of course, makes both education and welfare a moral task of the state (and as such the grounds for coercion through taxation). See *Metaphysical Elements of Justice* 326.
32. Lenore E. Walker, *The Battered Woman Syndrome* (New York: Springer, 1984).

This section began with a question about the relations among Kantian views of autonomy, rationality, and agential separateness. There has been no attempt to deny that autonomy and rationality are deeply connected and that both are the condition of our moral and practical capacities. On the other hand, the tremendous practical importance of autonomy and rationality in understanding the kind of agent we are does not force us to view ourselves as, from the moral point of view, wholly or essentially or even ideally rational. As we are practical agents—human agents—we are constituted by our needs, our interests, our beliefs, and our connections to others. Different aspects of our agency will be peculiar to our "natural" condition, our social circumstances, and our particular histories. We will be free human agents—ones whose actions express autonomy—as the actual conditions of our agency allow us to deliberate and act according to a conception of the Good that is constructed not only by moral requirements but also by the pursuit and critical attention to interests that we understand to be part of a good life.

10

Leaving Deontology Behind

IT SEEMS to me now incontrovertible that the chief source of misunderstanding of Kantian ethics is the almost universal commitment to treating it as a moral theory without a notion of value as its fundamental theoretical concept. It is a sign of the strength of this commitment that there is so little hesitation in the face of the *Groundwork*'s resonant opening. Kant may begin his argument with the announcement, "There is no possibility of thinking of anything at all in the world, or even out of it, which can be regarded as good without qualification, except a *good will,*" but the tradition holds fast to the idea that the goodness of the good will is a secondary or derivative matter of motivation, a function of attachment to prior and independent principles of right. In opposition to the tradition, I want to take seriously the claim that the *Groundwork* begins in "ordinary rational knowledge of morality" and that the task of philosophical ethics is not to correct ordinary knowledge, but to understand how it is possible.

Were we able to set aside the canon that sorts all moral theories as deontological or teleological[1]—with Kant the defining exemplar of the former—we might recognize in this opening sentence a variant on the familiar first move of classical ethics.[2] Indeed, I think an open-minded

---

1. This canon, like all others, has a history. The term "deontology" was coined by Jeremy Bentham as "a fit term to represent in the field of morals, the principle of Utilitarianism" (*Deontology,* 1834, p. 21). In the 1870s "deontology" was used by the idealists to translate *Pflichtenlehre* (duty-teaching), a term of art in German textbooks for the ethical teachings of the stoics. J. H. Muirhead is the first to use it in a two-part division of all ethical theories: the teleological (ethics of ends) and the deontological (ethics of duties and rules); see his *Rule and End in Morals* (Oxford: Oxford University Press, 1932). Muirhead argued that the history of ethics had a watershed in the stoics' misinterpretation of Aristotle's "rule of right reason," so that "a Rule according to which men should direct their conduct tended to take the place of the idea of an End or form of goodness to be realized in life." It is this "loss of vision" that becomes "the deontological point of view" (p. 6).

2. Kant explicitly endorses the classical *Nihil appetimus, nisi sub ratione boni* in the

reading of the first two paragraphs of the *Groundwork* would place their point and argument alongside the comparable first paragraphs of the *Nicomachean Ethics*. Both texts argue that the subject matter of ethics is the good (all action is for some end taken to be good), and that if anything is conditionally good (good for some things and not others, good in some circumstances and not others), there must be something that is unconditionally good (a final end). The primary object of ethical inquiry is this unconditioned good. At this point, the texts part company. Although pressing the details of the comparison is instructive—about Kant, but also about Aristotle—the point of insisting that the two texts can be compared is to make it easier to see the *Groundwork* embarking on a familiar path of inquiry into the nature of the good. Tradition aside, there is no good reason to suppose that the project of the *Groundwork* is best understood by discounting the claim of value with which it begins.[3]

I also believe that, understood this way, Kant begins just where one should. It is simply implausible to suppose that a moral theory could persuasively do its work without a grounding concept of value. According to canonical deontology, once we find out that some action x is morally required there is no sense to a further question: is it good (or of value) to do x? Surely this is a natural question. Perhaps the Kantian insistence that the condition for accepting moral requirements not be that they promote some other (and nonmoral) end is sometimes extended into the implausible claim that morality is without end or point at all. Such a move may even seem unavoidable given certain preconceptions about the possible answers to value questions.

Some may think that canonical deontology gets it right about Kant because no moral principles subtended from a concept of value can explain obligation: obligation requires practical necessitation independent of desire, and value guides action only through actual desire.[4] But Kant directs our attention to the concepts of obligation and duty because they hold the key to elucidating the concept of the unconditioned good (G397). While it is

---

Critique of Practical Reason, subject to the caveat that it be understood to mean "we desire something because we represent it to ourselves as good" (KpV59n).

3. The conclusion of the main argument of the *Groundwork* confirms this. Having introduced in his first chapter the idea of the good will as the only possible unconditioned good, and shown that the unconditioned good is possible only if there can be an interest-independent motive for action that takes lawfulness itself as a final and sufficient reason, Kant argues in the second chapter that a rational will could be so motivated only by an unconditioned rational principle (law)—the Categorical Imperative. What the CI is and how it relates to morality and judgment is explored through a set of formulations of the one principle. Kant then concludes: "We can now end where we started in the beginning, viz. the concept of an unconditionally good will. That will is good which cannot be evil, i.e., whose maxim, when made into a universal law, can never conflict with itself" (G437).

4. Of course some, following Hume, think this just shows that Kant and other deontologists get it wrong about obligation.

true that it is acting from the motive of duty that provides a perspicuous instance of good willing, this compromises the connection between obligation and value only if one accepts a Humean story about value, motives, and desire. Kant does not.

The claim I want to make is quite straightforward. Whatever it is that makes Kantian ethics distinctive, it is *not* to be found in the subordination of all considerations of value to principles of right or duty. In this sense, Kantian ethics is not a deontology.[5] Although principles of right constrain our pursuit of particular conceptions of the good, this does not amount to the absolute "priority of the right" in the canonical sense. Kant's project in ethics is to provide a correct analysis of "the Good" understood as the ultimate determining ground of all action.[6] This is an essential part of the critique of practical reason. His criticism of past moral philosophy is that in failing to see the importance of the necessitation involved in moral obligation, it mistakes the nature of the good. Kant's focus on the good will, both as the formal final end *and* as the ultimate internal condition of rational agency, can be understood as seeking a way between the poles of naturalism and metaphysical realism about value. Slotting Kantian ethics as deontological both mistakes its philosophical ambition and saddles it with implausible moral presuppositions.

I

The price of accepting the deontological view of Kant (or the deontological view of anything) has been very high. Without a theory of value, the rationale for moral constraint is a mystery. It is hardly sufficient to reject "why" questions by asserting that such questions reveal a misunderstanding of moral constraint: the constraint that does not need to answer any "why" questions. Moral skepticism seems to be a reasonable response to morality presented in this way. Moreover, without a theory of value it is not at all clear how we are to make the reasoned comparative judgments necessary

5. "Deontology" has recently been used to identify theories that reject value maximizing: they reject the premise that, for any good, more is necessarily better. In particular, theories of this sort dispute the idea that *instances* of what is good add. Deontology is also identified with taking the distinctions between doing and allowing, or intending and foreseeing, to be morally significant. In these weaker senses of deontology, Kant's ethics is deontological. Weak deontology, however, is a thesis about value, not a claim of independence from value.

6. Having said this, I should also say that Kant's philosophical interest in ethics is in part driven by issues central to the project of the critical philosophy as a whole. He is clear, though, about what belongs to the metaphysics of morals per se and what to the critique of practical reason (see the preface to *Groundwork*). For an interesting account of these issues, see John Rawls, "Themes in Kant's Moral Philosophy," *Kant's Transcendental Deductions,* ed. E. Forster (Stanford: Stanford University Press, 1989), pp. 102–113.

for deliberation in circumstances containing competing moral considerations. The resolution of conflict is sometimes thought to be possible through intuitions about cases or else through some intuited hierarchy of principles. But the first option leaves us in the dark about why the conflict is to be resolved in a given way; the second merely moves the opacity up a level.

This sort of difficulty about conflict resolution—serious enough in its own right—signals the presence of a more fundamental problem. In order for agents to read the moral facts of the world, they require recognitional resources that render these facts perspicuous. Both rules and standard cases introduce possibilities of pattern recognition, but neither offers the agent the kind of rationale that could support full deliberative judgment. The questions we need to ask are too hard, the moral data too complex. If our reading of the moral data is crude, the moral problems we encounter will to that degree be less tractable, the resolutions less convincing. Lack of suppleness in basic moral categories leads to epicycles of ad hoc exceptions and conditions or to a desire either to limit or to explain away deontological constraints. Neither move produces a stable outcome.

Thomas Nagel goes some of the way toward working through this problem.[7] He takes as the datum in need of explanation the fact that there are clear cases where deontological prohibitions are felt to be both irrational *and* compelling. This is especially so where we must harm an innocent person to promote some greater good or prevent some greater harm. We believe we should act, but we feel a constraint that needs to be overridden. The task is then to articulate some important moral insight of deontology that explains the legitimate strain in such situations. Nagel's conjecture is that deontology captures the idea that one must not allow oneself to be guided by evil. The source of this is in the points of view of both agent and victim when one intentionally harms an innocent person, even as a means to some greater good.

But this explanation through judgmental perspective itself requires explanation. Nagel supposes that we have some base-line intuition that one must always act for (or not against) the good of those intentionally affected by what we do, and that victims have complaint *beyond* their injury when we intentionally act against their good (regardless of the goodness of our further ends). But why we should be or feel constrained by our intentionally affecting another's good—why in acting against their good we are "led by evil"—remains unexplained. Now in fairness to Nagel, this is not the question he needs to ask. For his purposes, the inquiry stops when he has identified a plausible origin of deontological constraints in the intuitions of the subjective point of view. But if we are to understand the putative moral authority of deontological constraints, we need to know why the subjective

7. In *The View from Nowhere* (New York: Oxford University Press, 1986), pp. 175–185.

view has a deontological construction. Moreover, nothing here follows about whether or when other considerations—ones based in the "objective" point of view—take precedence.

One might (Nagel does not) regard the deontological constraint as a kind of moral insurance: a restriction on permissible means as the necessary or legitimate cost of protecting ourselves from the real temptation to do very wrong things in pursuit of perceived (and real) goods. This is not implausible. What we must not overlook if we are drawn to this sort of account is the practical effect of accepting an explanation of moral requirements in terms of some kind of characterological fallibility.

If we say that we may not cause pain to innocents in pursuit of the good because, like recovering alcoholics, we have no middle ground between abstinence and abuse, we have drawn the explanation to an end. But at some cost. We would have to acknowledge grounds for the "sober" to do what "we" may not. And even if there are none who are so strong that they may permit themselves to do what we cannot, we are left with the unwelcome conclusion that there is nothing the matter with what we want to do—what we can plainly see would be best to do—only we cannot risk doing it, given what we are like and what we might therefore do next. And then what does one say to the next rebutting foray that claims that we *can* do limited amounts of *x* without becoming addicted to excessive *x*? Assent only makes the dilemma more acute.[8] It is hard to see how morality so conceived could promote self-respect.

There are, to be sure, other ways of explaining deontological constraints. What I have wanted to make plain here is that deontology *does* require defense of a certain sort and that the conditions of adequacy for that defense involve the place of morality in our self-conception as practical agents. Negotiating the casuistry is not enough.

For purposes of clarity and the possibility of fresh thinking, I would like to let go of the term "deontology." I am convinced that the *combination* of its root meaning emphasizing rule and principle with the idea that moral requirements are not based in conceptions of value or of goodness makes inaccessible just those theoretical options I find necessary for an accurate accounting of Kantian ethics. Part of Kantian ethics' appeal is in its claim to make sense of the special demands that morality makes in our practical lives.[9] Canonical deontology can provide no such explanation. While its denial that pursuit of the good is the foundation of morality implies that

---

8. One might describe these problems as arising from a tension between act and rule deontology.

9. I am not here thinking of answers to some "Why be moral?" question, calling for a rebuttal of moral skepticism. On the other hand, an answer to the question I am taking seriously goes some distance in explaining why the skeptic's question cuts less deep than is often supposed.

morality must have a special place in our lives, that denial also makes it impossible to explain the place that morality does have.

The most plausible accounts of Kantian moral theory look to a connection with *rationality* to establish the pride of place of moral requirements. And surely rationality offers the right kind of explanation: principles of theoretical rationality have regulative priority without appeal to special concerns or interests. But as is well known, the formal explanatory advantage gained from appeals to rationality is lost when practical rationality is explicated along Humean or instrumentalist lines.[10] The value of conformity to Humean principles of practical rationality resides in the contingent connection between the principles and the means to interest satisfaction in general. Humean practical rationality has no desire-independent authority. For the alignment of morality with rationality to enable us to understand the special demands of morality—the ones I believe are misrepresented in the language of deontology—it must reveal the sense in which rationality as a regulative norm represents a distinctive conception of value. It will not do merely to connect rationality with some value; that would only replicate the Humean difficulty. We need to understand rationality as a value, not the value of rationality.

II

Let us then see what follows from taking the *Groundwork* opening at face value. We will take it that for Kant the subject of philosophical ethics is the unconditioned good—something of ultimate and ubiquitous value. It is ultimate in the sense that it provides the final court of judgment about the goodness of actions, states of character, and such; it is ubiquitous because the goodness of any action or state of character depends on it. Kant's claim, of course, is that the only possible unconditioned good is the good will.

Two things follow from locating unconditioned goodness in the good will: (1) the goodness of the good will is in its willing, not in the effects it brings about, and (2) the goodness in willing derives from the relation of the will (through its principle) to practical reason. I take these claims to signal the introduction of a set of distinctive assumptions about the nature of value. The domain of "the good" is rational activity and agency: that is, willing.[11] Objects and events are not possible bearers of value. They can be

10. See Christine M. Korsgaard, "Skepticism about Practical Reason," *Journal of Philosophy* 83 (1986), 5–25.

11. To speak intelligibly of "the will" and "willings" does not require positing any special capacities or faculties. We can take "the will" to represent the psychic organization of a rational agent determining itself to act for reasons. If we are to assess action or the adoption of ends *as willed,* we must represent the action or end adoption through the agent's justifying reasons.

thought of as good only insofar as they are possible ends of rational willing. They are judged good just in case the determination to act for them (here and in this way and for this purpose) is good. Actions *as events* (as effects of willing) cannot be the object of moral or practical assessment. Actions are called good because of the manner in which they are willed. Faculties and states of character are said to be good just in case they are conducive to action or choice judged to be good (as willed). Reflection on pretheoretical intuitions about standard examples is to confirm this.

The two claims thus mark out a metaphysics of value. The activity of rational willing brings value into a world that, absent rational beings, could have none.[12] Each agent, insofar as she is rational, acts in ways she takes to be (in some sense) good. She acts with and from the belief that her choices and reasons for choosing *are* good. Choices and reasons for choosing are good if and only if they are justified. The analytic task of the metaphysics of value (and by inclusion the metaphysics of morals) is to provide the principles and standards of justification for willings. This is the program of the second chapter of the *Groundwork,* worked out in the apparatus of imperatives and principles of practical rationality.

There is nothing un-Kantian in the identification of the role of imperatives as providing norms of value or goodness. Kant defines imperatives as principles that "say something would be good to do or refrain from doing . . . to a will that does not always therefore do something simply because it has been presented to the will as something good to do" (G413). In this light we should understand the *Groundwork* to be arguing that choice (and so action) is justified—that is, good—just in case our willings satisfy the conditions expressed in the principles of practical rationality, and we will as we do for that reason.

The principles of practical rationality introduce a complex, ordered set of conditions of goodness or choice-worthiness. We are familiar with this claim in the language of imperatives: maxims of action are rational if and only if they satisfy the principles of the imperatives that govern them: the hypothetical or technical means-end principle, the principles of prudence, and the principle of the Categorical Imperative. Elaborated in the less-familiar language of value we should say: according to the principle of the Hypothetical Imperative, the willing of an action is not good—not choice-worthy—if the willed action is not suited to bring about the end for whose sake it is taken. The willing of an action is conditionally good if the action

---

12. The things we call good that are not possible objects of rational willing—a good lion and other exemplars of species characteristics; good *x* where *x* is the kind of thing useful to a nonrational being (good watering hole)—are called good in a derivative or extended sense. This might be explained as the effect of projection onto the causal activity of nonrational wills or by the imputation of purpose to nature as a rational system.

is an effective means *and* it is chosen for that reason. It is only conditionally good because there are further principles that govern the willing of actions and ends. Likewise, the adoption of an end (also an act of will) is conditionally good if acting for or having that end will not interfere with other ends that are of equal or greater importance. The final condition on willing—of actions and ends—is set by the principle of the CI: actions and ends are not good if the agent's principles of choice (willing) are such that they could not (not "would not") be accepted as choice-worthy by all rational beings.[13] Actions and ends willed in conformity with the principle of the CI are unconditionally good.[14]

Although the principles of practical rationality can provide norms of assessment or justification, that fact in itself does not make it the case that they represent a conception of value. Rules or principles or laws can be used as a basis of assessment independent of any conception of value they contain. (That is, after all, what canonical deontology asserts.) It is thus necessary to ask for the sense in which the formal constraints of rationality could be said to introduce a standard of value. In particular, one wants to know how or in what sense refraining from acting in a way that rational beings could not accept is in any way *good*. Here we must not ask for some other good that this way of acting promotes or brings about—asking, that is, for some further standard of justification. This misses the point. It is the distinctive claim of Kantian theory that there is no further condition of justification—of goodness—on actions or ends (willings) than the full set of principles of practical rationality. So the right question to ask is whether a standard of practical rationality provides a real answer to the problem of deontology: can formal rational constraints be or constitute a conception of *value*?[15]

Care must be taken in how we approach this question so that it is not determined at the outset that, whatever goodness is, it cannot be or be equivalent to conformity to rational principle. If, as I claim, Kant is offering a radical critique of traditional conceptions of value—not just moral

---

13. A condition of choice that could not be accepted by all rational beings would be: doing *x* where the possibility of *x*-ing depends on other rational beings similarly situated not doing *x*. This is the condition standardly found to be the ground of choice of the deceitful-promise maxim.

14. Not every willing that is unconditionally good in this sense has moral worth (say, permissible actions willed on condition that they are permissible). There is also a difference between a willing that is *unconditionally* good and one that is *completely* good. It is desirable (and indeed the "highest good") to act on maxims that morality permits *and* that involve the satisfaction of a settled array of subjectively appropriate ends. But the principles commending the integration of ends in a fully rational conception of happiness are not violated when one's reason for abandoning an end is that it or its pursuit is impermissible.

15. The positive answer to this question is what Rawls calls Kantian constructivism. See his "Themes in Kant's Moral Philosophy," pp. 95–102.

goodness—then we need a neutral approach to the question of what value is. I think that the best approach is through an examination of the role a conception of value is to play in action and judgment. If Kantian principles of rationality can perform this role effectively, we can fairly conclude that they constitute a conception of value.[16]

As noted earlier, one of the failings of traditional deontology is in the fact that it fails to give a reason or rationale for moral constraint. The absence of a rationale is significant for two connected reasons. First, a rationale renders moral action intelligible to the moral agent, making possible the reasoned integration of morality into one's system of ends and commitments. Second, it introduces a framework for reasoned deliberation necessary to the stable resolution of morally complex situations. A grounding conception of value could provide this rationale by offering an explanation of the wrong- or right-making characteristics of action that renders moral requirements intelligible in a way that is then able to guide deliberation. A conception of value that is effective in this way may be called *didactic*—in the original sense of "intended to instruct."

We will have good reason to accept the claim that the Kantian set of rational constraints expresses a conception of value if it can perform both didactic tasks. In teleological theories, the didactic role is played by a conception of the good that is a natural or a perfectionist end of human activity. One way of putting the question to Kantian ethics is to ask whether the unconditioned good—the good will—can play the didactic role of a (the) final end.

Since good willing is willing in conformity with the principles of practical rationality, we are asking whether these principles can be a final end. There is nothing suspect about casting principles as ends. Accepting any standard as regulative over a domain of activity is to adopt the standard as an end. Principles are not routine ends of action in the sense that we do not typically initiate action in order to satisfy them, although we can. But if we accept that the defining feature of ends is that they are sources of reasons that shape action, then principles can be ends. The obvious peculiarity of the claim that the principles of practical rationality can be a *final* end is that they are formal and so, like principles of inference, neither fully nor independently reason-giving.[17]

When Kant says that the principles of practical rationality are formal (or better, "purely" formal), we are tempted to conclude that they have no

---

16. Showing that *x* is a conception of value is not to answer the question, "Why is *x* good?"

17. Of course the second formulation of the CI calls for the treatment of "humanity" as a regulative and possibly final end: an end-in-itself. This is confirming of the strategy of interpretation I am developing only if the second formulation adds no independent value content to the idea of conformity to the principles of practical rationality. I think it does not. There is more about its role in section IV.

substantive content—they are empty.[18] We think this because we suppose that while something can have form *and* content, if there were something that was merely or purely formal it could not, by definition, have content. But this opposition between form and content misses a key distinction that Kant makes: a purely formal principle is one that is *not material,* not one that is empty or without content (KpV21–27).

In distinguishing material and purely formal practical principles, Kant is sorting the different kinds of reasons agents may have. Reasons supported by material practical principles are contingent: dependent on the desires and interests of particular agents.[19] Purely formal principles, by contrast, are said to give reasons that are necessary and universally valid, reasons that hold in virtue of features that are constitutive of our rational natures. Purely formal principles do not have *no* content; they have *noncontingent* content.[20]

Since in Kantian theory formal principles are norms of maxims—principles that describe actions as they are willed—Kant's theory of action is the obvious arena in which to work out the connection between formality and reasons. In the next section I will take up the much-contested question of maxim content. Its resolution is the key to understanding how formal principles apply to maxims, which is the necessary first step in identifying Kant's distinctive views about value.

III

In the most basic kind of voluntary action, a rational agent determines a course of action appropriate to promote or bring about a state of affairs she has adopted as an end. In so acting we say the agent acts for reasons; Kant says the agent has a maxim of action. Maxims of action express what an agent wills: her action and intention as understood to be good and chosen because good. Strictly, Kant says that maxims are agents' subjective principles in acting (G400n, 421n), to be contrasted with objective principles according to which agents ought to act. The contrast is between a conception of an action as taken to be (believed to be) good and one that is

18. I take this to be the source of Hegel's claim that no moral content can be derived from the application of formal principles of rationality.

19. Contingency is relative to our rational nature. To say that a desire or inclination is contingent is to say, in effect, that it is not constitutive of the kind of being we are—a kind of rational being. Shared appetites are still contingent: we would not cease being rational agents if we did not need food. For a useful discussion of contingent and necessary interests, see Andrews Reath, "Hedonism, Heteronomy, and Kant's Principle of Happiness," *Pacific Philosophical Quarterly* 70 (1989), 42–72.

20. Formal principles with noncontingent content play a role in practical judgment analogous to the role that the "forms of intuition" (space and time) play in empirical judgment.

objectively good. Those maxims are objectively good that conform to the principles of practical rationality. In this sense, the principle of an objectively good maxim—not the end or way of acting—is valid for every rational being.

The fact that maxims present actions as they are or are believed to be good has for the most part been ignored in the Kant literature. There are various explanations for this. One, of course, is the deontology assumption itself, which makes considerations of value appear marginal in Kant's work. This in turn explains the concentration on moral worth as the kind of goodness that actions can have: a kind of goodness supposedly introduced by a special motive (the motive of duty) *after* the evaluation of an action as required by duty. Looking at moral worth this way masks the difference between an action being good (having moral worth) and a maxim having content that includes a conception of an action or end as good. It is then hard to make sense of the fact that Kant says two things: actions have moral worth when done from the motive of duty, and actions have moral worth when their maxims have moral *content* (G398). This double claim suggests that moral worth does not come from a special motive external to the agent's morally correct maxim (a maxim that could equally be acted on from nonmoral motives), but when the maxim includes a particular conception of the action in its principle to which the motive of duty is attached. That is: moral worth marks a unity of motive and maxim content.

One might worry that it is futile to introduce arguments that depend on subtleties of maxim content when it is not clear that the idea of a maxim's content is well defined. This is the "action-description problem." The success of Kantian theory in producing either determinate or acceptable moral results is thought to hang on there being a non-question-begging way to construct *the* maxim of an action to be presented for assessment by the CI. The history of attempts to find a method for determining the unique and correct descriptions of actions—either in general or for Kant—is not filled with encouraging success.[21] Although I do not in the end think Kant's ethics vulnerable to the action-description problem, looking at the attempts to resolve or deflect it is a good way to initiate a more promising account of maxims, maxim content, and the connection between will and value that maxims present.

---

21. I do not think there is or could be a solution to the action-description problem. Descriptions are driven by the purposes for which they are solicited. If our moral theory looks to actual consequences, the action descriptions of interest will need to capture causally relevant features; those descriptions will not do if the theory assesses intentions, *not* because they are wrong but because they are not relevant. One resource not used in solutions to Kant's action-description problem is the value content of maxims. As we shall see, its inclusion alters what it is reasonable to count as an acceptable solution.

Two strategies dominate recent efforts to solve the action-description problem for maxims. Maxims have been identified either with the agent's "specific intention" in acting[22] or with "underlying intentions" and "rules of life" *(Lebensregeln)*.[23] The clear advantage of the first strategy is that it most naturally supports the notion that maxims are the vehicle for *action* assessment. The advantage can be brought home, however, only if there is a method of generating a privileged action description from the agent's intention. Some success can be had in eliminating erroneous descriptions through a method of counterfactual questioning.[24] One argues: if an agent would have done the same action in the absence of feature d in her present circumstances of action, then d was not part of the agent's intention, and it is not a relevant component of the action description. But the removal of irrelevant description does not guarantee that the remaining terms of description are appropriate.

The natural source of descriptive terms for an intention is the end that is regulative of the agent's activity. But what am I doing in walking out the door, checking the oil, and putting the keys in the ignition? Is it getting on the road? or going downtown? or meeting Jane for lunch? We might say it is the last, since that is the success condition for all the previous activity. If the rest of the activity would not get me to lunch with Jane, it is without point for me. Now if this is the right way to select intentions in acting, and I think it is, it is not a successful method for describing actions for purposes of assessment. We need to be able to assess component elements of what is intended (sometimes as means, sometimes as aspects, perhaps sometimes as foreseen consequences), which will not be picked out by the regulative end. Suppose that among the things I do in heading off to meet Jane is to hurt Dick's feelings. Description derived from the action intended as means to an end will not include that. And since I would, as it happens, meet Jane regardless of the effect on Dick, counterfactual questioning misleads.

A reasonable response to this problem is to construct maxims for each intentional aspect of an action and to hold that an action is impermissible if any of the maxims of its intentional aspects is rejected by the CI.[25] Hurting Dick, which is something I mean to do, is now registered in a separate maxim. The gain in inclusiveness, however, is had at the expense of the idea

22. See Onora (Nell) O'Neill, *Acting on Principle* (New York: Columbia University Press, 1975), chap. 2.

23. This view is argued for in Rüdiger Bittner, "Maximen," in *Akten des Kongresses,* ed. G. Funke and J. Kopper (Berlin: de Gruyter, 1975), pp. 485–498; Otfried Höffe, "Kants kategorischer Imperativ als Kriterium des Sittlichen," in *Ethik und Politik,* ed. Otfried Höffe (Frankfurt: Suhrkamp, 1979), pp. 84–119; and Onora O'Neill, "Consistency in Action," in *Constructions of Reason* (Cambridge: Cambridge University Press, 1989), pp. 83–89.

24. See O'Neill, *Acting on Principle,* pp. 71–72.

25. This is O'Neill's suggestion in *Acting on Principle,* chap. 2.

that a maxim represents the agent's willing. The proliferation of maxims to match intentional aspects of actions undermines the very idea of *a* maxim of action and with it, I think, the idea of moral assessment of action.

The second strategy attempts to give direct expression to the idea that maxims represent willings. It holds that a maxim describes the agent's underlying or standing motivational state, or the intentional position from which she deliberates (something suited to be the major premise in a practical syllogism).[26] This strategy in effect bypasses the action-description problem: agents do not have an indefinite or even very large array of rules of life, and the ones they do have can be reasonably well inferred from the patterns of deliberation and justification they employ. It protects the apparatus of the moral theory by blocking description-tailoring moves and by bringing to the CI procedure the kind of general maxims it seems able to handle best. The chief cost of using underlying intentions or *Lebensregeln* is that moral assessment is then not of actions but of an agent's moral worthiness or character. It is of course true that character assessment is often occasioned by an agent's intentional actions, since it is through particular actions that one gives expression to *Lebensregeln* or brings into focus an underlying intention. But this identification of maxims—as objects of moral assessment—with *Lebensregeln* elides action and agent assessment in a way that ignores relevant moral particulars of deliberative activity. Where, for example, the moral problem with an action is incidental to the life-rule or underlying intention, it would not register in the agent's maxim and thus would be inaccessible to moral assessment.

I do not think that appeals to text help with this: the maxims Kant uses are at all levels of generality. And if maxims come in all sizes, neither of the two strategies can be right. In lieu of a third interpretation, it is tempting to try an inclusive account that emphasizes the relations between levels of maxims. One might construct a tiered set of maxims, with maxims of action at the bottom and higher-order maxims operative as "background conditions" as we move to the volitional top of the heap.[27] We do often view our practical activity this way: in virtue of having such and such a general commitment I adopt lower-order strategies or plans and then, as opportunities arise, formulate intentions to act. (It will not matter whether my reasoning follows this pattern: I may recognize that I have a higher-order commitment only by identifying a pattern in my actions that is best ex-

---

26. The more particular principles describing intentional action ("To run every morning before breakfast") are not properly maxims, but *Vorsätze*—subordinate practical rules—derived from maxims given particular circumstances of action (the conclusions of practical syllogisms).

27. Henry Allison suggests this, given the inconclusive outcome of his review of contemporary discussions of maxims in *Kant's Theory of Freedom* (Cambridge: Cambridge University Press, 1990), pp. 89–94.

plained by it. Of course some actions are not best explained by higher-order commitments.) Furthermore, Kant sometimes speaks of a highest-order maxim (or *Gesinnung*) through which a fundamental choice for good or evil informs our subsequent choices and maxims. Though this kind of account is attractive for its inclusiveness—it captures a fuller sense of what willing is—it still leaves undetermined the content of the maxim of an action or the maxim of any other level of willing.

If the textual evidence is insufficient to settle the issue, we should accept an account of maxims that makes best sense of Kant's conceptions of morality and agency together. The account of maxims that is best, as I see it, is both obvious and unorthodox. If in willing an action an agent proceeds as she judges her action and her purpose to be good, then the maxim of action that represents her willing should contain *all* the aspects of the action and end that make them choice-worthy for her. The convention of regarding maxims of action as represented by schemata of the form "To do *a* in circumstances *c* in order to bring about *e*" (where *a* is an action and *e* an end, a state of affairs) has made it appear that the only evaluative component represented *in* the maxim is in the supposed causal fit between action and end. There is no reason for this restriction. It is true that Kant believes that all actions are taken for ends; it does not follow that the only sense of an action's goodness (choice-worthiness) that we have is its suitability to promote an end. If the maxim is to represent the way an agent wills—how, to put it somewhat dramatically, she sets herself to change the world for what she takes to be good reasons—the maxim should include all aspects of both action and end that the agent would offer as justification for her acting as she intends to act.

An agent may choose to act for an end because of her interest in it or because the end contributes to some further goal. And she may choose to act in a particular way because that action produces collateral effects also of interest to her. (Some means are more enjoyable than others.) If her choice is made on the basis of this rich background of value, then her maxim should include all of the aspects that determine choice-worthiness.

For this reason we must look to the agent's motives if we are to describe the action-as-willed.[28] If the end of an action is the state of affairs the agent would bring about, the motive explains what it is in the state of affairs that is attractive. We do not see what the agent wills until we see her action and end in the way she sees them as good.

---

28. The account of action that Kant works with is more complex still. Agents have incentives *(Triebfedern);* they act from motives. An agent's incentives are all the sources of reasons for action that apply to her in virtue of her own desires and interests *and* in virtue of her rational agency. We say that an agent acts from motive *m* when she has an incentive that supports *m* and she takes *m* to provide good reasons for action.

Furthermore, when an agent accepts a norm of justification, this also affects her sense of the choice-worthiness of her actions and ends. Different agents acting the same way for the same purpose (state of affairs) will have different maxims as they accept different norms as conditions of willing (justificatory norms such as permissibility, but also ideals).

The agent who acts to help because she is drawn by the need of others acts on a different maxim than the one who acts to help on condition that her action is permissible. The agent whose helping action is chosen out of the recognition that it is morally required acts on a different maxim still. The three maxims have two things in common. First is an action-end pair: in each, the agent would do a as a means to helping Y. Second is the regulative belief that a is a suitable means to helping Y.[29] Where the maxims differ is in the set of regulative conditions of goodness that the agents accept and act from. The first agent sees her action as good, we stipulate, because she accepts the fact of her feelings being aroused by Y's plight as giving sufficient reason for action. The second is similarly moved, we suppose, but judges her action good only as it satisfies the further condition of permissibility. Since this is the way she determines the goodness of her action, the full description of the willed action should reflect that regulative belief. The maxim of the third agent contains a different description of the end (as adopted because morally required) and so a different understanding of the choice-worthiness of the action-end pair. From the point of view of what they will—what good they would bring about—the three agents each do very different things as they act to bring about the same state of affairs. We should not accept any story about maxims that obscures the way that different conceptions of goodness affect an agent's conception of what she does.

The views I am rejecting would have us imagine each of our agents acting on the same maxim of action under the jurisdiction of different higher-order principles. The location of the standards of assessment is *external* to the agent's maxim of action, or, as is often said, the standards are *applied* to the maxim of action. While there is nothing impossible about a conception of action and agency that is represented through discrete, hierarchically ordered maxims under the regulation of normative principles, it does not seem to be Kant's.

Following Kant we will say that regulative principles give maxims their *form*. When an agent accepts a regulative principle (or principle of justification), she *can* look to it as an external standard: asking, in effect, "Here's what I will, now how did I do?" But this is not the normal role of a regulative principle. Usually we adapt our projects to the norms we accept as we go

---

29. There could be a maxim of the same action-end pair where the agent had a very different sense of the connection between doing a and Y's receiving help. Nothing is lost here by ignoring this and similar variants.

along. Our standards give our actions and projects a form they would not have otherwise: they reveal the sense in which our actions and ends are chosen because we judge them to be good. Descriptions of action that omit the regulative principles that shape our choices are for this reason seriously incomplete.

We should not suppose that this kind of account is unique to moral choice. Value commitments of other sorts—aesthetic, economic, and such— equally affect descriptions in maxims as they determine the features of actions and ends that make them worthy of choice. Maxims then are as thin or as thick as agents' grounds of choice are simple or complex.

The integration of will and value explains the puzzle in the account of moral worth. The maxims of morally worthy actions have moral content as a function of the form or principle of the agent's willing; yet the content of a maxim of action must be the described action and its end. For a morally worthy maxim to have moral content in virtue of its principle (its form), we must see the principle in the adoption of ends and determination of means. Actions and ends are chosen as they are seen to be good: as satisfying or giving expression to rational principle. The good-making characteristics of the action-end pair, its principle, must therefore be a constitutive element of the maxim's moral content.

We need to take up one further issue about maxim content. Since maxims express willings, content is determined by what an agent takes to be the good characteristics of her action and choice. But if part of what makes an action or choice seem good is its fit with desires or interests, it may only be after a pattern of action has emerged that the agent can recognize what maxim she has been acting on. There may be subjective elements at work which the agent is not consciously attending to, some that would be brought forward easily on reflection, and some that might become available only through a kind of practical therapy. The effect of this opacity is that the maxim the agent sincerely takes herself to be acting on may not be the maxim she does in fact act on. This seems to me to be the right outcome. Maxim specification is a dynamic process that the agent will be drawn into as her actions *as she describes them* seem at once justified and in conflict with principles she accepts.[30]

It does not follow from this that we sometimes act on unconscious maxims. Not, that is, if by unconscious we mean outside the arena of deliberative rationality. There are no such maxims. We may have, as Kant puts it, "secret incentives of our actions" that appear in the guise of more respectable motives. Nonetheless, our maxims are shaped by our beliefs about

---

30. Cultural evaluations that shape judgment but that appear as facts (as when what appears as physically or conceptually impossible is instead the reflection of prevailing racist or sexist categories) do not defeat maxim construction, but foreclose deliberation in those areas.

our circumstances of action—outside of and within ourselves. Fear, embarrassment, or carelessness can lead us to believe things about our motives and ends that are not so. To varying degrees, such faults can be corrected. A moral theory can provide reasons to understand ourselves better; it is not a failure of a theory that self-knowledge is a task, not a given.

Packing everything into the maxim may make it seem to be an unwieldy instrument for practical assessment. Whether it is or not depends on how one thinks practical assessment proceeds. Certainly, if one were to take some very thickly described maxim of action to the CI procedure, asking of the maxim whether it could be willed a universal law without contradiction, there is virtually no chance of obtaining a determinate (or even a coherent) result. Detailed descriptions have always defeated universalization tests. But if we set aside assumptions about the method of moral judgment in Kantian ethics and instead think about what we want "from the bottom up," having a rich and value-laden action description is the sort of thing that ought to make moral judgment more accurate. For if an agent takes herself to be acting in such and such a way because it is good, and what is good is a function of principles of rational choosing, then one would need to have the full description of an action's choice-worthy features to determine whether the action *is* good.[31]

Let us at this point accept as part of Kant's conception of rational agency that principles of practical rationality are at least partially determining of the value content of maxims. Rational principles represent conceptions of the good, providing at once norms of assessment or judgment *and* the forms of willing that shape the maxims of agents committed to their authority. What remains to be explained is the sense in which a purely formal conception of rationality is not empty.

IV

If a rational agent adopts ends and determines how to act on condition that her ends and actions are good, and if the ultimate condition of goodness is set by the grounds of choice-worthiness for a rational being per se (the

31. Too many Kant interpreters take the structure of moral judgment to be obvious and locate the interpretive challenge in making it work. We will do better if we think of ourselves as developing an approach to the method of moral judgment that reflects all we understand about agency, judgment, and value. On the one hand we know that moral judgment will involve the CI procedure: actions whose maxims cannot be willed a universal law without contradiction are not permissible. On the other, we know that the method of judgment must fit the object of moral assessment: maxims containing the full description of the agent's grounds of choice. Moral judgment, then, cannot involve the straightforward application of the CI procedure to maxims. What is needed is a different model of moral judgment that fits the account of value and agency that Kant employs. This project is begun in Chapter 7.

principle of the CI), then there will be content derivable from purely formal principle(s) of practical rationality if there are any general conditions of willing that a maxim must satisfy, independent of agents' contingent ends.

This point may be clearer if put a different way. The Hypothetical Imperative gives every maxim a form, a condition of goodness; content—and so specific direction of the will—is derived from particular ends. The Categorical Imperative is said to give the will direction through form alone (G420). Since form constrains willings according to the principles of practical rationality, the CI could direct the will only if there is some thing or things that one must will (*as* a rational agent) if one wills anything at all. There would have to be noncontingent regulative facts of rational agency per se that function as conditions on all willing (or: that constrain what we may rationally will). What I will argue is that without an account of rational willing or agency robust enough to deliver content, the CI cannot be an effective principle of moral judgment.

The CI procedure's contradiction tests detect when a maxim fails to have universal form. As traditionally interpreted, the tests do not reveal which feature of the condemned maxim is salient in producing the contradiction. To this extent, the procedure functions as a black box. Because of the way the procedure is constructed, we have reason to accept its results as determinative of moral permissibility. But the construction is not itself didactic.

This fact is in part responsible for the puzzle maxims—such as "To always be first through the door"—which generate contradictions under universalization that are not morally significant. Each interpreter of the CI procedure must develop ways to set aside the puzzle maxims.[32] One could exclude results that depend on physical or logical impossibilities (requiring that failure be some kind of practical impossibility); one could argue that the "first through the door" maxim *is* impermissible since acting on it would involve violent means, such as shoving people out of the way; or one could exclude the maxim on grounds that it would not when fully stated satisfy the Hypothetical Imperative. These are all defensible strategies of exclusion that will work for a "first through the door" type of maxim. Other strategies will be needed to exclude other kinds (such as "To consume but never produce *x*"). But even a successful set of strategies of exclusion is problematically ad hoc because each countermove relies on independent knowledge of the correct results of applying the CI procedure. There is the possibility that our strategies of exclusion will be too crude. While it may be the case that

---

32. Those, like Bittner and Höffe, who argue that maxim stands for *propositio maxima* (the major premise of the practical syllogism) would claim that the puzzle maxims are not maxims at all. This is clearly an advantage of their view. Since it is had, I believe, at the cost of Kant's distinctive understanding of rational action, it seems preferable to remain open to the possibility of puzzle maxims.

for some x it is permissible to consume without producing, perhaps there are some y where it is not. What is missing is a *rationale* for the judgment of permissibility that warrants the development of a strategy of exclusion.

The absence of a rationale is not an obstacle only for resolving difficulties in judgment and maxim construction introduced by the puzzle maxims. Without it, the CI procedure—which expresses the basic conception of value in a deliberative method—cannot fulfill its didactic promise. The best way to see the force of this claim is to look at one of the standard interpretations of a CI procedure argument.

Consider the familiar *Groundwork* example of the deceitful promise. I am not concerned with the validity of Kant's argument. I want instead to try to understand how the conclusion he draws could be viewed as following from an argument that has didactic moral import. Let us then accept that the maxim of deceitful promising could not be or could not be willed a universal law without contradiction. We then ask for an interpretation of this result that gives its rationale: an explanation of the contradiction that reveals the wrong-making characteristic of the willing in the deceitful-promising maxim itself.

A familiar interpretation of this CI procedure argument locates the problem in the maxim of deceit in the agent's reliance on the fact that others do not promise deceitfully as a condition of practical success. The condition of this reliance is undermined in the universalization test: one cannot without contradiction will the original maxim in a world in which everyone deceives. The wrong-making characteristic is then taking advantage of others' not acting in the way one proposes to act. This at least has the form of an interpretation: it explains why the action (maxim) is wrong, the wrong-making characteristic is the cause of contradiction under universalization, and the account of the wrong-making characteristic is in terms that are useful to subsequent deliberation and judgment (say, by directing us to pay attention to situations in which we may be taking advantage of others).

I argued in Chapter 7 that this interpretation does not support the right results because it fails to distinguish cases of taking advantage that are legitimate and ordinary from those that are unfair. But even if it did not fail in this way, the interpretation does not account for the moral point—the rationale—of the interpreted requirement and thus fails as an interpretation. Knowing that a maxim is wrong when the success of acting on it depends on others not acting in the same way does not explain *why* such dependence should be a wrong-making characteristic. What is missing is not an explanation of how we know the action/maxim is wrong. That the maxim fails the CI procedure demonstrates its impermissibility (and nothing else could do that). What we want to know is why one should not take advantage of others' behavior and practices. In Kantian theory this should be answered by giving a reason why a principle of taking advantage conflicts with the principles of practical rationality. Or: why the willing in the maxim of deceit is inconsistent with principles that describe the nature of rational agency per se. If I am right about the ultimate sources of moral content in Kantian ethics, these are, as they should be, questions of value.[33] It is in making connections between content and value that moral theory adds to ordinary moral knowledge. An interpretation of the CI procedure that lacks the resources for this task fails to integrate the requirements it explains into a fully coherent and practically effective account of morality.

I want to argue that Kant provides the necessary interpretation through the sequence of formulations of the CI that follow the universal-law formula.[34] It has been remarked that each successive formulation of the CI shows the Moral Law from a different point of view: Universal Law takes the viewpoint of the agent acting; Humanity, the perspective of the person acted upon; Autonomy and the Kingdom of Ends, the place of the agent in a community of like persons. This is not all they do. The successive formulations interpret the arguments of the CI procedure in terms that reveal the aspects of rational agency that generate contradictions under universalization. These interpretations provide the requisite connection between formal principles and value; they show *how* content is derived from

33. This is why one cannot fix the interpretation, following Rawls, by introducing a publicity requirement in the procedure of assessment. The procedure would then not reject maxims of permissible advantage taking, supposing those are just the ones where persons have no reason to mind our taking advantage of their expectations or patterns of behavior. (Universal knowledge would not then undermine practical success.) But this solution would not make the procedure (through its interpretation) effectively didactic. The "fix" introduces a new locale of moral opacity. Why should publicity be determinative? What reason do we have for thinking that in satisfying publicity under universalization a maxim has universal form?

This is a question that Thomas Scanlon attends to in arguing for a general interpretation of Kantian ethics based on a value of public, mutual respect: an action is permissible if no one could rationally object to it. But note that the publicity requirement is then an expression of a more basic value claim.

34. The sequence of formulas, in the particular order that they are in, performs several key tasks in the *Groundwork*'s argument. At each introduction of a formula, Kant refines the key question for the metaphysics of morals: how is a Categorical Imperative possible? Attending the universal-law formulation is a footnote discussion of why the possibility question for the CI will be difficult—the CI must be able to "connect" substantive requirements on willings with the concept of the will of a rational being as such (G420n). The Formula of Humanity makes the next move by arguing that the above connection will only be possible if there is an "end-in-itself" which as such can "constitute an objective principle of the will and can hence serve as a practical law" (G429). The Formula of Autonomy adds to this the idea that a self-conception as an end-in-itself is only possible for a will that can regard itself as legislating universal law. Thus the CI is possible only if the will is self-legislating. (The third chapter of the *Groundwork* is designed to respond to the refined version of the possibility question.) In addition, and at the same time, the sequence of formulas constructs an interpretation of rational willing that presents its didactic content.

the constraint of universal form for willing. The CI procedure can then produce results that are didactic.

Returning to the deceitful promise, let us see what the interpretations add to our understanding of the CI procedure argument. Kant argues under the Formula of Humanity that the maxim of deceitful promising goes wrong because in acting on it one would prevent the person deceived from holding "the very same action as an end" (G430). The maxim is for this reason incompatible with rational nature as an end-in-itself.[35] The argument marks the feature of rational agency that the deceitful promise impermissibly exploits. Using deceit to control access to facts, one moves someone to deliberate on grounds she believes (falsely) she has assessed on their merits. When deceit is effective, it causes the victim to have the beliefs necessary for her to adopt ends and choose actions that serve the deceiver's purposes. The victim's will becomes an instrument of the deceiver's purposes—under the deceiver's indirect causal control. This is not an action the victim can hold as her end.

Interpreted through the Formula of Humanity, the argument of the CI procedure is then comprehensible in its claim that a maxim of deception contains a form of willing whose principle is not a possible principle of rational agency. A maxim of bringing the will of another under one's control misuses or mistakes the fact that one's actions affect another rational agent (here her deliberative activity). Explaining why a rational agent must not be used in this way is the task of the Formula of Autonomy.

The Formula of Autonomy tells us to regard a rational agent as self-legislating: one who can take herself (and, by the argument of the third chapter of the *Groundwork,* must take herself) to be acting for reasons "all the way down." Less metaphorically, this is to say that rational agents can fully determine their actions according to reasons. Indeed, the capacity to act for reasons all the way down is defining of rational agency. Kant calls it autonomy. It is what we respect in respecting a person as an end-in-herself. Because it is easy to misunderstand this feature of the claim of autonomy for rational agents, I want to spell it out in greater detail.

The ends of rational agents are adopted, not given. Something is a possible end if it can be brought about through action and is judged to be in some sense good. We should say: the adoption of an end is an activity of will undertaken for a reason. Many of our ordinary ends look to desires: they are adopted because we believe that acting in accordance with them or for their sake will satisfy the demand of some desire (or more complex interest).

---

35. The idea of rational nature as an end-in-itself is introduced in the *Groundwork* because the Moral Law cannot be the ultimate determining ground of a will unless it provides the will with an end that is a noncontingent condition of choice-worthiness or goodness. Rational nature as an end-in-itself is in this sense a final end.

The sense in which reasons go all the way down is this: even when we act for the sake of desire, desire is not the cause of our action. We act on such principles as desire satisfaction, or even this-desire satisfaction, is good. Our adoption of ends always has a principled basis. We act for reasons.

Evaluative questions concern the adequacy of the principles on which we act. The desire that is the occasion of a given willing is itself neither good nor bad; desires are not themselves proper objects of evaluation. (This is as true of the desire for happiness as it is of the desire for food or pleasure.) We may judge the satisfaction of some desire to be good because we believe it to be necessary to our well-being. We can be wrong about this. What would be "bad" is our adopting a principle of desire satisfaction as the ultimate determining ground of our willing. Kant calls this self-love: "the propensity to make the subjective determining grounds of one's choice into an objective determining ground of the will in general" (KpV74).

A being whose ultimate grounds of action were given—who truly acted from desire—would not act for reasons all the way down. Its desires would be causes of its actions. Such a being would not, in the end, have a reason for acting one way rather than another. Kant thinks of animals as having wills of this sort; perhaps he thinks of children this way as well—at least until their rational capacities become effective.

The rational will differs from the animal will not just in its capacity to act from a conception of the good, but more profoundly in the fact that the rational will contains principles of justification that provide a complete standard of goodness. (Action that is fully justified has a maxim that is unconditionally good.) It is for this reason that the willings of rational agents are open to full justification. And it is for this reason that interference with autonomous rational activity is condemned.[36]

The maxim of deception places the grounds of choice-worthiness of the victim's reasons in the deceiver's will. The victim cannot take the deceiver's action as good for the reasons that make it good (in the eyes of the deceiver) all the way down. In effect, the deceiver has a maxim of treating a rational agent as someone whose will may be brought under causal control—as one whose reasons do not go all the way down. Someone who is an end-in-herself—a rational agent with autonomy—cannot accept that as a principle of action. It violates the requirement that we regard reasons as coming to an

36. Nothing in the talk about interference is inconsistent with the strict construction of the rational will as a "noumenal" entity, outside the possibility of causal interaction. Noumenal wills cannot be hurt or threatened by anything we do to human beings. The principles of fully justified (good) willing set the conditions of respect for rational wills: an attitude that is required of us because we and those persons with whom we interact must be regarded as beings who act for reasons all the way down. Nonetheless, rational willing is a task for us. We can be harmed or aided in the attempt to bring our maxims into conformity with the principles of respect: respect for ourselves and for others *as* rational beings.

end in the will of each agent, separately. The moral problem is not *in* the will of the deceived, but in the maxim of the deceiver. Fault is therefore present independent of injury, regardless of whether the deceived person minds acting for the deceiver's end.

In this way the Formulas of Humanity and Autonomy give us the desired interpretation of the CI procedure's universalization test (the didactically relevant source of contradiction). The Formula of Universal Law shows *that* the maxim of deception is impermissible; the Formulas of Humanity and Autonomy explain *why* it is not good. The Formula of Universal Law can function alone, but it needs interpretation to make its results didactic. The Formula of Humanity provides interpretation, but it cannot function alone. It is only *after* we know that a maxim is impermissible (because it does not have the form of universal lawgiving) that we can ask how, in that maxim, we fail to treat rational nature as an end.

The interpretation identifies the aspect of rational agency that is subverted in the deceiving maxim's principle of willing. A law of rational agency that entails the causal control of one will over another implies that no will is a possible source of reasons all the way down. Such a law could not be a law of rational agency: a law describing the agency of ends-in-themselves. *Under universalization,* the maxim of deception produces a law of dissociated or dispersed and unfree agency. Or, as we might say, in transforming reasons into causes, universal deception violates the separateness of rational agents.

The argument that the universalized deceiving maxim is self-defeating is now didactic: a principle of manipulative control of another rational agent's will is not a form of willing consistent with principles constitutive of rational agency. We are thereby instructed not to will in such a way as to violate the separateness condition of rational wills.

This is what it looks like to derive a substantive moral result from a purely formal constraint of rational willing. What it amounts to in application will be the work of casuistry. But casuistry is here possible only because the interpretation of the Formula of Universal Law's contradiction is didactic: it explains the wrong-making characteristics of impermissible maxims in terms of the theory's conception of value.[37]

V

To this point I have been arguing two things: first, the principles of practical reason are principles of final justification that set the standard for which

---

37. As we shall see, this interpretation is deepened through the Formula of the Kingdom of Ends. I have set aside what this adds to moral judgment because the point here is not to construct the casuistry but to establish the source of moral content.

forms of willing (maxims) are fully good; second, although these principles are formal, they are not only not empty—substantive moral results can be had from them—they are also didactic. Under interpretation, the value the principles represent is elaborated in a conception of rational agency that makes moral judgment intelligible and, as we shall see, more complex deliberation possible.

What are we to make of the relatively rich conception of rational agency that emerges in the interpretation of the CI procedure argument? It seems to me a welcome development. Restriction of rationality to principles of logical consistency renders the CI procedure ineffective, and extension of the conception of rationality to "means-end" principles but no further, arbitrary. Part of the task of the moral theory is to explicate the conception of rationality necessary for morality to have content. It will be a separate question whether we are such rational beings. One might worry, however, that the arguments go too far in that they seem to depend on features unique to *human* agency. After all, deceit threatens "separateness" only for agents with rational wills of a certain sort: vulnerable to manipulation through control of information. If it is a special feature of human wills that they are separate, then the interpretation would have failed to show that the maxim of deceit subverts a principle of rational agency.

This objection mistakes the argument of the interpretation. Consistency with the conditions of separateness is the necessary form of all maxims for all rational beings. Separateness—being a source of reasons all the way down—is a constitutive feature of rational agency. What is contingent are the vulnerabilities that allow the conditions of separateness to be ignored. Thus, although the interpretation of the argument is in terms suited to the circumstances of human action (vulnerability to deceit), the principle of willing that is rejected violates a constitutive principle of practical rationality per se.

Likewise, although the argument rejecting the maxim of nonbeneficence makes use of the parochial facts that we are embodied and causally limited agents, dependent on others, the *form* of the argument is fully general: no rational agent can will a maxim to be a universal law without contradiction if the universalized maxim would threaten general conditions of *her* effective agency. The general conditions of effective agency will vary with the different possible natures of different kinds of rational beings *and* possibly will vary under different social settings for the same kind of rational being. (Human and nonhuman ethics would have the same foundations, but not the same duties or principles of casuistry.)

We may conclude that although the interpretations make use of facts specific to our kind of rational agent, they do not on that account appeal to less than fully general principles of rational willing. The interpretations specify the features of agency that cause contradiction in the CI procedure's arguments, thereby indicating the more general principle of rational willing that drives the contradiction.

There is no reason to object to this interplay between the pure and the empirical in arguments deriving duties. In both the *Groundwork* and the *Metaphysics of Morals* Kant speaks of two different studies that complete ethics: the metaphysics of morals, which derives the kinds of duties *we* have as rational agents, and a practical anthropology, needed because moral laws require "a power of judgment sharpened by experience, partly in order to distinguish in what cases they are applicable, and partly to gain for them access to the human will as well as influence for putting them into practice" (G389). And in the *Metaphysics of Morals* he says:

> Just as a metaphysics of nature must also contain principles for applying those universal first principles of nature as such to objects of experience, so a metaphysics of morals cannot dispense with principles of application; and we shall often have to take as our object the particular *nature* of man, which is known only by experience, to show in it the implications of the universal moral principles. (216)

The structure of moral theory that Kant had in mind is not obscure. Morality requires an a priori foundation that can only be had in the principles of pure practical reason: the Moral Law. Because the Moral Law applies to human beings with necessity and so independently of contingent interests, the ground of obligation must "be sought a priori solely in the concepts of pure reason" (G389). Nothing in the account of moral judgment and value that I have given disregards this. The *application* of the Moral Law cannot be carried out, however, without empirical knowledge of the object of application.

That the Moral Law is the foundation of morality tells us that we are to look to those aspects of activities which can conform to principles of practical reason—that is, willings. And it tells us that willings can only be good if they have a certain form. Our willings are justified only if they have a form that is possible for all rational beings to adopt. This much is generally acknowledged to be the argument of the *Groundwork*. But to understand why a certain form of willing cannot be adopted consistent with the principles of their rational agency by all human beings (and so a fortiori by all rational beings), we need to know how our maxims of action are to be seen as possibly containing principles of rational agency. We must therefore have a way of eliciting such principles from the actual practical concepts we use, when these concepts do not exhibit principles explicitly, and moreover are laden with the texture and detail of particular forms of practical life. This task is possible because the interpretations of the CI procedure arguments elaborate the aspects of our kind of rational agency that impermissible maxims misuse. They enable a project of empirical moral inquiry that is a necessary part of the activity of moral judgment. Throughout, though, the guide to this empirical ethical investigation has to be the "pure part" of ethics—the a priori grounding of moral principle in rational nature as such, interpreted in a way that sets terms for the empirical investigation of agency.

Which facts are the facts we need to know? What is the material form of rational nature? Not every fact about human nature counts. We need to know the facts about how persons live which are relevant to the empirical form of their rational agency. And we need to be able to identify the way these facts get taken up into our maxims as conditions of choice and action. (In the *Metaphysics of Morals* Kant speaks of a projected appendix necessary to complete the ethical system in which a method of application of the Categorical Imperative would be elaborated to take account of the specific circumstances of moral judgment and action such as a person's "age, sex, health, prosperity or poverty."[38])

Understanding how these and related facts engage with principles of practical rationality belongs to what I call "middle theory." It is so called because it lies between the high theory of value and the low theory of applications. Middle theory provides the missing link in a reconstruction of Kantian ethics.

Middle theory has several tasks. To it belongs, first of all, the project of articulating the contingent structure of rational agency. We are to apply a metaphysical and transcendental concept of pure practical rationality to the empirical selves we are. Knowing that the principles of rational agency per se describe a deliberative stance in which one acts "under the idea of freedom" with reason having "causality in reference to its objects" (G449), we know that we are to regard one another (and ourselves) as capable of acting for and from reasons all the way down. We must not act on maxims whose principle fails to acknowledge the fact of another's (or our own) rational agency as an independent and original locus of judgment and causality. We must therefore be aware of the array of possible interferences with this deliberative efficacy so as not to take wrongful advantage of the limits and weaknesses of human agency. Middle theory should have the resources to explain why, for example, bringing another to act as you want by means of information you believe to be true properly acknowledges the claim of agency, whereas the use of deliberate falsehood (or misleading partial truths) does not.

---

38. I was reminded of this and related discussions by Sally Sedgwick, "On the Relation of Pure Reason to Content," *Philosophy and Phenomenological Research* 49 (1988), 66. The principles of this method would *schematize* the pure principles of duty to present them "as ready for morally-practical use" (68).

Middle theory also investigates the contingent empirical situation of human agents in order to understand how some circumstances of deliberative activity make rational agency available for wrongful use. In addition to general vulnerabilities, there are historically particular situations, institutions, and social structures that may allow us to disregard or discount the deliberative standing of some persons. What modes of treatment in what circumstances amount to deceit or coercion is in part a contingent matter, conceptually dependent on our morally informed knowledge of institutions, practices, and their effects. What is not contingent is that if one acts on a maxim of deceit one is acting impermissibly; what is contingent are the ways of acting that are deceitful.

In even relatively simple exchanges in complex relationships, facts about dependency (both particular to the parties and more general social determinants of behavior and attitude) will alter what counts as deceitful manipulation. Those with authority or power cannot simply say they had no deceptive intention when the efficacy of their proposed maxims depends on their ability to control information. If the moral fault in such omissions is not exactly that of intentional (manipulative) deception, it is a very close relation, and one that often does the work of deception where functional authority is unequal. Control over information need not signal deception— think of parents giving nutritional advice to their children—but monopoly of information introduces a presumptive burden that one not prevent or block deliberative independence where that is possible (so we should explain about sugars and fats and not just rail against junk food as if its consumption were morally depraved). In Kantian terms, this is part of what it means to agree positively as well as negatively with rational nature as an end in itself. We agree negatively when we do not deceive, positively when our actions encourage competent deliberative independence. (The *Groundwork* examples are misleading in their suggestion that positive agreement with rational nature is restricted to matters of self-development and beneficence.)

Since moral judgment requires that agents identify the morally salient features of their circumstances of action, when facts such as the limits of knowledge and skill of another affect an agent's deliberations and choices, they must be included in maxims. Those who prey on the fears of the elderly or the trust of the naive surely act on maxims that connect these vulnerabilities with the rational agency of their victims.

General facts that are constitutive of effective rationality will have local variations. It is a morally relevant general fact about human rational nature that we are mortal and vulnerable to injury from each other. It is also relevant that we are averse to injury and death (at least to ourselves and those we care about). The fact that we were mortal and vulnerable would still matter if we did not care whether or when we died or whether we were injured, but its moral significance would be different: we would then not be vulnerable to coercion through threat of death or injury. But given *our* institutions, it is a morally relevant particular fact that the social construction of illness and dying makes determination of deliberative competence difficult. Hospital environments and the structure of medical authority infantilize patients, making suspect both our and their own views of their deliberative capacities.

We are embodied agents with limited powers. We require security and stability of possession if we are to have a suitable conception of ourselves as effective agents, as having a life whose shape is at least in important ways a function of our own agency. We live among others and must have mechanisms for living *with* others (institutions of public choice) if these requirements of effective agency are to be realized. Thus it is that the first half of the *Metaphysics of Morals* concerns the legitimate terrain of law, providing the morally necessary political framework without which our activities cannot give expression to our rational natures[39]—activity under the guidance of the second half of the *Metaphysics of Morals'* account of the duties of virtue.

This structure of a general fact constitutive of rational agency in a context-specific form will be found throughout Kantian casuistry. The requirements of beneficence are equally a function of the prevailing institution of property and the nature of the inequalities it permits or brings about. The moral relevance of need that is caused through misfortune or personal failings is different in kind than need that is a function of the intrinsic inefficiencies of a system of property. Since property (as a coercive public institution) is justified as it provides the necessary condition for effective action, those who are injured as a result of the particular institution's inefficiencies may have a direct welfare claim against public resources.[40] The fact of a given institution thus not only alters the obligations we have, but the terms in which we describe moral claims and responses to those claims. Whether we may refrain from aiding because of the cost to us—to our own needs and projects—could depend on the source of the need for which the claim is made.

---

39. Kant views the state of nature as a place in which we cannot exist as rational beings. Its role is as an analytic device that explains the necessity of the state and the legitimacy of juridical coercion.

40. When Kant notes that the occasions for charity are themselves the product of unjustified inequalities of property (DV454), it does not follow that property per se or private property is vulnerable to moral challenge, or even that the particular institution of property that allows or possibly generates inequality is therefore illegitimate. The injustice that would show the illegitimacy of an institution of property—as opposed to giving reason not to act as though one deserved one's relative wealth—would obtain when the institution of property systematically failed to provide the possibility of effective agency for a portion of the people. Real slavery and oppressive wage labor would be two such unjust institutions.

Through this sort of elaboration of basic concepts of moral judgment in significant contexts of application, middle theory expands the list of moral categories. It follows that the list is not closed, and complete moral knowledge is not possible. This is not a bad thing. The lack of completeness is not a function of detail and complexity or of our status as imperfect knowers. Moral knowledge cannot be complete because what must be known will change. The acquisition of new moral knowledge is thus a permanent feature of moral practice.[41]

Middle theory is the theory of the practice of moral judgment. It effects the translation of the basic conception of value in the principles of practical rationality into principles that fit the circumstances of human action, judgment, and deliberation. Because it is responsive to the facts of institutions and social organization, middle theory is dynamic: it both shapes and is shaped by practice.

VI

We began with the task of showing that purely formal principles of rationality can be expressions of a didactically effective conception of value. While the CI procedure's requirement that maxims have the form of universal law is sufficient to produce results—to rule some maxims out as impermissible—it is not by itself sufficient to pick out the wrong-making characteristic of an impermissible maxim. The results it gives are therefore without clear rationale and unable to guide deliberation in morally complex circumstances (where the CI procedure itself is unable to generate determinate results). I have argued that the succeeding formulations of the CI provide interpretations of the CI procedure's arguments that resolve this difficulty.

The Formula of Humanity interprets the requirement that our maxims have the form of universal lawgiving as setting rational nature as a final end. This directs an inquiry into the nature of rational agency in general and of human agency in particular so that we can determine when, in our maxims, our treatment of others is not compatible with their status as rational agents: persons whose actions we are to regard as following from reasons, all the way down.

Through the Formula of Autonomy we discover that the only condition in which a rational agent can conceive of herself acting for reasons all the way down (as an end-in-herself) is if she is self-legislating. That is, we regard ourselves and are to regard others as "first causes" of reasons for action.

41. Where circumstances are very stable, one might be led to think that agents possess moral knowledge of a kind that we lack. It is just as likely that they are not taxed to respond constantly to new arrangements and emerging demands.

The ultimate ground of our reasons—and so any regulative norms of willing—must therefore be internal to the will.[42]

The Kingdom of Ends formula introduces the idea of a social plurality of autonomous beings who conceive of themselves and others as persons who act for reasons all the way down. This sets what Kant calls an Ideal of reason: the realm that reason would bring forth if it had sufficient power over the will (KpV44). It also implies, I believe, that insofar as we are social beings, rules and institutions that may be necessary for social life can be justified only if they are consistent with each person being regarded as an equal and autonomous member.

The upshot of the sequence of interpretations is a robust conception of embodied, social—that is to say, human—rational agency. Actions whose maxims have the form of universal law express respect for rational agency by taking the fact that all rational agents are ultimate sources of reasons to be a regulative norm for action.

If we accept that rational nature is reason-giving in this strong regulative way, it must have value of a special magnitude or kind. This idea is expressed in the *Groundwork* passage that follows the last formulation of the Categorical Imperative which speaks of the value—dignity—that we have as rational agents in virtue of our autonomy. I take Kant to be explicitly asserting that what emerges from the fully interpreted CI procedure is a distinctive conception of value. Understanding what is claimed to be of value and in what sense it is of value is the essential last step in appreciating the radical nature of Kant's claims.

We therefore should not regard the discussion of dignity and price as a bit of flowery value talk curiously placed after the last of the formally austere formulations of the CI. It is rather the last step in the argument of the second chapter of the *Groundwork*. Having shown that the CI's formal requirement of universalizability is possible just in case we are *as* ends-in-ourselves self-legislating and so sovereign members of a kingdom of ends, Kant concludes that "morality and humanity, insofar as it is capable of morality, alone have dignity" (G435). This conclusion is doubly significant. It provides the last step in the explanation of the unconditioned goodness of the good will *by* showing how it is that the principles of practical rationality constitute a conception of value.

We can now put together a complete argument. Needing to explicate the idea of a good will as a will that is unconditionally good and good in virtue of its principle of willing, Kant argues that there is only one principle that could be the principle of good willing: the CI's requirement of universal lawgiving. In requiring that the principle of one's maxims be possible laws

---

42. A much fuller argument for this sort of view has been made in Andrews Reath, "Autonomy of the Will as the Foundation of Morality," manuscript.

for all rational agents, the CI makes consistency with the constitutive principles of rational nature a limiting condition on our actions and willings. Rational nature is then the regulative and unconditioned *end* of willing—that is, a final end, an end-in-itself. Now rational nature is a possible end-in-itself only if it contains *as its own principle* the ultimate determining ground of action. This can be the case only if the will is autonomous, having the capacity to be its own original source of reasons.[43] (Since the only possible self-given principle is the CI, autonomy is the capacity to act morally.) Expressed in terms of value: as an end-in-itself, rational nature contains the conditions of its own goodness, goodness not dependent on any further end. Kant concludes that rational nature therefore has a unique kind of value "insofar as it is capable of morality": a particular kind of worth, *Würde*, a status notion, translated as dignity.

This conception of dignity completes the *Groundwork*'s critique of value. In the formal Kantian sense of critique, it is an argument to defeat the claims of sufficiency of empirical practical reason (heteronomy of the will).

The good will, in accepting the regulative authority of the CI, takes rational nature as its final end: actions and ends are judged to be good on condition that they are willed in conformity with the principles of practical reason. The goodness of the good will resides in the principle of its willing, not in any special efforts or virtues that allow it to make the principle of good willing the principle of all its maxims. (Those efforts and virtues have value as means.) The person with a good will is of no greater value than one with an ordinary will; she has no greater amount of dignity. As rational agents, we each have the capacity to bring our wills into conformity with the principle of good willing, and so each has all the dignity there is to have. Dignity is not, of course, security for either moral virtue or moral worth.

As the final end of rational willing, rational nature as value is both absolute and nonscalar. It is absolute in the sense that there is no other kind of value or goodness for whose sake rational nature can count as a means. It is nonscalar in the sense that (1) it is not the highest value on a single inclusive scale of value, and (2) it is not additive: more instantiations of rational nature do not enhance the value content of the world, and more instances of respect for rational nature do not move anything or anyone along a scale of dignity. There is no such scale.

If beings with dignity do not have relative value, either in the sense of one having more dignity than another *or* in the sense of many having more dignity than a few, casuistical principles that involve "counting heads" are not possible because they take no account of the fact that what is counted are not things but final sources of reasons. The resolution of situations

---

43. Whether the will is autonomous is the subject of the *Groundwork*'s third chapter; the argument of the second chapter assumes autonomy for its analytical purposes.

apparently calling for the sacrifice of one for another or one for many requires a return to middle theory. We will need to frame the deliberative *question* in terms of principles that direct us to act against one for the sake of another (say, against an aggressor for the sake of his victim) that are consistent with the full regard for both as rational agents.[44] That hard cases require the evolution of middle theory if they are to be correctly understood seems to me exactly the right result. We have no reason to suppose that our moral theory timelessly contains all the concepts we will ever need for deliberation and judgment.

VII

It remains to be asked whether and in what sense we have left deontology behind. I have argued: (1) we can understand the formal requirements of practical reason as a conception of value; (2) the various formulations of the one principle of morality articulate the concept of rationality that is the conception of value and spell out the sense in which it is reason-giving; and (3) we can expect a greater degree of success in our employment of the CI procedure when we interpret its arguments in terms of this conception of value. Still one might think it misleading to conclude from this that Kant's ethics has been shown to be based on value. After all, what I am calling "value" is just the same old principle of practical reason, albeit interpreted in a way that permits it to do the practical work one thought could be done only by a conception of value. But this is just the point. We cannot understand what practical reason is without understanding it as a conception of value. The sense in which I think we must leave deontology behind does not require that we argue for an independent conception of value as the foundation for practical reason. Rather, insofar as practical reason is the principle of obligation, it is and must be a conception of value.

Kant's place in the history of ethics is identified with the denial that the concepts of obligation and value can be separate. Taking this to be a claim for deontology—the strong priority of the right—mistakes Kant's insight. While many familiar notions of moral value that mark the goodness of persons *are* defined in terms of conceptually prior principles of practical reason, these notions do not exhaust the role of value in Kant's ethics. We need to understand Kant as arguing both that if there is unconditioned goodness it can only be in a principle of practical reason *and* that if reason is practical its principles describe a conception of value. The critique of

---

44. The aggressor acts on an impermissible maxim that she is under obligation to abandon. We do not fail to respect her as an autonomous person in interfering for that purpose. The victim may have a duty to resist aggression that permits our support.

practical reason is, in part, Kant's contribution to the philosophical study of value.

In leaving deontology behind, we liberate resources that enable Kantian ethics to support an effective model of moral judgment. The practical efficacy of the CI procedure is secured through interpretations of its arguments in terms of a robust conception of rational nature as a final end. Because its arguments are given value content, the CI procedure is didactic—able to explain the wrong-making features of impermissible willings in a way that can guide subsequent deliberation. The conception of value has no separate derivation; it is articulated through analyses of the conditions of rational willing provided by the remaining formulations of the Categorical Imperative. The formulations together construct a basis for moral content that makes possible what I call middle theory: the translation of a formal conception of value into terms suitable to the particular contexts of human action and deliberation.

Credits · *Index*

Credits

Chapters 7 and 10 are published here for the first time. Permission from the publishers to reprint all or parts of the other eight chapters is gratefully acknowledged.

1. "On the Value of Acting from the Motive of Duty," *Philosophical Review* 90 (1981), 359–382.

2. "Integrity and Impartiality," *Monist* 66 (1983), 233–250; "Rules, Motives, and Helping Actions," *Philosophical Studies* 45 (1984), 369–377.

3. "Mutual Aid and Respect for Persons," *Ethics* 94 (1984), 577–602. © by The University of Chicago. All rights reserved.

4. "The Practice of Moral Judgment," *Journal of Philosophy* 82 (1985), 414–436.

5. "What Happens to the Consequences?" in *Pursuits of Reason,* ed. Paul Guyer, Ted Cohen, and Hilary Putnam (Arlington: Texas Tech University Press, 1992).

6. "Murder and Mayhem: Violence and Kantian Casuistry," *Monist* 72 (1989), 411–431.

8. "Obligation and Performance," in *Identity, Character, and Morality,* ed. Amélie Rorty and Owen Flanagan (Cambridge: MIT Press, 1990).

9. "Agency, Attachment, and Difference," *Ethics* 101 (1991), 775–797. © by The University of Chicago. All rights reserved.

Index